Lectures on the Theory and Application of Modern Finance with R and ChatGPT

World Scientific Lecture Notes in Finance

ISSN: 2424-9939

This series provides high quality lecture note-type texts in all areas of finance, for courses at all levels: undergraduate, MBA and PhD. These accessible and affordable lecture notes are better aligned with today's classrooms and are written by expert professors in their field with extensive teaching experience. Students will find these books less formal, less expensive and also more enjoyable than many textbooks. Instructors will find all the material that they need, thus significantly reducing their class preparation time. Authors can prepare their volumes with ease, as they would be based on already existing, and actively used, lecture notes. With these features, this book series will make a significant contribution to improving the teaching of finance worldwide.

Published:

Vol. 10 *Lectures on the Theory and Application of Modern Finance with R and ChatGPT*
by Carlo A Favero (Bocconi University, Italy) and
Claudio Tebaldi (Bocconi University, Italy)

Vol. 9 *Behavioral Finance: Beyond the Basics*
edited by Itzhak Venezia (Academic College of Tel-Aviv-Yaffo, Israel), and Rachel Calipha (Academic College of Tel-Aviv-Yaffo, Israel)

Vol. 8 *Lecture Notes in Entrepreneurial Finance for the Digital Economy*
by Peter Joakim Westerholm (The University of Sydney Business School, Australia)

Vol. 7 *Lecture Notes in Risk Management*
by Yevgeny Mugerman (Bar-Ilan University, Israel) and
Yoel Hecht (College of Management Academic Studies, Israel)

Vol. 6 *Options — 45 years since the Publication of the Black–Scholes–Merton Model: The Gershon Fintech Center Conference*
edited by David Gershon (The Hebrew University of Jerusalem, Israel),
Alexander Lipton (Abu Dhabi Investment Authority, UAE &
The Hebrew University of Jerusalem, Israel),
Mathieu Rosenbaum (École Polytechnique, France) and
Zvi Wiener (The Hebrew University of Jerusalem, Israel)

World Scientific Lecture Notes in Finance – **Vol. 10**

Lectures on the Theory and Application of Modern Finance with R and ChatGPT

Carlo A Favero
Bocconi University, Italy

Claudio Tebaldi
Bocconi University, Italy

World Scientific

NEW JERSEY • LONDON • SINGAPORE • GENEVA • BEIJING • SHANGHAI • TAIPEI • CHENNAI

Published by

World Scientific Publishing Co. Pte. Ltd.
5 Toh Tuck Link, Singapore 596224
USA office: 27 Warren Street, Suite 401-402, Hackensack, NJ 07601
UK office: 57 Shelton Street, Covent Garden, London WC2H 9HE

Library of Congress Control Number: 2025000060

British Library Cataloguing-in-Publication Data
A catalogue record for this book is available from the British Library.

World Scientific Lecture Notes in Finance — Vol. 10
LECTURES ON THE THEORY AND APPLICATION OF MODERN FINANCE WITH R AND CHATGPT

ISBN 978-981-98-1159-5 (hardcover)
ISBN 978-981-98-1160-1 (ebook for institutions)
ISBN 978-981-98-1161-8 (ebook for individuals)

For any available supplementary material, please visit
https://www.worldscientific.com/worldscibooks/10.1142/14268#t=suppl

Desk Editors: Nambirajan Karuppiah/Catherine Domingo Ong

Typeset by Stallion Press
Email: enquiries@stallionpress.com

Preface

These lecture notes are thought for Master courses in Finance, Fintech and Quantitative Finance programs. We fully subscribe to the philosophy that Master students should be offered courses that are really at the cutting edge of the technologies and advances that are disrupting the financial industry and delve deep into topics such as AI, machine learning, and their importance for Asset Management. in these notes the illustration of the theory of Finance is paired with practical applications to real-life asset allocation problems. A hands-on approach is proposed to construct and manipulate databases to build portfolios, assess their performance and manage their risk. The course begins with a section on the fundamentals on individual choice, to then move from individual choice to market valuation, covering the traditional Markowitz mean-variance approach, market-based asset pricing and Arbitrage-based pricing theory.

Empirical modeling in finance is then introduced by illustrating its working and its historical evolution. The translation of financial theory into action on data is driven by building predictive models for asset prices and returns. Basic models are explored, and programming emerges as an essential prerequisite for data manipulation. Readers can acquaint themselves with the statistical software R and exhibit the application of theoretical concepts to financial data, illustrated by sample programs, exercises, and corresponding solutions.

The main focus is on the hands-on implementation of this approach using actual data, utilizing specific models to exemplify its practicality. The text also shows how Chat GPT could be used to help in doing Empirical Finance with R. The interaction with chat GPT is illustrated via live session entitled “Ask Chat GPT”, which provide guidance to efficient interaction with Chat GPT to write codes designed for specific tasks and adapt and debug them, if necessary.

The Lectures are meant to provide a background for flipped classrooms and interactive teaching with the demonstration and discussion of R codes, in which students are expected to engage in real-time coding on their laptops and group discussions.

About the Authors

Carlo Favero holds a D.Phil. from Oxford University, where he was a member of the Oxford Econometrics Research Centre. He has been professor of Econometrics at Bocconi University from 1994 to 2001 and professor of Economics since 2002. In 2009 he joined the newly formed Dept of Finance at Bocconi University, where he taught Econometrics. Since 2023, he holds a dual affiliation with the Department of Economics and the Department of Finance. He has published in scholarly journals on the econometric modelling of bond and stock prices, applied econometrics, monetary and fiscal policy and time-series models for macroeconomics and finance. He is a research fellow of CEPR in the International Macroeconomics programme, and a fellow of the Innocenzo Gasparini Institute for the Economic Research and the newly formed Institute for European Policymaking at Bocconi University. He is advisor to the Italian Ministry of Treasury for the construction of a stock-flow consistent econometric model of the Italian economy. He has been consulting the European Commission, the World Bank and the European Central Bank, on monetary policy and the monetary transmission mechanism and bond markets. He couthored with A.Alesina and F.Giavazzi the book "Austerity. When it Works and When it Doesn't" (Princeton University Press 2019). The book has been translated in Chinese, Spanish and Italian and in May 2020 was awarded the Hayek Book Prize by the Manhattan Institute.

Claudio Tebaldi holds a D. Phil in Statistical Mechanics and an M. Phil in Complex Systems from the International School of

Advanced Studies Trieste, an M. Phil in Economics and Finance from Venice International University and is currently Professor of Quantitative Methods for Economics, Finance, and Insurance. He is a member of the Department of Finance at Bocconi University, a fellow of Baffi-Centre for Economics Finance and Regulation, of the Innocenzo Gasparini Institute for the Economic Research and of the newly formed Institute for European Policymaking at Bocconi University. He is currently the Scientific Director of the Bocconi Fintech Lab and the Editor-in-Chief of Quantitative Finance. His research is mainly focused on financial risk management, asset and derivative pricing and has been featured on many high impact journals in the field of quantitative methods for economics and finance and two of his papers have been awarded as Best Paper in Finance of the Swiss Econometrics and Finance Society 2007 and Best Paper in Derivatives of the Northern Finance Association 2019. Acknowledgments: C.T. thanks to the past members of the Theory of Finance Course teaching team P. Colla, G. Gurioli, M. Navone, L. De Felice, D. Di Virgilio, G. Occhipinti and contributed with their valuable workand their insights to the refinement of the arguments presented in this book. The usual disclaimer applies.

Contents

Preface v

About the Authors vii

1 Individual Choice **1**

1.1 Different Paradigms for Decision Theory 2
1.1.1 Decision theory under certainty 2
1.1.2 Second: Decision theory under uncertainty . . . 3
1.1.3 Third: Decision theory under uncertainty, asymmetric information and strategic interaction 5
1.2 A Paradigm for Rationality 6
1.3 Decision Theory Under Uncertainty 8
1.4 Risk Aversion 12
1.4.1 Quantifying risk aversion 16
1.4.2 Certainty equivalent and risk premium 18
1.5 Insurance Pricing Principle 19
1.6 The Portfolio Problem 21
1.6.1 Two securities and two states of the world . . . 21
1.6.2 The case with N assets 23
1.7 Subjective Valuation 25
1.7.1 A numerical example 29
1.8 Expected Utility Reloaded 33
1.8.1 Step 1: Choice over binary actions 35
1.8.2 Step 2: Deriving the expected utility representation in a generic state space with S states 37

1.9 Deviations from Expected Utility 40
1.9.1 Independence axiom and the Allais paradox 40
1.9.2 The paradox of Ellsberg and the distinction between ambiguity and risk 42
1.9.3 Preference for temporal resolution of uncertainty 44
1.9.4 Anomalies observed by Khanemann and Tversky 46
1.9.5 Individual choice and collective decisions 49

2 From Individual Choice to Market Pricing 51

2.1 The Markowitz Mean–Variance Approach 52
2.1.1 A bit of terminology 54
2.1.2 Minimum variance portfolio 55
2.1.3 Risk parity portfolios 55
2.1.4 The M–V model with two risky assets and no risk-free 56
2.1.5 Optimal allocation when a risk-free security is available 61
2.1.6 The general solution to the N risky assets and no risk free 63
2.1.7 The general solution in the presence of a risk-free security 69
2.1.8 The FOC for a mean–variance investor when a risk-free asset is present 72
2.2 Market-Based Asset Pricing 73
2.2.1 The capital asset pricing model 73
2.2.2 The market portfolio 74
2.2.3 The capital market line 75
2.2.4 The security market line 75
2.2.5 SML and CML 76
2.2.6 Market price as the present value of cash flows 78
2.2.7 The zero-beta CAPM (Black) 79
2.2.8 The Roll's critique 81
2.3 A Structural Interpretation 82
2.4 Arbitrage-Based Pricing Theory 85
2.4.1 The linear factor model 85

2.4.2 Arbitrage portfolios 87
2.4.3 The Ross (1973) arbitrage pricing argument 89
2.4.4 Economic interpretation of the λ coefficients 91
2.4.5 APT when the risk factors are portfolio excess returns 91
2.4.6 APT and CAPM 92
2.4.7 APT tests and factor-mimicking portfolios . . . 93
2.5 APT and Risk-Neutral Valuation 95
2.5.1 CAPM and SDF 97

3 Empirical Tests of Asset Pricing Models 101

3.1 The View from the 1960s: Efficient Markets and Constant Expected Returns 101
3.2 The Cross-Sectional Evidence: CAPM Verification . . 102
3.2.1 Black, Jensen, and Scholes (1972) and portfolio aggregation 104
3.2.2 Capital market efficiency and the two-step Fama–McBeth (1973) procedure 106
3.3 The Frazzini and Pedersen (2014) BAB Factor Construction 109
3.4 Empirical Tests of APT, Anomalies and Fama and French (1993) 112
3.5 Direct Construction of Traded Portfolios 114
3.6 Time-Series Analysis of Returns 116
3.6.1 The behavior of returns at high-frequency . . . 116
3.6.2 A more realistic description 117
3.7 Time Series Anomalies 118
3.8 Returns at Different Horizons and the Dynamic Dividend Growth Model of Shiller (1981) 118
3.9 Conditional Asset Pricing with Predictable Returns 120
3.10 Predictive Models in Finance 122

4 From Theory to Practice 125

4.1 The Econometric Modeling Process 126
4.2 The Challenges for Financial Econometrics 127
4.3 Returns 128

4.3.1 Simple and log returns 128
4.3.2 Statistical models for asset prices and returns 129
4.3.3 Multi-period returns and annualized returns 130
4.3.4 Working with returns 131
4.4 Stock and Bond Returns 134
4.4.1 Stock returns and the dynamic dividend growth model 134
4.4.2 Bond returns: Yields-to-maturity and holding period returns 138
4.5 Going to the Data with R 142
4.5.1 Getting started 143
4.5.2 Data objects in R 144
4.5.3 Data handling in R 146
4.5.4 Data exploration and graphics 148
4.5.5 Interacting with Chat GPT 157
4.6 Appendix: The Data 165

5 The Constant Expected Return Model 169

5.1 Model Specification 169
5.1.1 Stocks for the long run 171
5.2 Model Estimation 173
5.2.1 Parameters estimation in a linear model 174
5.3 Model Simulation 176
5.4 The CER Model at Work with R 177
5.4.1 Asset allocation with the CER 177
5.4.2 Model simulation: Backtesting and VaR 182

6 Factor Models 189

6.1 Time-Series Representation 189
6.2 Cross-Sectional Representation 191
6.3 Factor-Based Portfolios and Factor Exposures 191
6.4 Asset Allocation with the CER and the CAPM in R 192
6.5 Validating Factor Models 199
6.5.1 Which factors? 200
6.6 Factor Models with Predictability 200
6.6.1 An illustration with R 205

7 Models for Risk Measurement 211

7.1 Risk Measurement 211
7.1.1 Value at risk (VaR) 211
7.2 VaR without Predictability 212
7.2.1 VaR with the CER 212
7.2.2 VaR with the CAPM 212
7.3 The Evidence from High-Frequency Data 213
7.4 A General Model for High-Frequency Data 214
7.4.1 GARCH models for heteroscedasticity 214
7.4.2 GARCH properties 215
7.4.3 GARCH forecasting 215
7.4.4 Testing for GARCH 215
7.5 Estimation of GARCH Models 216
7.5.1 Quasi MLE estimation 217
7.6 From GARCH to VaR 218
7.6.1 GARCH with factors 218
7.7 Measuring Risk: An Illustration with R 218
7.8 Backtesting VaR 223
7.8.1 Unconditional coverage testing 224
7.8.2 Independence testing 225
7.8.3 Conditional coverage testing 226
7.8.4 Backtesting VaR in R 226

Bibliography 229

Index 233

Chapter 1

Individual Choice

One of the statutory goals of financial economics is the provision of disciplined answers to practical questions that naturally arise in everyday life, when we are forced to make decisions regarding wealth management. For example, in the context of personal finance and portfolio management, this means finding rational answers to simple questions like:

(1) Given a level of initial wealth, how do we make relevant investment decisions?
(2) Will my current savings provide sufficient pension benefits when I retire?
(3) Given an amount of savings and a basket of assets, how can I choose how much to invest in each of these assets?
(4) Do I need a financial advisor? How can I verify that she/he is doing a good job with my money?
(5) How can I construct the best portfolio for my clients? My client will be happier with a 50% stocks and 50% bonds portfolio or with a 30% stocks and 70% bonds portfolio?
(6) How can I assess whether the price of a security is appropriate?

Despite their apparent simplicity, the road toward satisfactory answers to these questions is bumpy. The problem is that preferences about actions are not directly observable. Helping individuals tackle financial decisions and improving their financial literacy has recently emerged as a social goal. It is key to promote people's well-being and more sustainable economic development. In the following, we first consider the point of view of a single investor and introduce the basic terminology and definitions that categorize the problem of choice in different environments of increasing complexity.

1.1 Different Paradigms for Decision Theory

A primary empirical problem is the so-called elicitation of the agent's preference from the decision-maker's actions and observable information. The advent of social media and big data technologies has dramatically increased the amount of data that might be used in principle to reconstruct investor preferences. The following three frameworks are usually considered when analyzing individual choice.

1.1.1 *Decision theory under certainty*

In a world where there is no uncertainty, decision theory is simplified. There is a one-way strict correspondence between action and consequences:

$$c = f(a) \in C \quad \Rightarrow \quad a \in A$$

Here, f is a function that describes the outcome c of any action a an agent may choose among the array A of possible actions. In this simple framework, every single time that I take action a, I get the consequence c: there is no uncertainty about the effects derived from my action.

Hence, if I can rank consequences, I can also rank the actions. For instance, given actions a_1, a_2, and a_3 and their consequences $c_1 = f(a_1)$, $c_2 = f(a_2)$ and $c_3 = f(a_3)$:

$$c_1 \succeq^c c_2 \succeq^c c_3 \Rightarrow a_1 \succeq a_2 \succeq a_3$$

where $\succeq$ ($\succeq^c$) means "is weakly preferred to" and is a binary relationship in the set A (C). So, if I know that my client prefers consequence c_1 to consequence c_2, I know that he will prefer action a_1 to action a_2 or will be indifferent among the two.

Example 1. Let's give an example: if I know with certainty that next year T-Bill will yield a return of 4.5% and IBM a return of

15%, I can find the terminal value of 10$ invested in three different portfolios

Portfolio	Return (%)	TV ($)
100% T-Bill	4.5	104.5
50%TB - 50%IBM	9.75	109.75
100% IBM	15	115

Remember that there is no uncertainty about the asset's returns. Under this condition, I know that my customer, who prefers more to less, will prefer the portfolio composition that produces the greater final wealth. The best portfolio for my client will be 100% IBM.

1.1.2 *Second: Decision theory under uncertainty*

If the consequence of an action is not uniquely determined, the description of the decision process becomes more interesting:

- Consequences depend both on my actions and on the "state of nature" ω:

$$c = f(a, \omega) \quad \Rightarrow \quad a \in A,\ \omega \in \Omega$$

  The state of nature is an exogenous state that is unknown to and not controlled by the decision maker, who can only observe it ex-post.
- To each action it is associated with a vector of consequences that collects all the possible outcomes that can be realized in different states of nature. Consider the simplest description of uncertainty where there are S states of the world $\Omega = \{\omega_1, \ldots, \omega_S\}$ and two possible actions a and b. Then each action results in a vector of S consequences

$$a \Longrightarrow [c_{a,1}, \ldots, c_{a,S}]$$
$$b \Longrightarrow [c_{b,1}, \ldots, c_{b,S}]$$

- Now it may happen that $u(c_{a,1}) > u(c_{b,1})$ but $u(c_{a,2}) < u(c_{b,2})$. The state of nature may affect the preference for consequences and, in this way, complicate the preference for actions.

Example 2. Consider now the previous problem when it is possible trade a risky security

	Market ↑		Market ↓	
Portfolio	Return (%)	TV	Return (%)	TV
100% T-Bill	4.5	104.5	4.5	104.5
50%TB-50%IBM	12.25	112.25	−2.75	97.25
100% IBM	20	120	−10	90

We can see that the first portfolio has the lowest return if the stock market goes up but the highest if the market goes down.

In our discussion, we will assume that the relevant uncertainty can be completely described within a simple, yet complete, stand-alone probabilistic model. The key assumption in this framework is that the description of uncertainty is reduced to the analysis of probabilistic scenarios described by a probability measure that can be ex-ante estimated and is known to all the investors.

To consider a probabilistic description of uncertainty, it is necessary to introduce the notion of probability space. In this chapter, we will discuss the relevant financial economic principles in a finite state probability space which is defined by the triple $(\Omega, \mathcal{A}, \mathbb{P})$ where[1]:

- Ω is a non-empty set, each element $\omega \in \Omega$ is a state and provides a complete description of the outcomes that occur once that uncertainty is completely resolved and ω is verified to be the true state.
- $\mathcal{A} \subset \mathcal{P}(\Omega)$ is an algebra of events, i.e., a properly selected subset $\mathcal{A}$ of the set of parts of Ω, $\mathcal{P}(\Omega)$, that verifies the following two properties:
  (i) If $A, B \in \mathcal{A}$, then also their union $A \cup B \in \mathcal{A}$.
  (ii) If $A \in \mathcal{A}$, then also its complement $\Omega \backslash A \in \mathcal{A}$.
- $\mathbb{P}$ is a set function that associates to each event its probability: $\mathbb{P} : \mathcal{A} \to [0, 1]$ that satisfies the following two conditions:

[1]The definition of those probability spaces where the space of all possible states is not finite is non-trivial. For a general introduction, see, e.g., Billingsley (2017).

(i) The probability of mutually exclusive events must be equal to the sum of the probabilities of each of these events.
(ii) $\mathbb{P}[\Omega] = 1$.

When possible, we will consider the simplest realization of a probability space, the one where only two possible states can occur. It is defined as follows:

- $\Omega^B := \{up, down\}$ is the state space.
- $\mathcal{A}^B := \mathcal{P}(\{up, down\}) = \{\varnothing, \{up\}, \{down\}, \Omega^B\}$.
- Assume $\mathbb{P}[\{up\}] := \pi > 0$, hence by the normalization condition $\mathbb{P}[\{up, down\}] = 1$ and by the property i), we conclude that $\mathbb{P}[\{down\}] = 1 - \pi$.

To gain intuition, we may think that it describes the uncertainty faced by an investor who is willing to invest in an economy and estimates the probability of an expansion π and that of a recession $1 - \pi$.

1.1.3 *Third: Decision theory under uncertainty, asymmetric information and strategic interaction*

The way uncertainty affects choice is more complicate and cannot in most cases be described relying on a unique, publicly known probabilistic model. Here follow two examples of elements of complexity:

(1) In the real world, uncertainty is not the same for everybody. Usually, someone has a better knowledge about future states of nature (so-called *insider*). The theory in this field studies how asymmetric information changes the equilibrium outcomes.
(2) In the real world, I know that my action will generate a reaction by other people and this will affect my result: $c = f(a, \Gamma(a), s)$, where $\Gamma(a)$ is the reaction of the other agents triggered by my action, i.e. When selecting an optimal action it is necessary to take into account the strategic interaction among decision makers.
For example, if I'm the CEO at IBM and I own 100 M\$ of IBM ordinary stocks, and I decide to sell part of these stocks, I have to consider the possible market reaction to my action.

This third framework is a more realistic picture of the real world but it is very difficult to build portfolio selection tools under these assumptions. Traditional analysis of financial markets does not consider asymmetric information and strategic interaction at the individual level: following this practice we will concentrate on decision theory under uncertainty and develop portfolio selection models that will work in this simplified context, assuming that an exogenously specified probabilistic model exists and is sufficiently informative about price behavior. Usually this simplification is a good approximation if we are (or if we face) small investors that do not have private information and cannot influence stock prices. Of course, if you face (or if you are) an insider or a large stake owner, you cannot neglect the implications of your action on other decisions.

For the interested reader, it is worth recalling that this (over-)simplified analysis of competitive behavior in financial markets should be grounded on rigorous analysis of a solution concept for a game with strategic interaction where agents form their expectations and take decisions in an interactive situation, form conjectures by putting themselves in the shoes of other intelligent agents. For a nice introduction to game theory and strategic thinking, see Battigalli *et al.* (2023).

1.2 A Paradigm for Rationality

In the absence of uncertainty, the investment decision is simplified. The following assumptions summarize a minimal set of consistency conditions that underlie the notion of economic rationality and are usually assumed to describe choice in the absence of uncertainty

A.1 The preference relation is **complete**: that means that given two consumption bundles a and b (or two consequences in our previous terminology) we can always say that either $a \succeq b$ is true, or $b \succeq a$ is true or they are both true (the agent ranks all the relevant actions). In this case, we will say that the investor is indifferent between the two choices, $a \sim b$.

A.2 The preference relation satisfy the property of **transitivity**: if $a \succeq b$ and $b \succeq c$, than it must follow that $a \succeq c$.

A.3 The preference relation is **continuous**: let $\{x_n\}$ and $\{y_n\}$ be two sequences of consumptions bundles, such that $x_n \longmapsto x$ and $y_n \longmapsto y$ (the first consequence converges to x and the second converges to y). If $x_n \succeq y_n$ for all n, then the same relationship is preserved in the limit: $x \succeq y$.

We are now ready to introduce the following formal definition:

Definition 3. A preference relation is rational if it is complete and transitive, i.e. it satisfies properties A.1 and A.2. A preference over actions A is represented by a utility function $u : A \to \mathbb{R}$ if for any $x, y \in A$ such that $x \succeq y \Rightarrow u(x) \geq u(y)$.

Then we can state:

Theorem 4. *A preference can be represented by a utility function it only if is rational.*

Proof. See Mas-Colell *et al.* (1995) Chapter 1. □

Theorem 4 states that rationality is a necessary condition for a preference to be representable by a utility function. However, rationality without continuity of the preference is not a sufficient condition for the existence of a utility representation. To show this fact, it is useful to find a counter-example.

Example 5. The so-called lexicographic preference order in $\mathbb{R}_+ \times \mathbb{R}_+$ is defined as follows: $x := (x_1, x_2) \in \mathbb{R}_+ \times \mathbb{R}_+$ dominates $y := (y_1, y_2) \in \mathbb{R}_+ \times \mathbb{R}_+$, i.e., $x \succeq_{lex} y$ if:

$$x \succeq_{lex} y \text{ if } \begin{cases} x_1 > y_1 & \text{or} \\ x_1 = y_1 & \text{and} \quad x_2 \geq y_2 \end{cases}$$

This is the usual way words are ordered in a dictionary. It is a simple exercise to prove that $\succeq_{lex}$ defines a rational preference. On the other hand, it is also possible to show that it cannot be represented by any utility function. This can be proved as follows: suppose by contradiction that there exists a utility function u representing lexicographic preferences, e.g., over two goods. Then $u(r, 1) > u(r, 0)$ must hold, so the intervals $[u(r, 0), u(r, 1)]$ must have a non-zero width. Moreover, since $u(r, 1) < u(p, 1)$ whenever $r < p$, these intervals must be disjoint for all $r \in \mathbb{R}_+$. This is not possible for an uncountable set of r-values in $\mathbb{R}_+$. Notice that a lexicographic preference does not verify A.3. Indeed, set $x_1^n = 1/n$, $x_2^n = 0$, and $y_1^n = 0$, $y_2^n = 1$ then for any n: $x^n = (x_1^n, x_2^n) \succeq y^n = (y_1^n, y_2^n)$, but $x^n \to (0,0) \preceq y^n = (y_1^n, y_2^n) \to (0,1)$.

Condition A.3 identifies a class of representable rational preferences. In fact:

Theorem 6. *Consider any rational preference that verifies* A.3. *Then there exists a continuous utility function* u *such that for any two actions* a, b *belonging to* A:

$$u(a) \geq u(b) \quad \text{if and only if } a \succeq b$$

Proof. See Mas-Colell *et al.* (1995, Chapter 3). □

In general, the utility function $u(.)$ that represents a specific preference relation $\succeq$ is not unique. In fact, we can easily find a new utility function which represents the same preference relation using the following trick: define a new utility function as $u^*(.) = G(u(.))$ where G is an increasing transformation (e.g. $G(x) = x^3$) then the increasing property implies that $u(a_1) \geq u(a_2)$ if and only if $u^*(a_1) \geq u^*(a_2)$ and therefore also $u^*(.)$ represents the same preferences, i.e., $a_1 \succeq a_2$ if and only if $u^*(a_1) \geq u^*(a_2)$. This observation proves that only the relative ranking of utility matters, while the absolute level of the utility index can be changed without altering the representation of agent preferences. A utility function unaffected by an increasing transformation is said to be *ordinal.*

1.3 Decision Theory Under Uncertainty

Decision theory under uncertainty analyzes the possible methods to describe a preference in the space of actions $a \in A$ starting from what we can observe and measure, i.e., the preferences on the domain of possible uncertain consequences C.

The decision criterion must be given by some statistical index $\mathbb{U}(a)$ over acts which aggregates preferences over consequences c_s^a in different states of nature $s = 1, \ldots S < +\infty$. Consider the following framework:

(1) We can associate to each action a a finite number of consequences, a vector of dimension $S > 0$ to each action:

$$a \to [c_1^a, \ldots, c_S^a] \in C^S$$

(2) We can assign a well defined probability $p_s := \mathbb{P}(\{\omega = s) > 0$ to the event that the final realized state ω is s. In this way, each action a can be associated to a random variable $c^a(\omega)$, which is the random function $c^a : \Omega \to \mathbb{R}$ defined by the relation $c^a(\omega) = c_\omega^a$, $\omega = 1, \ldots, S$.

As shown by the formal definition of rational choice under certainty, the definition of a rational choice over actions in the presence of uncertainty will require a careful investigation of the ordering relations in vector spaces and their representations. Since it is mathematically non-trivial and full of economic implications that are well beyond the goals of this book, we postpone its discussion to the end of this chapter, in Section 1.8.

In the meantime, we provide the mathematical definition of one specific example of rational choice criterion, the so-called expected utility:

Definition 7. We will say that an agent preference over an action $a \in A$, corresponding to the vector of consequences $c^a := [c_1^a, \ldots, c_S^a] \in C^S$, is represented by an expected utility functional $E^{\mathbb{P}}[u(\cdot)]$, if there exists a probability space $(C^S, \mathcal{A}, \mathbb{P})$ and a function $u : C \to \mathbb{R}$ such that:

$$\mathbb{U}(a) := E^{\mathbb{P}}[u(c^a(\omega))]$$

As an illustration of its use consider the following.

Example 8. Consider a lottery

Prize	Probability
500	0.2
100	0.8

and an individual with zero initial wealth. Assume that

$$u(Y) = \ln(Y)$$

Then the expected logarithmic utility of the lottery is defined by:

$$E\left[u\left(Y\right)\right] = 0.2 \cdot \ln\left(500\right) + 0.8 \cdot \ln\left(100\right) = 4.927$$

Note that the logarithmic function is concave and increasing:

$$u' = \frac{1}{Y} > 0$$

$$u'' = -\frac{1}{Y^2} < 0$$

Hence, the utility from the expected prize is given by:

$$u\left(0.2 \cdot 500 + 0.8 \cdot 100\right) = u(180) = 5.193 > 4.927$$

which is larger than the expected utility derived from playing the lottery. According to this criterion, a sure amount of money equal to the expected prize is preferred to playing lottery.

At first glance, one may think that using a utility function $\mathbb{U}\left(\cdot\right)$ is an over-complication. Why don't we simply take the expected wealth as a measure of the "utility" of this portfolio? An intuitive answer to this question has been proposed by the eighteenth-century mathematician Daniel Bernoulli called the St. Petersburg paradox.

The St. Petersburg paradox: The St. Petersburg game is played by flipping a fair coin until it comes up tails, and the total number of flips, n, determines the prize, which equals $2^n\$$. Thus if the coin comes up tails the first time, the prize is $2\$ \cdot 1 = 2\$$, and the game ends. If the coin comes up heads the first time, it is flipped again. If it comes up tails the second time, the prize is $2\$ \cdot 2 = 4\$$, and the game ends. If it comes up heads the second time, it is flipped again. And so on. There are an infinite number of possible consequences (runs of heads followed by one tail) possible. The probability of a consequence of n flips ($P(n)$) is 1 divided by 2^n, and the expected payoff of each consequence is the prize times its probability.

The following table lists these figures for the consequences where $n = 1 \dots 10$:

n	$P(n)$	Prize ($)	Expected payoff ($)
1	1/2	2	1
2	1/4	4	1
3	1/8	8	1
4	1/16	16	1
5	1/32	32	1
6	1/64	64	1
7	1/128	128	1
8	1/256	256	1
9	1/512	512	1
10	1/1024	1024	1

Observe that in this valuation, the duration of the bet, i.e., the number of coin flipping, is not relevant to the utility assessment, the agent is assumed to be indifferent to the amount of time required to achieve the final bet outcome and the preference which is represented by the log-utility is a static one.

The game's expected value is the sum of the expected payoffs of all the consequences. Since the expected payoff of each possible consequence is $1, and there are an infinite number of them, this sum is an infinite number of dollars. A rational gambler would enter a game iff the price of entry was less than the expected value. In the St. Petersburg game, any finite price of entry is smaller than the expected value of the game. Thus, the rational gambler would play no matter how large the finite entry price was. But it seems obvious that some prices are too high for a rational agent to pay to play. Many commentators agree that "few of us would pay even $25 to enter such a game." If this is correct, then something has gone wrong with the standard decision-theory calculations of the expected value above. Bernoulli proposed to replace the sum of the expected payoff in dollars by the sum of the expected utilities of each consequence.

In light of the widely accepted principle that (roughly speaking) money has a decreasing marginal utility, he proposed the logarithm of the money amount as a realistic measure of the utility of money might be given. Here are the first few lines in the table for this gamble if $u\,(TW) = \log(TW)$:

n	$P(n)$	Prize ($)	Utilities	Expected utilities
1	1/2	2	0.301	0.1505
2	1/4	4	0.602	0.1505
3	1/8	8	0.903	0.1129
4	1/16	16	1.204	0.0753
5	1/32	32	1.505	0.0470
6	1/64	64	1.806	0.0282
7	1/128	128	2.107	0.0165
8	1/256	256	2.408	0.0094
9	1/512	512	2.709	0.0053
10	1/1024	1024	3.010	0.0029

The sum of expected utilities is not infinite: it reaches a limit of about 0.60206 (worth 4$, $u\,(W) = \log\,(W) \implies W = 10^{u(W)}$). The rational gambler, then, would pay any sum less than 4$ to play.

Summing up, the game offers the possibility of huge prizes. A run of forty would, for example, pay a whopping 1.1$ trillion. Of course, this prize happens rarely: only once in about 1.1 trillion times. Half the time, the game pays only 2$, and you're 75% likely to wind up with a payment of 4$ or less. Your chances of getting more than the entry price of 25$ are less than one in 25. Very low payments are very probable, and very high ones, are very rare. It's a foolish risk to invest more than 25$ to play.

1.4 Risk Aversion

We now proceed with the formalization of the above argument on a more systematic basis. Consider the following:

Definition 9 (Fair Game). Consider a lottery Z with prizes (payoff) $\{z_1, \ldots, z_S\}$ and initial cost p (price). The lottery is fair if its expected payoff is equal to the initial cost

$$E(Z) = \sum_{s=1}^{S} \pi_s z_s$$
$$= p$$

Definition 10 (Risk Aversion). We say that an individual is **risk averse** if she refuses to play a fair game at any level of initial wealth. Formally, let $Y^{(0)}$ be the individual initial wealth and $Y_k^{(1)} = Y^{(0)} + z_k - p$. Then an agent is risk averse if:

$$E\left[u\left(Y^{(0)} + Z - p\right)\right] = \sum_{k=1}^{n} \pi_k u\left(Y_k^{(1)}\right) < u\left(Y^{(0)}\right), \quad \text{for any } Y^{(0)}$$

i.e., the utility derived from the decision to play the fair lottery is always lower than the utility derived from not playing it.

This behavioral property has a direct implication on the expression of the utility index $u(\cdot)$ representing a risk averse agent. Let's further specialize the notion of a fair game and restrict our attention to fair binary lotteries like:

Prize	Probability
h	0.5
$-h$	0.5

Such a lottery is fair, in fact, the expected payoff is $\frac{1}{2}h - \frac{1}{2}h = 0$. Then a risk-averse individual endowed with initial wealth Y refuses to play such a game, hence

$$u(Y) > \frac{1}{2}u(Y+h) + \frac{1}{2}u(Y-h)$$

which is equivalent to

$$u(Y) - u(Y-h) > u(Y+h) - u(Y)$$

Since this property must hold for any Y in the domain of definition and for any $h > 0$, it implies that the marginal utility must be

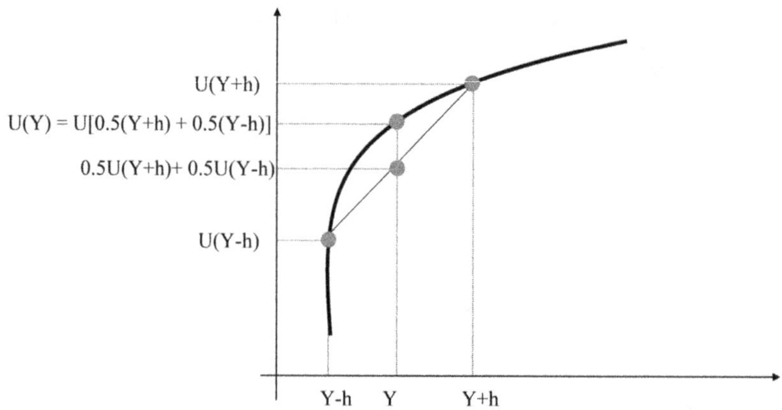

Figure 1.1. Illustration of the impact of concavity of the utility-based valuation of a fair lottery.

decreasing at any level of wealth, i.e. the utility function is concave in its domain of definition. Figure 1.1 provides a geometric illustration of the construction.

The relationship between risk aversion and concavity of the utility index u is two-way: in fact, concavity of u implies risk aversion. This is a direct implication of a well-known result known in probability as Jensen inequality. In our language, it states that given a concave $f(x)$ then, for any fair lottery L:

$$E[f(L)] < f[E(L)] \tag{1.1}$$

Consider the following example.

Example 11. A subject endowed with 100 with a utility function with the characteristics seen before can buy a ticket for the following lottery:

Prize	Probability
400	0.2
−100	0.8

Note that the lottery is fair, i.e., the expected prize of the bet is $0.2 \cdot 400 + 0.8 \cdot (-100) = 0$. Will the subject take the bet? To answer this question let's try to calculate the utility of the subject in two different scenarios, "bet" and "no bet". In the "no bet" scenario the subject has a fixed wealth of 100 and his utility will be $u(100)$

$$U(no\ bet) = u(100)$$

In the "bet" scenario his utility will be:

$$U(bet) = 0.2 \cdot u(500) + 0.8 \cdot u(0) = E[u(Y)]$$

The utility in the "no bet" scenario is exactly $u[E(Y)] = u(Y_0)$, and from the Jensen Inequality we know that for a subject with this utility function $E[u(Y)] < u[E(Y)]$, and so we can be sure that the subject will refuse to buy the ticket for this lottery.

Risk neutrality and risk propensity: We have seen that a risk-averse individual

$$u[Y + E(Z)] \geq E[u(Y + Z)]$$

for any initial wealth level Y. Nonetheless, agents can have a different attitude toward risk. For sufficiently regular utility indices, one can describe an alternative behavior of the subject by changing the assumption about (the second derivative of) the utility function:

- An agent with $u'' = 0$ is **risk neutral** and $E[u(Y)] = u[E(Y)]$: you don't care about risk. Consider a subject with the following linear utility function $u(Y) = \frac{1}{2}Y$:

$$u' = \frac{1}{2}x > 0$$

$$u'' = 0$$

$$E[u(Y)] = 0.2 \cdot \frac{1}{2} \cdot (500) + 0.8 \cdot \frac{1}{2}(100) = 90$$

$$u[E(Y)] = \frac{1}{2} \cdot (180) = 90$$

  A risk-neutral individual is perfectly indifferent about participating in a fair game: his utility in the "bet" scenario is the same as the one in the "no bet" scenario.
- An agent with $u'' > 0$ is **risk lover**. Consider a subject with the following exponential utility function $u(Y) = e^{aY}$, $a > 0$. In this case, $u''(Y) > 0$ for any Y and the risk lover individual will always

accept to participate in fair games: the Jensen inequality, in this case, can be applied with $f(x) = -u(x)$.

1.4.1 *Quantifying risk aversion*

Concavity characterizes the utility function of a risk-averse agent. Is it possible to quantify the degree of risk aversion? How can we confront two individuals and rank them based on their risk aversion?

A naive measure of risk aversion would be to look at $u''(Y)$, but unfortunately it doesn't work very well: consider two subjects with two different utility functions: $u(Y)$ and $g(Y) = B + Au(Y)$ with $A > 0$. Now these two functions describe the same preferences and rank different risky prospects exactly in the same way, but if we look at the second derivative we see that $u''(Y) \neq g''(Y) = Au''(Y)$ and we would say that the second agent is more risk-averse than the first one. To define a correct measure of risk aversion, it is necessary to introduce an index unaffected by an affine transformation. From now onward, we will assume non-satiation:

$$u' > 0 \tag{1.2}$$

The coefficient of absolute risk aversion (ARA) at the level of wealth Y is defined as

$$\mathrm{ARA}_u^Y = -\frac{u''(Y)}{u'(Y)}$$

The minus sign implies that the absolute coefficient of risk aversion is a positive number for a risk-averse agent. Now, we see that

$$\mathrm{ARA}_g^Y = -\frac{Au''(Y)}{Au'(Y)} = -\frac{u''(Y)}{u'(Y)} = \mathrm{ARA}_u^Y$$

The higher the level of ARA, the more concave will be the utility function and the higher the aversion to risk. An alternative measure of risk aversion is the so-called relative risk aversion coefficient which is defined as

$$\mathrm{RRA}_u^Y = \mathrm{ARA}_u^Y Y = -\frac{u''(Y)\,Y}{u'(Y)}$$

It measures the percentage of wealth increase an agent will require to accept a risky bet for a given initial wealth, Y. RRA_u^Y measures the elasticity of marginal utility with respect to marginal wealth. Indeed:

$$\mathrm{RRA}_u^Y = -\frac{Y}{u'} \cdot \frac{du'}{dY} = -\frac{d\ln(u'(Y))}{d\ln(Y)}$$

The basic examples of utility functions are determined by assuming constant ARA (CARA) and RRA (CRRA)

- CARA: $A \cdot (-e^{-aY}) + B \longrightarrow \mathrm{ARA}^Y_{\mathrm{ARA}} = a$.
- CRRA: $A \cdot (\frac{Y^{1-\gamma}}{1-\gamma}) + B \longrightarrow \mathrm{RRA}^Y_{\mathrm{CRRA}} = \gamma$.

Both these classes of utility functions can be obtained as limits of the so-called class of hyperbolic absolute risk aversion (HARA) utility functions:

$$\frac{\gamma}{1-\gamma}\left(\frac{aY}{\gamma} + b\right)^{1-\gamma}, \quad a > 0$$

that is defined for a range of wealth levels such that $\frac{aY}{\gamma} + b > 0$. Remarkably:

- When $\gamma = 0$, one recovers a linear utility corresponding to a risk-neutral investor.
- When $\gamma > 0$, $\gamma \neq 1$, $a = \gamma$ and $b = 0$ it describes a CRRA utility.
- When $\gamma \to 1$ the limiting expression recovers a logarithmic utility index $\log(aY + b)$.
- When $\gamma \to +\infty$ and $b = 0$ the limiting expression recovers the ARA utility function.

Usually, it is observed that the absolute risk aversion decreases with the level of wealth. Thus, the dollar amount invested in the risky asset tends to increase when the individual becomes wealthier

$$\frac{\partial \mathrm{ARA}_u^Y}{\partial Y} < 0$$

For this reason, constant relative risk aversion offers a more realistic description of normal behavior, i.e., utility of losses and gains are evaluated as a percentage of the wealth level.

1.4.2 *Certainty equivalent and risk premium*

We can define the certainty equivalent at the level of wealth Y of lottery Z as the quantity of money $CE_Y(Z)$ that gives to the investor the same level of satisfaction as the lottery itself. In other terms, it is determined by the solution to the equation:

$$E(u(Y+Z)) = u(Y + CE_Y(Z))$$

which is given by

$$CE_Y(Z) = u^{-1}(E(u(Y+Z))) - Y$$

Correspondingly, the difference between the expected prize of the lottery and its certainty equivalent

$$\Pi_Y(Z) = E(Z) - CE_Y(Z)$$

is the price discount or (risk premium) that an investor considers appropriate to sell (to buy) a lottery Z. In words, $CE_Y(Z)$ is the amount of (non-random) money that yields the same utility as the lottery Z while $\Pi_Y(Z)$ is the maximum amount of (non-random) money a risk averse investor is accepting to give up to receive, instead of the lottery Z, a cash amount equal to its expected value $E(Z)$. Note that for a zero-mean lottery, where the certainty equivalent for a risk-averse individual is negative, it holds $\Pi_Y(Z) = -CE_Y(Z)$. Thus, for a zero-mean lottery we have that $\Pi_Y(Z)$ is the amount of (non-random) money an investor is willing to pay to avoid the lottery Z, so that it captures the idea of the cost of risk.

Since risk aversion is equivalent to concavity of u, it follows immediately that for a risk-averse individual, the risk compensation is positive, $\Pi_Y(Z) > 0$, or equivalently the certainty equivalent is lower than the (lottery) expected value ($CE_Y(Z) < E(Z)$), as it happens in the example.

In the following, we aim to show that the above abstract considerations have important practical implications. In particular, they may be used to rationalize the institutional role of some financial intermediaries and some industry practices typical of the financial sector.

1.5 Insurance Pricing Principle

The fact that for a risk-averse investor, the risk compensation is positive, $\Pi_Y(Z) > 0$, has several important implications. In particular, it lies at the basis of the insurance business. In the following, we show that a risk-neutral provider may profitably offer protection to non-systematic risk, i.e., a reimbursement contingent on the occurrence of an unfavorable outcome, to a pool of well-diversified investors.

To illustrate the general pricing principle, consider the following example: The insurer is assumed to be risk-neutral and will try to sell full coverage to car accidents to the largest possible well-diversified pool of car owners. Let's consider a simple example of casualty and property insurance where a homogeneous pool of individuals is planning to insure cars, each with a value of $Y_0 = 20$K\$ (unit K\$ corresponds to thousands of dollars). For simplicity, suppose that the car represents the only wealth for each individual. To avoid this risk, each individual will buy an insurance contract that, in case of an accident, will restore the initial car value. There is a 10% probability that an accident could reduce the property value to 5K\$. Diversification in this case requires that the likelihood that the pool of insured have an accident are approximately independent across different cars and in the limit of a large pool the estimated probability approximates the effective fraction of cars in the pool that will suffer a car accident and will have to be reimbursed by the insurance company. Hence, the insurance company estimates an expected payment per insured car of 1.5K\$ (15K\$ of damage and a probability of 10% to be involved in a car crash). Hence the minimum premium to be charged by the insurance to grant the coverage of each car and break-even is equal to 1.5K\$. A natural question arises: will the car owner be willing to pay an insurance premium higher than the expected damage? The higher the premium that the insurance company can charge, the higher the room for running a profitable business that improves welfare by reducing the overall risk exposures by pooling and diversification.

It is easy to verify that the maximum premium that a risk-averse individual will accept to pay is higher than the break-even premium of 1.5K$ observing that in a risky situation, the certainty equivalent is lower than the expected value. In fact:

$$E\left[u\left(Y\right)\right] < u\left[E\left(Y\right)\right]$$
$$0.9 \times u\left(20\right) + 0.1 \times u\left(5\right) < u\left[0.9 \times 20 + 0.1 \times 5\right]$$
$$0.9 \times u\left(20\right) + 0.1 \times u\left(5\right) < u\left[18.5\right]$$

Hence, if the insurance company charges a premium of 1.5K$, this still leaves the car owner with a higher utility than the utility she would achieve by driving the car without insurance coverage. If the insurance company wants to evaluate the maximum premium that can be charged, it should determine the certainty equivalent for the investor solving the equation

$$E\left[u\left(Y\right)\right] = u\left[CE_0\left(Y\right)\right] \tag{1.3}$$

The amount of money $CE_0\left(Y\right)$ generates for the investor the same utility that is derived from driving the car in the absence of insurance coverage. Hence, the maximum insurance premium that can be charged by the insurance company is determined by the difference between the initial car value and the certainty equivalent. This insurance premium can be decomposed into two parts: the expected loss EL and the risk compensation Π (or premium) received by the insurance:

$$EL = Y_0 - E\left(Y\right)$$
$$\Pi = E\left(Y\right) - CE_0\left(Y\right)$$

This last component is an additional amount of money, not justified by the expected loss of a car accident, that the car owner is accepting to pay in order to avoid the uncertainty deriving from the risk of suffering a car accident.

Assume that an individual has a negative exponential utility function with risk aversion equal to 0.1 (assuming that wealth is expressed in thousands of dollars K$. Then

$$E\left[u\left(Y\right)\right] = 0.9 \times -e^{-0.1 \cdot 20} + 0.1 \times -e^{-0.1 \cdot 5} = -0.182\,45$$

which is smaller than

$$u\left[E\left(Y\right)\right] = -e^{-0.1 \cdot 18.5} = -0.157\,24$$

The maximum insurance premium that the insurance company can charge for this contract is computed as follows. First, we determine the sure amount of money that generates for the investor the same utility as the car without insurance. It is given by 17.013K\$. In fact

$$\begin{aligned} u\left[CE_0\left(Y\right)\right] &= E\left[u\left(Y\right)\right] \\ -e^{-0.1x} &= -0.182\,45 \\ x &= 17.013\text{K\$} \end{aligned}$$

Then the insurance company can sell coverage to a large, well-diversified pool of car holders and charge up to a maximum premium equal to 20K\$ – 17.013K\$ = 2.987K\$. This amount can be decomposed into expected loss and risk compensation:

- $EL = Y_0 - E\left(Y\right) = 20\text{K\$} - 18.5\text{K\$} = 1.5\text{K\$}$.
- $\Pi = E\left(Y\right) - CE_0\left(Y\right) = 1.487\text{K\$}$.

The insurance company will set up a reserve with the amount of EL to be ready to reimburse the policyholder in case of a car accident. The residual amount Π is still available to cover the administrative costs and produce a profit. The exact insurance selling price will in general depend on the bargaining power that the two parties, the seller and the buyer of insurance coverage.

1.6 The Portfolio Problem

The standard expected utility model plays a central role in the formulation in the definition of the optimal portfolio allocation problem in a market where several securities with uncertain payoffs are traded. Let us start by considering the simplest framework.

1.6.1 *Two securities and two states of the world*

Let $E^{\mathbb{P}}\left[U\left(Y_1^a\left(\omega\right)\right)\right]$ represent the investor's preference, where U is a concave increasing function. Let Y_0 be her initial wealth, $\tilde{r}\left(\omega\right)$ is the return of the risky asset, r_f is the risk free return and a_0, (a) is the amount of money invested in the riskless (risky) asset. To find the optimal decision, the agent will maximize its expected utility conditional on the budget constraint

$$\begin{aligned}
&\underset{(a_0,a)}{\text{Max}}\ E^{\mathbb{P}}\left[U\left(Y_1^a\left(\omega\right)\right)\right] \\
Y_0 &= a_0 + a \\
Y_1^a\left(\omega\right) &= \left(1+r_f\right)a_0 + \left(1+\tilde{r}\left(\omega\right)\right)a
\end{aligned}$$

Let's write explicitly this optimization problem in the framework where the probability space is the simplest one with only two states of nature, *up*, which will correspond to an expansionary period, and *down* which will correspond to a recession. Let π be the probability of the expansion. Then we can express the objective function as

$$\begin{aligned}
E^{\mathbb{P}}\left[U\left(Y_1^a\left(\omega\right)\right)\right] &= \pi U\left(Y_1^a\left(u\right)\right) + \left(1-\pi\right)U\left(Y_1^a\left(d\right)\right) \\
&= \pi \times U\left[\left(1+r_f\right)Y_0 + \left(\tilde{r}\left(u\right) - r_f\right)a\right] \\
&\quad + \left(1-\pi\right) \times U\left[\left(1+r_f\right)Y_0 + \left(\tilde{r}\left(d\right) - r_f\right)a\right]
\end{aligned}$$

To maximize the expected utility we have to find the first-order condition (FOC). By the chain rule for derivatives: if $f\left(x\right) = h\left[g\left(x\right)\right]$ then $f'\left(x\right) = h'\left[g\left(x\right)\right] \cdot g'\left(x\right)$

$$\pi \times U'\left(Y_1^{a,u}\right) \times \frac{dY_1^{a,u}}{da} + \left(1-\pi\right) \times U'\left(Y_1^{a,d}\right) \times \frac{dY_1^{a,d}}{da} = 0$$

Since

$$\frac{dY_1^i\left(a\right)}{da} = \left(r^i - r_f\right)$$

you can rewrite the optimality condition as

$$\pi \times U'\left(Y_1^{a,u}\right) \times \left(r^u - r_f\right) + \left(1-\pi\right) \times U'\left(Y_1^{a,d}\right) \times \left(r^d - r_f\right) = 0$$

and the optimal allocation a^* is determined by the FOC equation:

$$E^{\mathbb{P}}\left[U'\left(Y_1^{a^*}\left(\omega\right)\right) \cdot \left(\tilde{r} - r_f\right)\right] = 0 \tag{1.4}$$

where U' denotes the marginal utility. This is the fundamental equation of portfolio choice. Consider a logarithmic utility function

$$U\left(Y\right) = \ln\left(Y\right), \quad U'\left(Y\right) = \frac{1}{Y}, \quad U''\left(W\right) = -\frac{1}{Y^2}$$

$$\pi = \frac{1}{2}, \quad r_f = 2\%, \quad r^u = 7.3\%, \quad r^d = -3\%, \quad Y_0 = 10\text{K\$}$$

Then the FOC reads:

$$\pi \times U'\left(Y_1^u\right) \times \left(r^u - r_f\right) + (1-\pi) \times U'(Y_1^d) \times \left(r^d - r_f\right) = 0$$

$$\frac{1}{2} \times \frac{1}{(1+0.02) \times 10 + 0.053 \times a} \times 0.053$$
$$+\frac{1}{2} \times \frac{1}{(1+0.02) \times 10 - 0.05 \times a} \times (-0.05) = 0$$

Solving the equation, you can verify that the optimal strategy corresponds to invest, out of an initial endowment of 10 K\$, 5.7736 K\$. in the risky asset.

1.6.2 *The case with N assets*

It is useful to extend the above argument to the case with S states of the world and $N+1$ securities (a risk-free asset and N risky securities). The corresponding problem becomes

$$\underset{a_i}{\text{Max}} E^{\mathbb{P}}\left[U\left(Y_1^a\left(\omega\right)\right)\right]$$

$$\sum_{n=0}^{N} a_n = Y_0$$

$$\tilde{Y}_1^a\left(\omega\right) = a_0\left(1 + r_f\right) + a_1\left(1 + \tilde{r}_1\left(\omega\right)\right)$$
$$+a_2\left(1 + \tilde{r}_2\left(\omega\right)\right) + \cdots + a_N\left(1 + \tilde{r}_N\left(\omega\right)\right)$$

where a_n is the amount of dollars invested in stock n. Security 0 is the risk-free one and its terminal value does not depend on the realized state of the world. We can maximize this function, under the budget constraint using the standard Lagrangian equation

$$L = E^{\mathbb{P}}\left[U\left(Y_1^a\left(\omega\right)\right)\right] + \lambda\left(Y_0 - a_0 - a_1 \cdots - a_n\right)$$

The set of FOC is the following

$$\pi_1 U'\left(Y_1^a(1)\right) \frac{dY_1^a(1)}{da_n} + \pi_2 U'\left(Y_1^a(2)\right) \frac{dY_1^a(2)}{da_n}$$
$$+ \cdots + \pi_S U'\left(Y_1^a(S)\right) \frac{dY_1^a(S)}{da_n} = \lambda$$

for $n = 0, \ldots, N$. Hence, the resulting FOC are:

$$E\big[U'\big(Y_1^a(\omega)\big)\big](1 + r_f) = \lambda$$
$$E\big[U'\big(Y_1^a(\omega)\big)(1 + \tilde{r}_n)\big] = \lambda, \quad n = 1, \ldots, N$$

and their difference implies the FOC:

$$E\big[U'(Y_1)(\tilde{r}_n - r_f)\big] = 0, \quad n = 1, \ldots, N \tag{1.5}$$

This condition can be interpreted as follows: the optimal allocation in security n is determined by the condition that at the optimum the variation of utility determined by a marginal change of the allocation is zero. Indeed, if $E[U'(\tilde{Y}_1)(\tilde{r}_n - r_f)] < 0$, one could increase the expected utility by selling some amount of n and investing the proceeds in the risk-free asset, and if $E[U'(\tilde{Y}_1)(\tilde{r}_n - r_f)] > 0$ one could increase the expected utility by doing the opposite.

The resulting equation is very informative and provides important information about the optimal allocation of an expected utility maximizer. Consider the case of a single risky asset. Then:

Theorem 12. *For a non-satiated risk-averse investor* $E(\tilde{r} - r_f) > 0$ *if and only if* $a > 0$.

Proof. Consider that the FOC says that we will invest in a risky asset only if the marginal utility produced by this change is positive. We can consider the case of a risk-averse individual with a portfolio 100% risk-free. This subject will refuse to take a long position if and only if

$$E\left[U'(Y_0(1 + r_f))(\tilde{r} - r_f)\right] \leq 0$$

Since the initial wealth is non-stochastic, one can rewrite the above expression as

$$U'[Y_0(1 + r_f)] \times E[(\tilde{r} - r_f)] \leq 0$$

By non-satiation, $U'[Y_0(1 + r_f)] > 0$ hence $E[(\tilde{r} - r_f)] \leq 0$. □

This result indicates that, whatever the level of risk aversion and the level of wealth, it is always optimal to invest a fraction of wealth in a risk investment with a positive expected return. When compared with empirical evidence, this conclusion generates a puzzle. In fact, a large fraction of the population does not participate in capital markets even in the presence of robust statistical evidence showing that the risk premium of a simple investment in the stock market index produces a positive risk premium.

1.7 Subjective Valuation

The above considerations show that the first-order condition selects the optimal allocation, i.e. optimal quantities of securities to be held in the portfolio of a rational investor. Remarkably, the same condition shapes also a key equation for valuation theory. In particular, consider the subjective valuation of a random cash flow by a rational investor. First of all, it is useful to recall the accounting relationship that sets the relationship between the future cash-flows $\delta_1(\omega)$ and the current price P_0 under the historical measure $\mathbb{P}$. The simple random return is defined by

$$\widetilde{r}(\omega) = \frac{\delta_1(\omega)}{P_0} - 1 \tag{1.6}$$

Then, taking the $\mathbb{P}$-expectation:

$$\mu := E^{\mathbb{P}}[\widetilde{r}(\omega)] = \frac{E^{\mathbb{P}}[\delta_1(\omega)]}{P_0} - 1$$

that can be rearranged as the present value relationship:

$$P_0 = \frac{E^{\mathbb{P}}[\delta_1(\omega)]}{1+\mu}$$

This equation relates the discounted future expected cash flows to the current price. Now, we show that assuming the investor selects the optimal allocation a^* relying on the first-order optimality condition, it is possible to derive an alternative valuation equation. From eq. (1.5) it is immediate to derive the following relation:

$$\frac{E^{\mathbb{P}}\left[U'\left(Y_1^{a^*}(\omega)\right)(1+\tilde{r})\right]}{E^{\mathbb{P}}\left[U'\left(Y_1^{a^*}(\omega)\right)\right]} = (1+r_f)$$

It is then useful to introduce a random variable m, which is usually called *pricing kernel* or *price deflator* associated to the utility U.

It is defined for each state of nature by

$$m^U(\omega) := \frac{U'\left(Y_1^{a^*}(\omega)\right)}{E^{\mathbb{P}}\left[U'\left(Y_1^{a^*}(\omega)\right)\right]}$$

For a non-satiated investor, (positive $U'\left(Y_1^{a^*}(\omega)\right) > 0$) the definition implies $m^U(\omega) > 0$ and

$$E^{\mathbb{P}}\left[m^U(\omega)\right] = 1$$

These two properties imply that for each selection of a price deflator, it is possible to define a new measure

$$\mathbb{Q}^U(\{\omega\}) := m^U(\omega)\,\mathbb{P}(\{\omega\})$$

It is usually named the subjective risk-neutral measure. In fact, the FOC implies that:

$$E^{\mathbb{Q}^U}[\tilde{r}] = E^{\mathbb{P}}\left[m^U\tilde{r}\right] = r_f \tag{1.7}$$

i.e., the expected return under the newly defined measure $\mathbb{Q}^U$ for each security equals the risk-free rate of return.

Note that the probabilities $\mathbb{Q}^U$ embed the real historical probabilities $\mathbb{P}(\{\omega\})$ and a preference dependent factor $m^U(\omega)$. Inserting again the accounting identity (1.6) in eq. (1.7), it is immediate to conclude that the first order condition (1.4) is equivalent to the so-called (subjective) risk-neutral valuation formula:

$$P_0 = \frac{E^{\mathbb{Q}^U}[\delta_1(\omega)]}{1+r_f}$$

which is the so-called risk-neutral discounted valuation formula. Notice that by construction the two valuation formulas are equivalent. In this way, we proved the following:

Theorem 13. *Consider a probability space $(\Omega, \mathcal{A}, \mathbb{P})$ and a security producing a cash flow $\delta_1(\omega)$ at time 1. Then the price of the security is given by the discounted cash flow formula:*

$$P_0 = \frac{E^{\mathbb{P}}[\delta_1(\omega)]}{1+\mu}$$

Assume an investor selects the allocation according to a utility maximization principle. Then Eq. (1.4) *implies that the price of each security is also equal to the risk-neutral discounted cash flow formula:*

$$P_0 = \frac{E^{\mathbb{Q}^U}\left[\delta_1\left(\omega\right)\right]}{1+r_f}$$

In the $\mathbb{P}$-discounted cash flow formula, the price depends on the $\mathbb{P}$-expectation of the cash flows and on the $\mathbb{P}$-expectation of the security rate of return. In the $\mathbb{Q}$-discounted cash flow formula, the FOC produces sufficient information to compute the subjective price for each security belonging to the investor's opportunity set as a function of a unique rate of return, the risk-free one and a positive random variable, the pricing kernel, which is proportional to the marginal utility of the investor. Hence, the price computed relying on the risk-neutral valuation formula depends on subjective preference.

In the next chapters, we will discuss the additional assumptions required to guarantee that the resulting price is fair, i.e., it is compatible with a real market transaction between a buyer and a seller accepting to exchange the security.

To better understand the mechanics of computation of the pricing kernel, let's go back for a minute to the simplified scenario with two states of the world (u, d). In this case, we have that:

$$E^{\mathbb{P}}\left[m\left(1+\tilde{r}\right)\right] = \left(1+r_f\right)$$
$$\pi^u \times m^u \times \left(1+r^u\right) + \pi^d \times m^d \times \left(1+r^d\right) = \left(1+r_f\right)$$

where $\pi^d = 1 - \pi^u$ and

$$m^u = \frac{U'\left(Y_1^u\right)}{E^{\mathbb{P}}\left[U'(\tilde{Y}_1)\right]} \quad \text{and} \quad m^d = \frac{U'\left(Y_1^d\right)}{E^{\mathbb{P}}\left[U'(\tilde{Y}_1)\right]}$$

where $E^{\mathbb{P}}\left[U'(Y_1)\right] = \pi^u \times U'\left(Y_1^u\right) + \pi^d \times U'\left(Y_1^d\right)$. It is very easy to verify that

$$E^{\mathbb{P}}\left[m\right] = 1$$
$$\pi^u \times m^u + \pi^d \times m^d = 1$$
$$\frac{\pi^u \times U'\left(Y_1^u\right)}{\pi^u \times U'\left(Y_1^u\right) + \pi^d \times U'\left(Y_1^d\right)} + \frac{\pi^d \times U'\left(Y_1^d\right)}{\pi^u \times U'\left(Y_1^u\right) + \pi^d \times U'\left(Y_1^d\right)} = 1$$

Let's focus now on the economic interpretation of m_s: this is the ratio between the marginal utility of wealth in the state of the world s and the average marginal utility of wealth in all the states of the world. A large number would show that for me wealth is particularly "valuable" in this state of the world. Given the decreasing marginal utility of wealth implied in the concavity of the utility function, we know that in state s we are relatively poorer and any additional marginal amount of wealth has a significant impact on our utility. We can now define a new quantity $q_s = m_s \pi_s$. We know that

$$\sum_{s=1}^{S} q_s = \sum_{s=1}^{S} m_s \pi_s = 1$$
$$m_s \pi_s \geq 0 \quad \forall s = 1, \ldots, S$$

So, we can interpret q_s as a new probability measure of the state of the world s. The characterizing feature of this probability measure is that when I calculate the expected return for every risky asset I get the risk free rate:

$$\pi^u \times m^u \times (1 + r^u) + \pi^d \times m^d \times (1 + r^d) = (1 + r_f)$$
$$q^u \times (1 + r^u) + q^d \times (1 + r^d) = (1 + r_f)$$

How is this possible? We can understand this apparent contradiction remembering that:

- A risky asset can be seen as a vector of payoffs in the different states of the world.
- We give more importance (and so we are willing to pay more) to securities that pay high payoffs in states of the world where the marginal utility of wealth is higher.
- These securities will have higher prices and lower expected returns just for this differential preference for wealth in different states of the world.
- Preferences for wealth in different states of the world are included in the risk-neutral probabilities that you use to weigh the different states of the world.
- The resulting risk-neutral expectation must be discounted using the risk-free rate prevailing in the market.

Finally, we define the quantity

$$AD_s := \frac{m_s \pi_s}{(1 + r_f)}, \quad s = 1, \ldots, S$$

It is the price (positive for a non-satiated investor) that the investor is willing to pay for a security that generates a marginal increase in wealth in state of the world s and no change of wealth in other states of the world. These assets are called "Pure Securities" or "Arrow–Debreu Securities".

1.7.1 *A numerical example*

An investor (with a logarithmic utility function) has a portfolio of real assets (for example real estate properties) whose next period value has the following distribution:

S	Y_1^s
u	10000
d	7000

The two states of the world have the same probability. The investor can buy one of the two listed risky assets (A and B) whose terminal values follow the following distribution:

S	A_1^s	B_1^s
u	1	0.5
d	0.5	1

Problem 14. *How much is the investor willing to pay for the two assets?*

We can see how the expected utility of the investor changes when the two assets are added to the initial portfolio.

If we consider the initial risky situation the expected utility is:

$$E^{\mathbb{P}}\left[U\left(Y\right)\right] = \frac{1}{2}\ln\left(Y_1^u\right) + \frac{1}{2}\ln\left(Y_1^d\right)$$
$$E^{\mathbb{P}}\left[U\left(Y\right)\right] = \frac{1}{2}\ln\left(10000\right) + \frac{1}{2}\ln\left(7000\right) = 9.032003$$

and the certain equivalent is

$$E^{\mathbb{P}}\left[U\left(Y\right)\right] = U\left(CE\right)$$
$$9.157660 = \ln\left(CE\right)$$
$$CE\left(Y\right) = \exp\left(9.032003\right) = 8366.600$$

Now let's consider what happens if the investor buys the security A

$$E^{\mathbb{P}}\left[U\left(Y + A\right)\right] = \frac{1}{2}\ln\left(10001\right) + \frac{1}{2}\ln\left(7000.5\right) = 9.032089$$
$$CE\left(Y + A\right) = \exp\left(9.032089\right) = 8367.317$$

We can consider the marginal price of A as the additional amount that the investor is willing to pay in addition to its original wealth to buy the bet. It is given by the difference between the two certain equivalents:

$$P_A = CE\left(Y + A\right) - CE\left(Y\right) = 0.717$$

For security B we have that

$$E^{\mathbb{P}}\left[U\left(Y + B\right)\right] = \frac{1}{2}\ln\left(10000.5\right) + \frac{1}{2}\ln\left(7001\right) = 9.032099$$
$$CE\left(Y + B\right) = \exp\left(9.032099\right) = 8367.407$$
$$P_B = CE\left(Y + B\right) - CE\left(Y\right) = 0.807$$

The investor is willing to pay more for security B because the payoff distribution reduces the volatility of the terminal wealth. Security B can be seen as an insurance asset since it reduces the risk of the initial endowment.

Given these prices, we can calculate the expected returns of the two risky assets

$$\begin{aligned} E^{\mathbb{P}}(r_A) &= \pi^u \times \frac{A_1^u - P_A}{P_A} + \pi^d \times \frac{A_1^d - P_A}{P_A} \\ &= \frac{1}{2} \times \frac{1 - 0.717}{0.717} + \frac{1}{2} \times \frac{0.5 - 0.717}{0.717} = 4.583\% \end{aligned}$$

$$\begin{aligned} E^{\mathbb{P}}(r_B) &= \pi^u \times \frac{B_1^u - P_B}{P_B} + \pi^d \times \frac{B_1^d - P_B}{P_B} \\ &= \frac{1}{2} \times \frac{0.5 - 0.807}{0.807} + \frac{1}{2} \times \frac{1 - 0.807}{0.807} = -7.037\% \end{aligned}$$

Remark. Do not be surprised that the expected returns are, sometimes, negative. These results stem from the choice of the logarithmic utility function and even if they seem to be a bit unrealistic they still can be used in our demonstration.

Problem 15. *How can we estimate the risk-neutral probabilities in this system?*

We know that

$$\begin{aligned} q^u &= \pi^u \times m^u \quad \text{and} \quad q^d = \pi^d \times m^d \\ q^u &= \pi^u \times \frac{U'(Y^u)}{E^{\mathbb{P}}[U'(Y)]} \quad \text{and} \quad q^d = \pi^d \times \frac{U'(Y^d)}{E^{\mathbb{P}}[U'(Y)]} \end{aligned}$$

given the logarithmic utility function we have that

$$\begin{aligned} U'(Y^u) &= \frac{1}{10000} = 0.000100 \\ U'(Y^d) &= \frac{1}{7000} = 0.000143 \\ E^{\mathbb{P}}[U'(Y)] &= \frac{1}{2} \times 0.0001 + \frac{1}{2} \times 0.000143 = 0.000\,121 \end{aligned}$$

Hence, we conclude that

$$m^u = \frac{0.0001}{0.000\,121} = 0.824 \quad \text{and} \quad m^d = \frac{0.000143}{0.000\,121} = 1.176$$

As it should be expected, the relative value of one extra dollar is higher in the recessionary state:

$$q^u = \frac{1}{2} \times 0.824 = 0.412$$

$$q^d = \frac{1}{2} \times 1.176 = 0.588$$

The new probabilities incorporate the different marginal utility of wealth in the two states of the world. When you calculate average returns or payoff under the new probability measure you give more importance to what is paid in the state of the world d because in that scenario, you are poorer and give a greater value to wealth.

Problem 16. *What is the expected return of the two assets under the new probability measure?*

$$\begin{aligned} E^{\mathbb{Q}}(r_A) &= q^u \times \frac{A_1^u - P_A}{P_A} + q^d \times \frac{A_1^d - P_A}{P_A} \\ &= 0.412 \times \frac{1 - 0.717}{0.717} + 0.588 \times \frac{0.5 - 0.717}{0.717} = -1.569\% \\ E^{\mathbb{Q}}(r_B) &= q^u \times \frac{B_1^u - P_B}{P_B} + q^d \times \frac{B_1^d - P_B}{P_B} \\ &= 0.412 \times \frac{0.5 - 0.807}{0.807} + 0.588 \times \frac{1 - 0.807}{0.807} = -1.569\% \end{aligned}$$

We see that under the new probability measure the two assets have the same return.

Problem 17. *How can we interpret the return of the assets under the risk-neutral probability measure?*

Let's consider a risk-free asset that produces a next-period value of 0.75 in every possible state of nature. The price of this asset is

$$E^{\mathbb{P}}[U(Y + RF)] = \frac{1}{2}\ln(10000.75) + \frac{1}{2}\ln(7000.75) = 9.032094$$

$$CE(Y + RF) = \exp(9.032094) = 8367.362$$

At the margin, its price will be

$$P_{RF} = CE(Y + RF) - CE(Y) = 0.762$$

and the corresponding return is:

$$rf = \frac{RF - P_{RF}}{P_{RF}} = \frac{0.75 - 0.762}{0.762} = -1.569\%$$

As expected, the return of the risky assets under the risk-neutral probabilities are equal to the return of a risk-free asset.

The above computation highlighted that in the limit of small amounts (in the limit where the bets do not affect the total wealth of the investor) the marginal valuations of the agent can be used to define the corresponding subjective risk-neutral probability.

1.8 Expected Utility Reloaded

The past sections have shown that the characterization of a single behavioral feature, risk aversion, as represented by the degree of concavity of the utility index u within the expected utility functional $\mathbb{U}$, may provide a lot of insights on how agents take their financial decisions and shape market reactions to new information about cash-flows.

It is important to understand that the intuitive approach we have previously adopted in this chapter is not satisfactory from a scientific point of view. In fact, the assumption that the expected utility provides an appropriate description of agents' behavior is at present not properly motivated and hard if not impossible to be tested empirically.

The proper framework to fill this gap is provided by decision theory, the branch of social science that explores the theoretical underpinnings of human decision-making and its quantitative description.

While you cannot directly observe the shape of the utility function, you may try to elicit preference orders by observing the agent's choice. After the preference order, if any, is properly characterized, you can address the problem of providing a representation of the corresponding order in terms of a utility function. then a satisfactory model of choice is produced when both these goals are met.

J. Von Neumann and O. Morgenstern in 1953, see Von Neumann and Morgenstern (2007), were able to produce a proper axiomatic foundation for the use of the expected utility functional identifying the (behavioral) properties that a preference relationship must possess to be represented by an expected utility function. In the following, we sketch their construction. Despite its formal complexity, we stress that it is necessary to relate the information that can be collected to individual preferences by adopting an expected utility function within a quantitative model of the financial decision process. As a first step, let us associate a finite probability space with a finite number of outcomes to a space of lotteries and introduce an operation of composition of lotteries as follows:

Definition 18. A simple lottery is defined by a vector $L := (p_1^L, \ldots, p_S^L) \in \mathbb{R}^S$ where $p_s^L \geq 0$ for any $s = 1, \ldots, S$ and $\sum_{s=1}^S p_s^L = 1$.

- A simple lottery L_k^B is said to be a binary lottery when no more than two outcomes have a non-zero probability.
- A K-compound of simple lotteries is defined by: $(L_1, \ldots, L_K, \alpha_1, \ldots, \alpha_K)$ a collection of K simple lotteries and a collection of probabilities $\alpha_1, \ldots, \alpha_K, \alpha_k \geq 0$, and $\sum_{k=1}^K \alpha_k = 1$ such that the simple lottery $L_k := (p_1^k, \ldots, p_S^k)$ is played with probability α_k.

Observe that the K-compounding of simple lotteries $(L_1, \ldots, L_K, \alpha_1, \ldots, \alpha_K)$ is an operation that is internal within the set of simple lotteries. In fact, the simple lottery resulting from K-compounding will be denoted by

$$L^{\text{Comp}} := \sum_{k=1}^K \alpha_k L_k$$

and is the one defined as follows:

$$L^{\text{Comp}} = \left(p_1^{\text{Comp}}, \ldots, p_S^{\text{Comp}}\right)$$

$$p_s^{\text{Comp}} := \sum_{k=1}^K \alpha_k p_s^k \quad \text{for any } s = 1, \ldots, S$$

Then, it is straightforward to show that:

Lemma 19. *Any simple lottery L can be always represented as the K-compounding of simple binary lotteries:* $L = \sum_{k=1}^K \alpha_k^B L_k^B$.

This conclusion will turn to be very useful to simplify the representation of the preference. It shows that, provided an agent is able to efficiently manage the probabilistic implications of *K-compunding*, her attitudes toward choice among a finite number of alternatives are revealed by her decisions over binary lotteries.

We are now ready to build an expected utility representation for a preference with respect to actions in the presence of uncertainty considering a construction that is inspired by the one proposed originally by Von Neumann and Morgenstern (1953). The final goal is to consider an expected utility representation over acts $a \in A$ of the form:

$$\begin{aligned}\mathbb{U}[a] &= \sum_{\omega \in \Omega} E^{\mathbb{P}}[u(c^a(\omega))] = \sum_{s=1}^{S} \mathbb{P}[\{\omega = s\}]\, u(c^a(\omega)) \\ &= \sum_{s=1}^{S} p_s u(c_s^a)\end{aligned}$$

To achieve this result, we need to complete the following two steps:

(1) We develop an expected utility representation over special "simple" binary actions $a^B \in A^B \subset A$ that can be represented as a simple a binary lottery where the two outcomes are associated to prizes corresponding to two consequences $x,\ y \in C$.
(2) The expected utility representation for a generic action, $a \in A$, when the underlying state space has S states, is derived imposing linearity of the utility representation with respect to the decomposition of generic actions in simple binary actions a^B.

1.8.1 *Step 1: Choice over binary actions*

The notation $a^B := (x, y, \pi)$ will represent an act whose consequence is $x \in C$ with a probability π and $y \in C$ with a probability $1 - \pi$. Then, in order to develop a coherent decision approach for this model, the following properties are assumed to hold:

P1 $(x, y, 1) = x \in C$.
P2 $(x, y, \pi) = (y, x, 1 - \pi)$.
P3 Let (x, y, π) be a binary act and $z = (x, y, \tau)$, then $(x, z, \pi) := (x, y, \pi + (1 - \pi)\tau)$ (see Fig. 1.2).

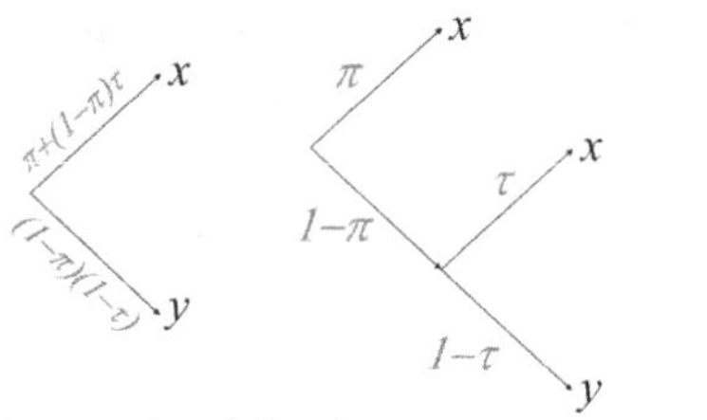

Figure 1.2. Lotteries which are equivalent under assumption P3.

This last assumption informs us that agents are concerned only with the cumulative probability of each outcome. Following Von Neumann and Morgenstern, we assume that preference relations on binary acts satisfy:

C.1 The preferences are complete and transitive.
C.2 The preferences are continuous.
C.3 The preferences satisfy the property of independence of irrelevant alternatives: $y \succeq z$ if and only if $(x, y, \pi) \succeq (x, z, \pi)$.
C.4 We also assume that in the world of possible acts there exists a best outcome b and a worst outcome w.

From C.1–C.4 we can draw two very important consequences:

C.I Let x, k, z be binary actions for which $x \succeq k \succeq z$. Then there exist a probability π such that $(x, z, \pi) \sim k$ ($\sim$ denotes indifference).
C.II Let $x \succ y$ ($\succ$ denotes strict preference), then $(x, y, \pi_1) \succeq (x, y, \pi_2)$ if and only if $\pi_1 \geq \pi_2$.

We are now ready to prove the following:

Theorem 20. *If* C.1 *to* C.4 *are satisfied, then there exists a utility function defined on the binary actions space such that*

$$\mathbb{U}\left[(x, y, \pi)\right] = \pi u(x) + (1 - \pi) u(y) \tag{1.8}$$

where u is a utility index over consequences.

Proof. Since any $x \in C$ is a special binary act by C.1, we know that continuity and transitivity imply the existence of a utility index $u(x)$ over sure consequences. Without loss of generality we denote by b the best lottery and by w the worst lottery and without loss of generality normalize $\mathbb{U}[b] = 1$, $\mathbb{U}[w] = 0$. Then by C.I and C.II for any binary act z there exists a unique π_z such that:

$$\mathbb{U}[z] = \pi_z \mathbb{U}[b] + (1 - \pi_z) \mathbb{U}[w] = \pi_z$$

Note that by definition of a binary act, there exist $x^z, y^z \in C$ such that $z = (x^z, y^z, \pi)$. Then there exist π_{x^z} and π_{y^z} such that:

$$\begin{aligned}(x^z, y^z, \pi) &\sim ((b, w, \pi_{x^z}),\ (b, w, \pi_{y^z}), \pi) \\ &\sim (b, w, \pi\pi_{x^z} + (1 - \pi)\pi_{y^z})\end{aligned}$$

hence,

$$\mathbb{U}[(x^z, y^z, \pi)] = \pi_z = \pi u(x^z) + (1 - \pi) u(y^z)$$

and Theorem 20 for binary actions is proved. □

1.8.2 *Step 2: Deriving the expected utility representation in a generic state space with S states*

Consider the following:

Definition 21. A utility function over lotteries has an expected utility representation if there exist $(u_1, \ldots, u_S)$ such that

$$U(L) = \sum_{s=1}^{S} p_s^L u_s$$

for any simple lottery L.

Then you can prove:

Proposition 22. *A utility function over lotteries has an expected utility representation if and only if it is linear in the space of simple lotteries, i.e., for any K-compounding $L^{\text{comp}} = (L_1, \ldots L_K, \alpha_1, \ldots, \alpha_K)$:*

$$U(L^{\text{comp}}) = U\left(\sum_{k=1}^{K} \alpha_k L_k\right) = \sum_{k=1}^{K} \alpha_k U(L_k)$$

Proof. See Mas-Colell *et al.* (1995, Chapter 3). □

Observe that the linear decomposition property with respect to compounding of lotteries, is an extension to a generic lottery of the property $P3$. This result highlights also that the property to be an expected utility functional over lotteries is a property that is not ordinal, i.e., it is not preserved by any increasing transformation, but it is *cardinal*, i.e., it depends and implies the existence of a linear vector space structure in the space of the lotteries. For this reason, this property is preserved only by linear affine transformations in the same space. Summarizing the above considerations, we are now able to state:

Theorem 23. *Consider a preference over binary actions $\succeq_B$ that verifies* P1–P3 *and* C.1–C.4. *By Theorem* 20, *it has an expected utility representation $\mathbb{U}^B : A^B \subset A \to \mathbb{R}$. Then $\mathbb{U}^B$ admits a linear extension $\mathbb{U}$ to A such that, for any $a \in A$ associated to the vector of consequences $[c_1^a, \ldots, c_S^a]$:*

$$\mathbb{U} : A \to \mathbb{R}$$

$$\mathbb{U}[a] := E^{\mathbb{P}}\left[u\left(c^a\left(\omega\right)\right)\right] = \sum_{s=1}^{S} p_s u\left(c_s^a\right)$$

Then $\mathbb{U}$ is the **expected utility** *representation of the preference $\succeq_B$ and $u(\cdot)$ is the associated utility index over (deterministic) consequences $c_s^a \in C$.*

Remark 24. $\mathbb{U}(a)$ is a cardinal representation of the preference relation, i.e., it is unique up to a positive affine transformation $H\mathbb{U}(a) + K$ with $H > 0$ and $K \in \mathbb{R}$.

Proof. Any action a can be considered as a simple lottery with a prize $c_s^a \in C$, uniquely associated to each outcome $s = 1, \ldots, S$. We want to construct an expected utility representation over lotteries of the form:

$$U(L) = \sum_{s=1}^{S} p_s^L U_s$$

that is a linear extension of the expected utility representation $\mathbb{U}^B$ over binary actions in (1.8). In light of the theorem's assumption, the restriction of the to a binary action A^B generates a representation of the preference $\succeq_B$. Then, the expected utility representation for lotteries $U(L)$ is an extension of $\mathbb{U}^B$ to the full set of actions $a \in A$ if and only if $U_s = H\mathbb{U}^B[(c_s^a, w, 1)] + k_s = Hu(c_s^a) + k_s$ with $H > 0$ and $k_s \in \mathbb{R}$ for $s = 1, \ldots, S$. This implies that the unique class of linear extensions to A of $\mathbb{U}^B$ must be given by a function $\mathbb{U} : A \to \mathbb{R}$ such that:

$$\begin{aligned}\mathbb{U}[a] &:= \sum_{s=1}^{S} p_s^L U_s = H \sum_{s=1}^{S} p_s u(c_s^a) + \sum_{s=1}^{S} p_s k_s \\ &= H \sum_{s=1}^{S} p_s u(c_s^a) + K,\end{aligned}$$

i.e. the expected utility representation $\mathbb{U}$ over generic actions is defined by its restriction on binary actions up to a positive affine change of variables, i.e., it is a cardinal representation of the preference, and the result of the theorem is proved. □

In conclusion, the utility of action a is the expected utility of the results that stem from the interaction of the action and the selection of the states of nature and preferences on actions are the weighted average of the utilities on the possible consequences of the actions.

Note that linearity of the representation in the lottery space, does not imply linearity of the utility function with respect to monetary amounts. This is easily verified in the following:

Example 25. We can consider an example with three possible states of the world

Return	TW	π_i
−10%	90	0.1
+5%	105	0.6
+20%	120	0.3

Then $E(TW) = 108$ but $\mathbb{U}(a_{TW}) \neq u(108)$. The expected utility of a_{TW} is given by

$$\begin{aligned}\mathbb{U}(a) &= E[u(c^a(\omega))] = \pi_1 \cdot u(c_{a,1}) + \pi_2 \cdot u(c_{a,2}) + \pi_3 \cdot u(c_{a,3}) \\ &= 0.1 \cdot u(90) + 0.6 \cdot u(105) + 0.3 \cdot u(120)\end{aligned}$$

The above sophisticate mathematical construction offers a good illustration of the complexities that arise when you try to create a formal framework to describe the way people make their decisions and correlate them to their beliefs, as represented by the probabilities of different outcomes, and their tastes, as represented by the preference relations.

1.9 Deviations from Expected Utility

The starting point of the previous argument is a list of behavioral axioms that, at least in principle, is expected to describe the real choice of market investors.

Modern decision theory and financial economics have highlighted several important systematic violations of the original assumptions on preferences by Von Neumann and Morgenstern that might be relevant for understanding the financial market outcomes as determined by the investor's decisions. In the following, we briefly identify the main deviations documented by experimental economists.

1.9.1 *Independence axiom and the Allais paradox*

As stated, C.3 is the most controversial of the axioms of choice under uncertainty, as evidenced by the famous Allais paradox that now we are going to illustrate. Choose a favorite between the two lotteries:

- Lottery **A**: 1000 € are won with probability 1.
- Lottery **B**: win 5000 € with probability 0.1, 1000 € with probability 0.89 or 0 with probability 0.01.

Choose now between the lotteries:

- Lottery **C**: 1000 € are won with probability 0.11 or nothing with probability 0.89.
- Lottery **D**: 5000 € win with probability 0.1 or nothing with probability 0.9

Experimental evidence shows that when faced with these choices the most frequent answer is $A \succeq B$ and $D \succeq C$, in clear violation of the axiom of independence. We can prove this by changing the representation of the two first lotteries as follows:

$$\begin{aligned} E(u(A)) &= u(1000) = 0.89u(1000) + 0.11u(1000) \\ E(u(B)) &= 0.89u(1000) + 0.1u(5000) + 0.01u(0) \\ &= 0.89u(1000) + 0.11\left[\frac{10}{11}u(5000) + \frac{1}{11}u(0)\right] \end{aligned}$$

and therefore the axiom of independence jointly with the first choice $A \succeq B$ implies that the lottery: $\frac{10}{11}u(5000) + \frac{1}{11}u(0)$ is dominated by $u(1000)$, a lottery with a certain outcome of winning 1000 €:

$$u(1000) > \left[\frac{10}{11}u(5000) + \frac{1}{11}u(0)\right]$$

but lotteries C and D can be decomposed as follows:

$$\begin{aligned} E(u(C)) &= 0.11u(1000) + 0.89u(0) \\ E(u(D)) &= 0.1u(5000) + 0.9u(0) \\ &= 0.11\left[\frac{1}{11}u(0) + \frac{10}{11}u(5000)\right] + 0.89u(0) \end{aligned}$$

hence the revealed preference $D \succeq C$ jointly with the axiom of independence imply:

$$u(1000) < \left[\frac{10}{11}u(5000) + \frac{1}{11}u(0)\right]$$

incurring a contradiction. This paradox signals a willingness in decisions to outweigh certain events even in violation of the independence axiom.

Salience

Allais paradox shows that violating the independence axiom of expected utility theory, decision-makers shift from risk-loving to risk-averse choices among two lotteries after a common consequence is added to both.

Bordalo *et al.* (2012) propose a new psychologically founded model of choice under risk, which naturally exhibits the systematic instability of risk preferences and accounts for this and other puzzles. In their model, risk attitudes are driven by the *salience* of different lottery payoffs. In the psychological literature, Taylor and Thompson (1982) put it: *Salience refers to the phenomenon that when one's attention is differentially directed to one portion of the environment rather than to others, the information contained in that portion will receive disproportionate weighting in subsequent judgments.*

Intuitively, a lottery payoff is salient if it is very different in percentage terms from the payoffs of other available lotteries in the same state of nature. Bordalo *et al.* (2012) focus on the salience of a payoffs (not on the underlying probabilities) and consider two assumptions that they label *ordering* and *diminishing sensitivity*: The *ordering* prescription specifies that decision-makers attend to differences rather than absolute values, while the *diminishing sensitivity* property states that changes are perceived on a log scale (Weber's law). Relying on these assumptions, they show that it is possible to reconstruct a choice function that reproduces the inversion of preference described by the Allais paradox. For a review of the empirical and theoretical financial-economic literature building on salience, see the recent review Bordalo *et al.* (2022).

1.9.2 *The paradox of Ellsberg and the distinction between ambiguity and risk*

In a Von-Neumann Morgerstern framework, the quality of information about the distribution of a lottery does not have an impact on the individual decisions. Ellsberg observes that empirically the opposite is true: decision-makers in general show a preference for those situations in which the quantification of uncertainty is more accurate: they prefer risk over ambiguity.

We consider an urn with 90 marbles of which 30 are red (R) and the other 60 are black (B) or yellow (Y) in unknown proportions. Faced with the choice between the two lotteries:

- Lottery **A**: win 1000 € if you extract a red marble (R) otherwise none ($B \cup Y$),
- Lottery **B**: win 1000 € if you extract a black marble (B) otherwise nothing ($R \cup Y$),

and the choice between

- Lottery **C**: win 1000 € if you extract a red or yellow marble ($R \cup Y$) otherwise nothing (B),
- Lottery **D**: win 1000 € if you pull a black or yellow marble ($B \cup Y$) otherwise nothing (R).

Agents usually respond $A \succcurlyeq B$ and $D \succcurlyeq C$ in breach of the principle of expected utility. In fact the choice consistent with $A \succcurlyeq B$ within VnM axioms of rationality would be $C \succcurlyeq D$. In fact, the first choice ($A \succcurlyeq B$) can be represented as follows:

$$\frac{1}{3}u(1000) + \frac{2}{3}u(0) > p(B)u(1000) + (1 - p(B))\, u(0)$$

Since $1000 > 0$, from assumption C.II, we know that the revealed preference implies that

$$p(R) > p(B)$$
$$\frac{1}{3} > p(B)$$

The second choice ($D \succcurlyeq C$), in turn, can be represented as

$$\frac{2}{3}u(1000) + \frac{1}{3}u(0) > (1 - p(B))\, u(1000) + p(B)u(0)$$

Again, since $1000 > 0$, from assumption C.II we know that the revealed preference implies that

$$\frac{2}{3} > 1 - p(B)$$
$$\frac{1}{3} < p(B)$$

Ambiguity aversion and variational representation of preferences

A fundamental feature pointed out by in Ellsberg (1961) is that there may be no single belief on the states of the world that the decision maker holds and that rationalizes her choices. Under standard expected utility, the decision makers have to be firmly convinced that the model they have adopted is the correct one. This is a strong requirement because agents may be aware of the possibility that their model is misspecified and consider as reasonable a set of priors. Maccheroni *et al.* (2006) introduce a class of decision functions, named a *Variational Representation of Preferences*, that, in addition to a utility function u on outcomes include also an ambiguity index c on the set of probabilities on the states. These decision functions are shown to produce the representation of the preference for decision makers that are aware that a single probabilistic prior might produce an imperfect description of the phenomenon in which they are interested and for this reason they take into account other possible models. These decision functions reproduce and rationalize the evidence resulting from the Ellsberg urn experiment discussed above.

1.9.3 *Preference for temporal resolution of uncertainty*

Kreps and Porteus showed a deviation from the axioms of individual rationality that occurs when the agent in a position to choose between tables having the same expected utility, shows a systematic preference for situations in which the resolution of uncertainty is anticipated (or postponed).

Consider for this purpose the two lotteries A and B shown in Fig. 1.3. If we consider the expected utility of the two tables, they are equivalent, in fact, according to basic axioms of expected utility the

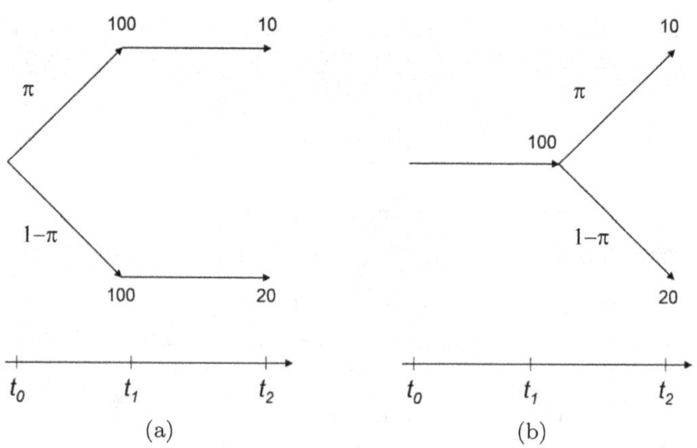

Figure 1.3. Early (A) and late (B) resolution of uncertainty.

agent is completely indifferent between the plan A where uncertainty is resolved at time 1 and the plan B in which the uncertainty is resolved at time 2. To distinguish between these two situations it is necessary to introduce a new function, which we call temporal aggregator of preferences: $W : \mathbb{R} \times \mathbb{R} \to \mathbb{R}$. The first argument of this function is the utility referred to a consumer who is known in the available information and the second argument relates to the certainty equivalent of future consumption. To illustrate the function of this aggregate consider a utility function specified by

$$
\begin{aligned}
U\left(c_1, c_2\left(\omega\right)\right) &= W\left(u\left(c_1\right), CE\left[u\left(c_2\left(\omega\right)\right)\right]\right) \\
&= \left(\left(1-\beta\right) u\left(c_1\right) + \beta E\left[u^{\alpha}\left(c_2\right)\right]^{1/\alpha}\right)
\end{aligned}
$$

where β is the weight assigned to the utility of the second node and α is an index that incorporates the preference for temporal resolution of uncertainty. In other words, the variation of α determines a different preference relation with respect to early or late resolution of uncertainty. Assuming a simple linear utility function ($u\left(x\right) = x$), let us value the utility index level of lottery A when $\alpha = 1/2$ and $\beta = 0.5$, $\pi = 0.7$:

$$
\begin{aligned}
U_0^A &= 0.5 \cdot [0.7 \cdot 100 + 0.3 \cdot 100] \\
&\quad + 0.5 \cdot [0.7 \cdot 10^{\alpha/\alpha} + 0.3 \cdot 20^{\alpha/\alpha}] \\
&= 0.7\left(0.5 \cdot 100 + 0.5 \cdot 10^{\alpha/\alpha}\right) \\
&\quad + (0.3)\left(0.5 \cdot 100 + 0.5 \cdot 20^{\alpha/\alpha}\right) \\
&= 0.7 \cdot 55 + 0.3 \cdot 60 = 56.5
\end{aligned}
$$

while the utility index of lottery B is given by

$$
\begin{aligned}
U_0^B &= 0.5 \cdot 100 + 0.5 \cdot \left[\left(0.7 \cdot 10^{0.5} + 0.3 \cdot 20^{0.5}\right)\right]^2 \\
&= 50 + 0.5 \cdot [(2.21.. + 1.34..)]^2 \\
&= 50 + 0.5 \cdot [3.55..]^2 = 56.31
\end{aligned}
$$

thus in this case the agent will prefer A (early resolution). The preference with respect to time resolution is quantified by index $1 - \alpha$: when this index is larger than 0, $1 - \alpha > 0$, the agent prefers early resolution, if it is negative the agent will prefer late resolution. As an exercise try to verify that in case $1 - \alpha < 0$ lottery B would be preferred to A (late resolution).

This is the simplest illustration of the problems that arise when individual choice under uncertainty may involve, a dynamic nature.

1.9.4 *Anomalies observed by Khanemann and Tversky*

At the end of the 1970s, Daniel Kahneman and Amos Tversky began studying human decision-making under uncertainty from the perspective of cognitive psychology. They isolated several deviations from the standard VnM model.

The reflection effect

A certain population was asked to choose between the following lotteries:

- Lottery **A**: win 4000 \$ with pr. 80% or nothing with pr. 20%,
- Lottery **B**: win 3000 \$ with pr. 100%.

The vast majority of the sample (80% of the subjects) chose lottery **B**, revealing that $B \succcurlyeq A$. The same subjects where later asked to choose between the following two lotteries:

- Lottery **C**: loose 4000 \$ with pr. 80% or nothing with pr. 20%,
- Lottery **D**: loose 3000 \$ with pr. 100%.

This time, faced with the possibility of losing money the vast majority of the sample (92%) chose lottery **C**, revealing $C \succcurlyeq D$. This combination may make sense at first sight but let's consider it from the point of view of our traditional expected utility model. The expected value of lottery **A** is 3200 \$, higher than the expected value of lottery **B** (3000 \$), so we can conclude that the investors who chose **B** over **A** must be risk averse. Looking at the second choice we observe that the expected value of lottery **C** is −3200 \$, lower than the expected value of lottery **D** (−3000 \$). In this case, the vast majority of the population has chosen a lottery with a lower expected value, indicating risk-loving behavior. *The authors conclude that investors have a changing risk aversion, showing a risk-averse* *behavior when facing possible gains and a risk-loving behavior when facing possible losses.*

Certainty effect

A certain population was asked to choose between the following lotteries:

- Lottery **A**: win 4000 \$ with pr. 80% or nothing with pr. 20%,
- Lottery **B**: win 3000 \$ with pr. 100%.

The vast majority of the sample (80% of the subjects) chose lottery **B,** revealing that $B \succcurlyeq A$. The same subjects were later asked to choose between the following two lotteries:

- Lottery **C**: win 4000 \$ with pr. 20% or nothing with pr. 80%,
- Lottery **D**: win 3000 \$ with pr. 25% or nothing with pr. 75%.

This time the majority of the sample (65%) chose lottery **C**, revealing $C \succcurlyeq D$. This combination cannot be explained from the perspective of our traditional expected utility model. In fact from the first choice, assuming $u(0) = 0$, we have that

$$u(3000) > 0.80u(4000)$$

while from the second we have that

$$0.25u(3000) < 0.20u(4000)$$
$$4 \times 0.25u(3000) < 4 \times 0.20u(4000)$$
$$u(3000) < 0.80u(4000)$$

The authors conclude that there is a preference for lotteries with sure outcome.

Prospect theory

Considering together reflection and certainty effects (as well as other violations not reported here) the authors propose an alternative to the expected utility model, the so-called prospect theory, characterized by

(1) Substitution of the traditional utility function (u) with a *value function* (v) defined over gains and losses with respect to the initial wealth and not over the terminal wealth. This function is concave on gains and convex on losses (see Fig. 1.4).

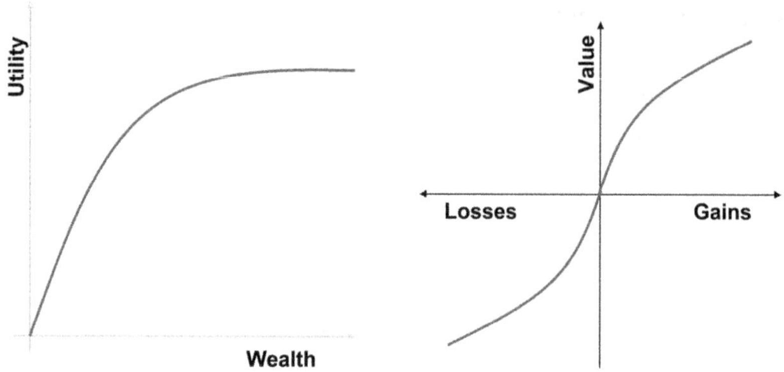

Figure 1.4. Illustration of the shape of a utility function compatible with prospect theory.

(2) Substitution of the traditional probabilities (p) with *decision weights* (π), a nonlinear transformation of the probabilities.

The mathematical formulation of their model is the following: let's consider a game that produces n possible outcomes (gains or losses) x_i with probabilities p_i. The Value (instead of expected utility) of the game is

$$V = \sum_{i=1}^{n} \pi_i v(x_i)$$

with a value function v defined as

$$v = \begin{matrix} x^{\alpha} & x \geq 0 \\ -\lambda(-x)^{\alpha} & x < 0 \end{matrix}$$

and the decision weights π defined as

$$\pi_i = \omega(p_i) - \omega(p_i^*)$$

and

$$\omega(p_i) = \frac{p^{\gamma}}{(p^{\gamma} + (1-p)^{\gamma})^{\frac{1}{\gamma}}}$$

where p_i is the probability that the game will yield a result at least as good as x_i and p_i^* is the probability that the game will yield a result strictly better than x_i. The authors also calibrate the following parametrization:

$$\alpha = 0.88; \quad \lambda = 2.25; \quad \gamma = 0.65$$

1.9.5 *Individual choice and collective decisions*

Axioms on individual rationality require that preferences are transitive. While these axioms of rationality are reasonable to describe the choice of a single agent, they can be inadequate to represent the preferences of a community. Think of the so-called Condorcet paradox: suppose that voters express their preferences on candidates in a pattern like this

- 1/3 of voters prefers $A \succ B \succ C$;
- 1/3 of voters prefers $B \succ C \succ A$;
- 1/3 of voters prefers $C \succ A \succ B$.

Collectively we have that $A \succ B$ by 2/3 of voters, $B \succ C$ by 2/3 of the electorate, $C \succ A$ from 2/3 of voters and thus a preference based on democratic norms, or the preference of the majority of voters violates transitivity and cannot be represented (otherwise we fall into contradiction because $A \succ A$ or A is strictly preferred to himself). Hence the aggregation of individual preferences to describe collective decisions will in general be a non-trivial process.

Chapter 2

From Individual Choice to Market Pricing

The previous chapter focused on individual choice and its financial implications, assuming that price uncertainty is set exogenously and is describable using lotteries with a finite set of possible outcomes. Even in this simplified framework, the solution of the optimal portfolio choice becomes soon intractable due to the nonlinear nature of the first-order conditions (FOCs) arising from the constrained utility maximization problem. In addition, utility-based price determinations are purely subjective and might be very different from transacted prices.

In this chapter, we follow the approach of Markowitz and introduce a simplified framework. Its key advantage is that it can be used to describe collective actions and thus offers the possibility to formulate valuation models that relate asset characteristics, their expected cash flows, to their *fair* prices. We recall that a price is said to be *fair or market-based* if it is considered as an acceptable price by agents that stay on both sides, supply, and demand, of the market.

We proceed in two steps. First, we introduce a framework for individual choice problems where the preference of individual investors over different securities with uncertain payoffs can be determined in terms of simple sufficient statistics that can be derived from the security price and payoff distributions. These are the security returns' expected means, variances and linear correlations. From a probability theory point of view, this corresponds to assuming that return fluctuations can be described within a Gaussian probability space.

In the second step, we consider security valuation models where the price determination embeds the feedback on prices of traders' buying or selling decisions. In particular, we analyze two frameworks: the general equilibrium Capital Asset Pricing Model and a partial equilibrium Arbitrage Pricing Theory. These approaches are explicitly designed to produce price assessments comparable with prices observed in an informationally efficient, frictionless public market.

2.1 The Markowitz Mean–Variance Approach

A mean–variance approach is applied when the expected return and the expected risk (the standard deviation) of the returns of an investment are considered sufficient statistics to characterize that allocation opportunity.

This is possible if the following two conditions are verified[1]:

(1) The selection of the optimal investment is scale-invariant, i.e., the optimal allocation will not depend on the absolute size of the investment.
(2) Fluctuations of financial asset *returns are properly described by a Gaussian distribution.*

Both these assumptions are known to have limited applicability. First, it is documented that in the market there exist dis-economies of scale related to the price impact of trades, i.e., bigger portfolios are harder to trade. Second, the conventional argument supporting the normal distribution hypothesis, the central limit theorem, offers limited support to the assumption in this specific case. It underestimates the profit and losses due to very infrequent but large-size price changes. Proper consideration of these "surprises" and their impact on the overall performance assessment requires a more sophisticated decision model. As a simple exemplification of the relevance of *rare events*, it is worth recalling the existence of a full category of hedge funds targeting those investment opportunities that are expected to capitalize most of the profits precisely on those infrequent "rainy days" when disasters or highly unlikely outcomes occur.

[1]These conditions are sufficient but not necessary. We will assume them throughout this chapter in order to produce a statistical description of the risk profile for a generic portfolio of securities.

A long position in these funds has a high insurance value since it limits draw-down risk. The utility of these financial instruments depends on their price. It will depend on the frequency of the rare outcome and the level of the expected loss conditional on the occurrence of this event. A precise joint assessment of these two quantities is impossible within a model where returns are assumed to follow an (unconditional) Gaussian distribution since they are closely connected with the information embedded in higher moments of the return's empirical distribution like skewness and kurtosis.

In the following, we assume that standardized returns of security p follow a standard normal random variable $\tilde{Z}$ so that

$$\tilde{Z} = \frac{\tilde{r}_p - \mu_p}{\sigma_p} \sim N(0,1)$$

thus $\tilde{r}_p = \sigma_p \tilde{Z} + \mu_p$ where the greek letter, $\mu_p := E^{\mathbb{P}}[\tilde{r}_p]$, denotes the expected return while $\sigma_p := E^{\mathbb{P}}\left[\tilde{r}_p^2 - E^{\mathbb{P}}[\tilde{r}_p]^2\right]^{1/2}$ denotes the standard deviation of a generic security p. Then, setting

$$E^{\mathbb{P}}[\hat{U}(\tilde{r}_p)] := E^{\mathbb{P}}[U(\tilde{Y})]$$

where $\tilde{Y} = Y_0(1 + \tilde{r}_p)$ denotes the final wealth, the expected utility is

$$E^{\mathbb{P}}\left[\hat{U}(\tilde{r}_p)\right] = \int_{-\infty}^{+\infty} \hat{U}(\sigma_p Z + \mu_p)\, n(Z)\, dZ$$

where $n(Z)$ is the density of the standard normal distribution $N(0,1)$. Recalling that by assumption the decision function is scale-invariant, this expression shows that the overall expected utility depends on the parameters (μ_p, σ_p) while higher moments do not play any role. For a non-satiated risk risk-averse agent, the expected utility is increasing in μ_p and decreasing in σ_p and the indifference curves are increasing and convex, i.e., the marginal rate of substitution between risk and return is positive and increasing. In light of the above considerations, it is possible to introduce a (local) quadratic approximation approximation of the expected utility functional:

$$E^{\mathbb{P}}[\hat{U}(\tilde{r}_p)] \approx A + B\left(\mu_p - \frac{\tau}{2} \cdot \sigma_p^2\right)$$

where τ is a measure of risk aversion (but not the Arrow–Pratt one). As expected $\tau > 0$ if $U' > 0$ and $U'' < 0$.

2.1.1 *A bit of terminology*

According to the standard mean–variance dominance criterion, we will say that portfolio A dominates portfolio B if, for a level of risk of A smaller or equal than the risk of B, portfolio A has an expected return that is higher than the expected return of B. Alternatively, we will say that portfolio A is dominated by portfolio B, if for a for a level of risk of A greater or equal than the risk of B, portfolio A has an expected return that is lower than the expected return of B. In the following, we will characterize the set of non-dominated portfolios that can be realized considering the set of possible allocations in a finite set of securities while satisfying a budget constraint. We will adopt the following taxonomy:

- **Feasible set:** The set of all the portfolios that can be built by combining the assets with different weights
- **Minimum variance frontier:** The set of all the portfolios that are obtained from the risk minimization condition.
- **Efficient frontier:** The set of minimum variance portfolios that are non-dominated.

If the market includes only two assets, then the feasible set and the minimum variance frontier coincide. When we consider N assets the situation is depicted in Fig. 2.1.

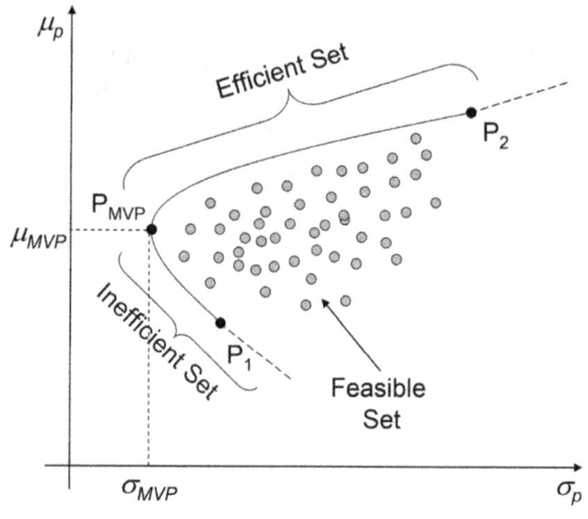

Figure 2.1. Mean–variance frontier with N assets.

2.1.2 *Minimum variance portfolio*

Let's denote with $\mathbf{r}$ the Gaussian distributed random vector of linear total returns from time t to time $t+k$ from a given menu of N risky assets for the interval $[t, t+k]$, $\mathbf{r} \sim \mathcal{N}(\mu, \Sigma)$, where μ, Σ denote respectively the vector of mean returns and the returns' variance–covariance matrix, $\mathbf{w}$ is the vector of weights given to the N risky assets in the portfolio and $\mathbf{e}$ is a (Nx1) column vector of ones. In case the target is to find the minimum variance portfolio:

$$\min_{\mathbf{w}}(\mathbf{w}'\Sigma\mathbf{w})$$

subject to

$$\mathbf{w}'\mathbf{e} = 1$$

the solution will be

$$\mathbf{w} = \frac{\Sigma^{-1}\mathbf{e}}{\mathbf{e}'\Sigma^{-1}\mathbf{e}}$$

In this case, only the second moment of the distribution of returns matters.

2.1.3 *Risk parity portfolios*

An alternative approach to building a portfolio is to choose weights in such a way that the contribution of each asset to the volatility of the portfolio is the same (risk parity). To determine optimal weights in this scenario, decompose the total variance of a portfolio in the sum of the contributions of each asset to the total portfolio variance:

$$\text{Var}[\mathbf{w}'\mathbf{r}] = \sum_{i=1}^{N} w_i \text{Cov}\left(r_i, \mathbf{w}'\mathbf{r}\right)$$

$$\mathbf{w}'\Sigma\mathbf{w} = \sum_{i=1}^{N} w_i (\Sigma\mathbf{w})_i$$

the risk contribution of each asset to total risk can then be written as follows:

$$\text{RRC}_i = \frac{w_i(\Sigma\mathbf{w})_i}{\mathbf{w}'\Sigma\mathbf{w}}$$

Risk Parity Portfolios are constructed by choosing weights so that:

$$\mathrm{RRC}_i = \frac{1}{N}$$

Figure 2.2 illustrates the difference between an equally weighted portfolio and a risk parity portfolio.

Note that weights in the risk-parity portfolio are uniquely determined by the variance–covariance matrix.

2.1.4 *The M–V model with two risky assets and no risk-free*

Let's consider first a market where only two risky securities are traded. By convention, we will assume that security P_1 is less risky and has a lower expected return than security P_2. The feasible set of portfolios can be represented as a curve in the mean-variance space

$$\mu_p = a\mu_1 + (1-a)\,\mu_2$$
$$\sigma_p^2 = a^2\sigma_1^2 + (1-a)^2\,\sigma_2^2 + 2a\,(1-a)\,\rho_{12}\sigma_1\sigma_2$$

where a denotes the allocation to the lowest risk security 1.

We know that for $\rho = 1$

$$\sigma_p^2 = a^2\sigma_1^2 + (1-a)^2\,\sigma_2^2 + 2a\,(1-a)\,\rho_{12}\sigma_1\sigma_2$$
$$\sigma_p^2 = a^2\sigma_1^2 + (1-a)^2\,\sigma_2^2 + 2a\,(1-a)\,\sigma_1\sigma_2$$
$$\sigma_p = a\sigma_1 + (1-a)\,\sigma_2$$

and the standard deviation of the portfolio is a linear combination of the standard deviations of the securities. In order to get the equation of the frontier we can solve for a:

$$\sigma_p = a\sigma_1 + (1-a)\,\sigma_2$$
$$\sigma_p = a\,(\sigma_1 - \sigma_2) + \sigma_2$$
$$a = \frac{\sigma_p - \sigma_2}{\sigma_1 - \sigma_2}$$

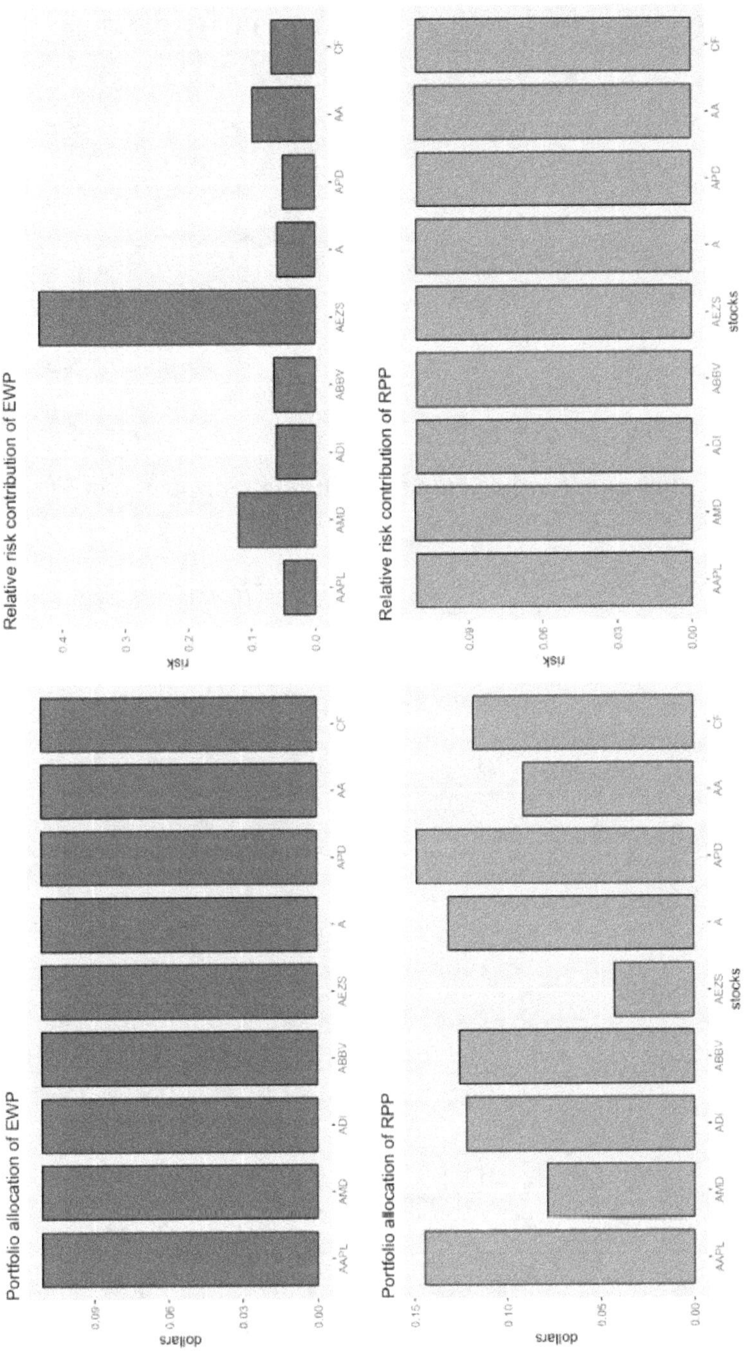

Figure 2.2. Portfolio allocation in equal weights portfolios (EWP) and risk parity portfolios (RPP).

and plug this value in the definition of the expected return

$$\begin{aligned}
\mu_p &= a\mu_1 + (1-a)\,\mu_2 \\
&= \frac{\sigma_p - \sigma_2}{\sigma_1 - \sigma_2}\mu_1 + \left(1 - \frac{\sigma_p - \sigma_2}{\sigma_1 - \sigma_2}\right)\mu_2 \\
&= \frac{\sigma_p - \sigma_2}{\sigma_1 - \sigma_2}\mu_1 + \frac{\sigma_1 - \sigma_p}{\sigma_1 - \sigma_2}\mu_2 \\
&= \frac{(\sigma_p - \sigma_2)\,\mu_1 + (\sigma_1 - \sigma_p)\,\mu_2}{\sigma_1 - \sigma_2} \\
&= \frac{(\mu_1 - \mu_2)}{\sigma_1 - \sigma_2}\sigma_p + \frac{\sigma_1\mu_2 - \sigma_2\mu_1}{\sigma_1 - \sigma_2}
\end{aligned}$$

The mean–variance frontier is the straight line represented in Fig. 2.3
For $\rho = -1$

$$\begin{aligned}
&\sigma_p^2 = a^2\sigma_1^2 + (1-a)^2\,\sigma_2^2 + 2a\,(1-a)\,\rho_{12}\sigma_1\sigma_2 \\
&\sigma_p^2 = a^2\sigma_1^2 + (1-a)^2\,\sigma_2^2 - 2a\,(1-a)\,\sigma_1\sigma_2 \\
&\sigma_p = a\sigma_1 - (1-a)\,\sigma_2 \text{ or } \sigma_p = -a\sigma_1 + (1-a)\,\sigma_2
\end{aligned}$$

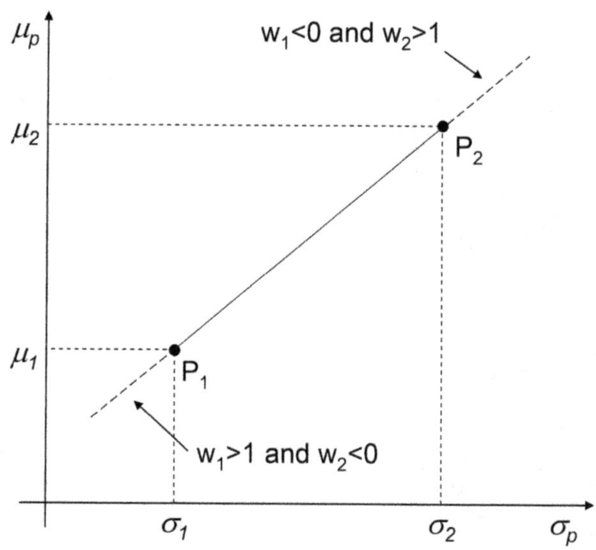

Figure 2.3. Mean–variance frontier with $\rho = 1$.

and we will consider the positive solution so

$$\begin{aligned} a\sigma_1 - (1-a)\,\sigma_2 &\geq 0 \\ a\sigma_1 - \sigma_2 + a\sigma_2 &\geq 0 \\ a &\geq \frac{\sigma_2}{\sigma_1+\sigma_2} \end{aligned}$$

So, we can say that

$$\sigma_p = \begin{cases} a\sigma_1 - (1-a)\,\sigma_2 & \text{if } a \geq \frac{\sigma_2}{\sigma_1+\sigma_2} \\ -a\sigma_1 + (1-a)\,\sigma_2 & \text{if } a < \frac{\sigma_2}{\sigma_1+\sigma_2} \end{cases}$$

We see that for $a \geq \frac{\sigma_2}{\sigma_1+\sigma_2}$ $\frac{d\sigma_p}{da} = (\sigma_1 + \sigma_2) \geq 0$. The increase in the weight of security one will increase the portfolio risk, while for $a < \frac{\sigma_2}{\sigma_1+\sigma_2}$ $\frac{d\sigma_p}{da} = (-\sigma_1 - \sigma_2) \leq 0$ and an increase in the weight will reduce portfolio risk.

Example 26. If we consider the following case: $\mu_1 = 0.05$, $\mu_2 = 0.1$, $\sigma_1 = 0.1$, $\sigma_2 = 0.2$, $\rho_{12} = -1$. Let's start with a portfolio fully invested in security 1. In this case

$$\begin{aligned} a = 1 > \frac{2}{3} &= \frac{\sigma_2}{\sigma_1+\sigma_2} \\ \sigma_p &= a\sigma_1 - (1-a)\,\sigma_2 \\ \sigma_p &= a0.1 - (1-a)\,0.2 \\ \sigma_p &= a0.3 - 0.2 \end{aligned}$$

When we decrease a moving money from security 1 to security 2 the portfolio risk decreases. The portfolio risk is a positive linear function of a. When $a = \frac{\sigma_2}{\sigma_1+\sigma_2} = \frac{2}{3}$ the portfolio risk $\sigma_p = 0$. From this point on if we persist in reducing a to values $a < \frac{\sigma_2}{\sigma_1+\sigma_2}$

$$\begin{aligned} \sigma_p &= -a\sigma_1 + (1-a)\,\sigma_2 \\ &= -0.3a + 0.2 \end{aligned}$$

the portfolio risk becomes a negative linear function of a and the investment in security 2 will increase the portfolio risk.

The corresponding minimum variance and linear efficient frontier ($\mu_p > \mu_{MVP}$) are shown in Fig. 2.4.

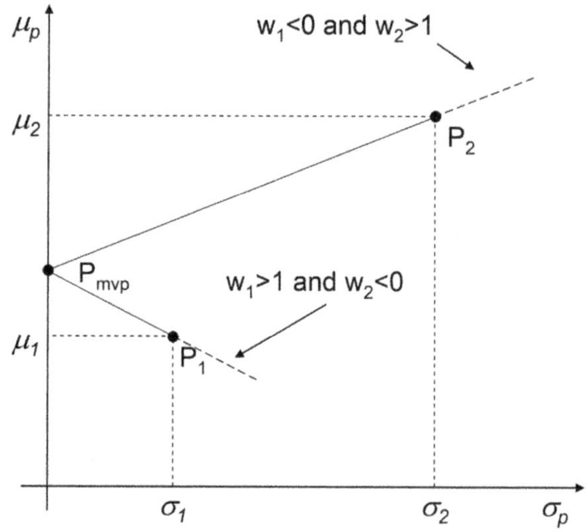

Figure 2.4. Mean–variance frontier with $\rho = -1$.

For $-1 < \rho < 1$ the portfolio risk is no longer a linear function of a. Let's derive the weights for the absolute minimum variance portfolio minimizing the portfolio variance:

$$\sigma_p^2 = a^2\sigma_1^2 + (1-a)^2\sigma_2^2 + 2a(1-a)\rho_{12}\sigma_1\sigma_2$$

over all possible allocations a without any constraint on the expected return. Then the FOC implies

$$\frac{d\sigma_p^2}{da} = 2a\sigma_1^2 - 2(1-a)\sigma_2^2 + 2\rho_{12}\sigma_1\sigma_2 - 4a\rho_{12}\sigma_1\sigma_2 = 0$$

$$2a\sigma_1^2 + 2a\sigma_2^2 - 4a\rho_{12}\sigma_1\sigma_2 = 2\sigma_2^2 - 2\rho_{12}\sigma_1\sigma_2$$

$$a^{\text{MVP}} = \frac{\sigma_2^2 - \rho_{12}\sigma_1\sigma_2}{\sigma_1^2 + \sigma_2^2 - 2\rho_{12}\sigma_1\sigma_2} \tag{2.1}$$

The minimum variance portfolio has a positive investment in the riskier security 2 when $a < 1$. Imposing the condition:

$$a = \frac{\sigma_2^2 - \rho_{12}\sigma_1\sigma_2}{\sigma_1^2 + \sigma_2^2 - 2\rho_{12}\sigma_1\sigma_2} < 1$$

one can verify that the possibility of achieving a risk lower than the risk of P_1 from a convex combination of P_1 and P_2 arises when the

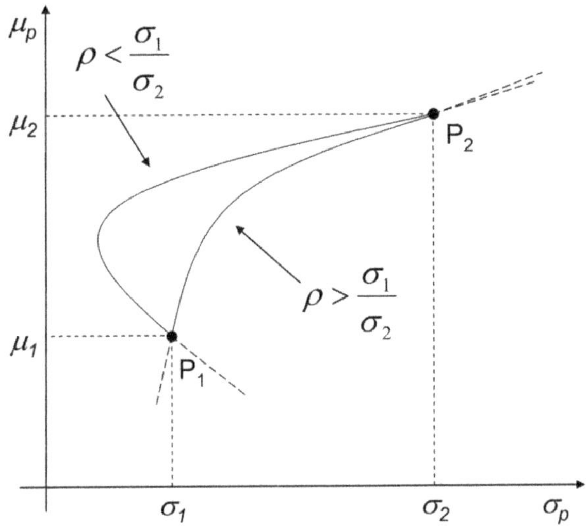

Figure 2.5. Mean–variance frontier for $-1 < \rho < 1$.

correlation between these two assets is sufficiently low, in particular, when

$$-1 \leq \rho_{12} < \frac{\sigma_1}{\sigma_2} \tag{2.2}$$

So, if the correlation is negative, the condition is always true regardless of the risk of the two securities. If the correlation is positive, let's say 0.5 we see that the marginal investment in the riskier asset is optimal only if $\sigma_2 < 2\sigma_1$. Above this level, the diversification effect is more than compensated by the higher average risk and the investment in the riskier asset never helps to reduce the portfolio risk. In Fig. 2.5 we represent the generic mean-variance frontier for $-1 < \rho < 1$.

2.1.5 *Optimal allocation when a risk-free security is available*

The next step is to derive an efficient frontier when investors can invest in a risk-free asset, an asset with a variance equal to zero and a fixed rate of return r_f. Without loss of generality, we can assume that the set of investable securities is formed by two risky assets and a risk-free investment. Denote by w_f the allocation in the risk-free security. Then, solving the budget constraint w.r.t. w_f:

$$w_f = 1 - w_1 - w_2$$

the constrained optimization problem can be written as follows:

$$\min_w \frac{1}{2}\left(w_1^2\sigma_1^2 + w_2^2\sigma_2^2 + 2w_1w_2\sigma_{12}\right)$$
$$\text{s.t.} \qquad w_1\left(\mu_1 - r_f\right) + w_2\left(\mu_2 - r_f\right) = \mu_p - r_f$$

where w_1 and w_2 are unconstrained. The corresponding Lagrangian is

$$\begin{aligned} L = {} & \frac{1}{2}\left(w_1^2\sigma_1^2 + w_2^2\sigma_2^2 + 2w_1w_2\sigma_{12}\right) \\ & + \lambda\left(\mu_p - r_f - w_1\left(\mu_1 - r_f\right) - w_2\left(\mu_2 - r_f\right)\right) \end{aligned}$$

The FOCs for the minimization problem are then:

$$\begin{aligned} \frac{\partial L}{\partial w_1} &= w_1\sigma_1^2 + w_2\sigma_{12} - \lambda\left(\mu_1 - r_f\right) = 0 \\ \frac{\partial L}{\partial w_2} &= w_2\sigma_2^2 + w_1\sigma_{12} - \lambda\left(\mu_2 - r_f\right) = 0 \\ \frac{\partial L}{\partial \lambda} &= \mu_p - r_f - w_1\left(\mu_1 - r_f\right) - w_2\left(\mu_2 - r_f\right) = 0 \end{aligned}$$

These conditions imply the following:

Proposition 27. *Let p^* denote the optimal portfolio solving the FOCs. Then for any security i traded in the market:*

$$\frac{\left(\mu_i - r_f\right)}{\sigma_{i,p^*}} = \frac{1}{\lambda} = \frac{\mu_{p^*} - r_f}{\sigma_{p^*}^2}$$

where σ_{i,p^*} denotes the covariation between asset i and p^*.

Proof. The first two FOC conditions imply

$$\begin{aligned} \lambda\left(\mu_1 - r_f\right) &= w_1^*\sigma_1^2 + w_2^*\sigma_{12} = \text{Cov}\left(R_{p^*}, R_1\right) \\ \lambda\left(\mu_2 - r_f\right) &= w_2^*\sigma_2^2 + w_1^*\sigma_{12} = \text{Cov}\left(R_{p^*}, R_2\right) \end{aligned}$$

where p^* denotes the optimal portfolio. Considering a convex combination of these two equations it is easy to show that the ratio between the excess return and the covariance with the optimal portfolio is constant for any admissible portfolio and equals $1/\lambda$. Then, the first two FOCs for the relevant weights imply

$$w_1 \frac{\partial L}{\partial w_1} = w_1^2 \sigma_1^2 + w_1 w_2 \sigma_{12} - \lambda w_1 (\mu_1 - r_f) = 0 \tag{2.3}$$

$$w_2 \frac{\partial L}{\partial w_2} = w_2^2 \sigma_2^2 + w_2 w_1 \sigma_{12} - \lambda w_2 (\mu_2 - rf) = 0 \tag{2.4}$$

and summing them up one gets

$$\sigma_*^2 - \lambda \left[w_1^* (\mu_1 - r_f) + w_2^* (\mu_2 - r_f) \right] = 0$$

$$\sigma_{p^*}^2 - \lambda \left[\mu_{p^*} - r_f \right] = 0$$

that implies

$$\frac{\mu_{p^*} - r_f}{\sigma_{p^*}^2} = \frac{1}{\lambda}$$

and the result is proved. □

This condition states that the ratio between the expected risk premium of every stock and the contribution of that stock to the portfolio risk, as measured by the covariance between the individual security and the optimal portfolio, must be the same. If this was not the case, we could increase the portfolio efficiency by selling part of the stock with worse performance (in terms of return to risk ratio) and investing in the stock with the highest performance.

This intuition is pretty similar to the FOC that we considered in the basic portfolio allocation framework discussed in the previous Chapter. A formal the connection between the two conditions will show up when discussing the more general framework of the Arbitrage Pricing Theory. The shape of the resulting efficient frontier is depicted in Fig. 2.6.

2.1.6 *The general solution to the N risky assets and no risk free*

In this section, we show that the solution of a mean–variance optimal allocation problem in a market with N risky securities can be reduced to the simpler case of a market with two risky securities only.

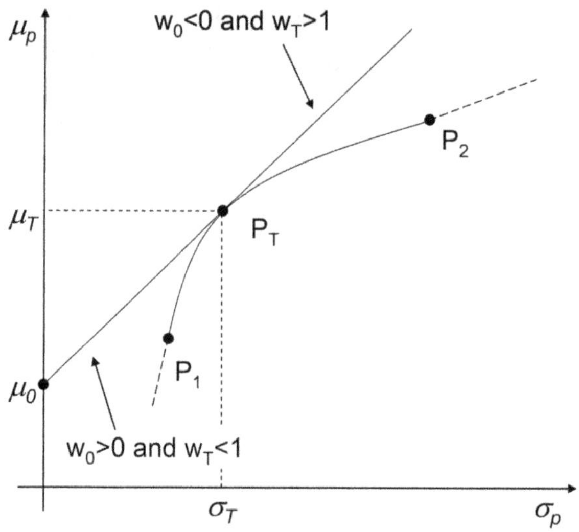

Figure 2.6. Efficient frontier when a risk-free security is traded in the market.

To be more precise, we show that the funds allocations that satisfy the FOCs for the N-securities problem and generate the minimum–variance frontier portfolios are linear combinations of only two risky funds. In fact, we can state the following:

Proposition 28. *Every frontier portfolio can be generated as a linear combination of the two funds:*

$$g = \frac{\left[B\left(V^{-1}\mathbf{1}\right) - A\left(V^{-1}\boldsymbol{\mu}\right)\right]}{D}$$

$$h = \frac{\left[C\left(V^{-1}\boldsymbol{\mu}\right) - A\left(V^{-1}\mathbf{1}\right)\right]}{D}$$

where the expressions of A, B, C, and D are given by Eqs. (2.14)–(2.17). *In particular, the allocation w_q producing the minimum variance frontier portfolio with expected return equal to μ_q is determined by the combination.*

$$w_q = g + h\mu_q$$

Corollary 29. *Every minimum variance portfolio can be generated as a linear combination of two distinct portfolios on the minimum variance frontier.*

Proof. We recall that a portfolio is a *frontier portfolio* if it has the minimum variance among portfolios that have a given target expected return μ_p. So a portfolio is a frontier portfolio if and only if the N-vector of portfolio weights $w \in \mathbb{R}^N$ are the solution to the following constrained quadratic minimization problem:

$$\min_w \frac{1}{2} w^\intercal V w$$

$$\text{s.t.}$$

$$w^\intercal \boldsymbol{\mu} = \mu_p$$

$$w^\intercal \mathbf{1} = 1$$

Where μ_p is the expected return for portfolio p, V is the variance–covariance matrix of the risky assets returns:

$$V := \begin{bmatrix} \sigma_1^2 & \sigma_{12} & \cdots & \sigma_{1n} \\ \sigma_{21} & \sigma_2^2 & \cdots & \sigma_{2n} \\ \vdots & \vdots & \ddots & \vdots \\ \sigma_{n1} & \sigma_{n2} & \cdots & \sigma_n^2 \end{bmatrix}$$

$\boldsymbol{\mu}$ is the column vector of the expected returns

$$\boldsymbol{\mu} = \begin{bmatrix} \mu_1 \; \mu_2 \; ... \; \mu_n \end{bmatrix}^T$$

$\mathbf{1}$ is the column vector of ones

$$\mathbf{1} = \begin{bmatrix} 1 \; 1 \; ... \; 1 \end{bmatrix}^T$$

This optimal control problem selects the allocation that minimizes the portfolio variance subject to the constraint that the portfolio expected return is equal to μ_p and that the sum of portfolio weights sum to 1. It can be restated as a free minimization problem introducing the Lagrangian

$$L(w, \lambda, \gamma) := \frac{1}{2} w^\top V w + \lambda \left(\mu_p - w^\top \boldsymbol{\mu} \right) + \gamma \left(1 - w^\top \mathbf{1} \right) \tag{2.5}$$

where γ and λ are two positive constants. The FOCs that are necessary and sufficient to minimize the value of the Lagrangian function over $(w, \lambda, \gamma) \in \mathbb{R}^{N+2}$ are

$$\frac{\partial L}{\partial w} = Vw - \lambda \mu_p - \gamma \mathbf{1} = 0 \tag{2.6}$$

$$\frac{\partial L}{\partial \lambda} = \mu_p - w^\top \boldsymbol{\mu} = 0 \tag{2.7}$$

$$\frac{\partial L}{\partial \gamma} = 1 - w^\top \mathbf{1} = 0 \tag{2.8}$$

Solving (2.6) with respect to w, one gets

$$w = \lambda \left(V^{-1}\boldsymbol{\mu}\right) + \gamma \left(V^{-1}\mathbf{1}\right) \tag{2.9}$$

and multiplying both sides by $\boldsymbol{\mu}^\top$, one gets

$$\boldsymbol{\mu}^\top w = \lambda \left(\boldsymbol{\mu}^\top V^{-1}\boldsymbol{\mu}\right) + \gamma \left(\boldsymbol{\mu}^\top V^{-1}\mathbf{1}\right) \tag{2.10}$$

Consider now (2.10) and (2.7) together. Then

$$\mu_p = \lambda \left(\boldsymbol{\mu}^\top V^{-1}\boldsymbol{\mu}\right) + \gamma \left(\boldsymbol{\mu}^\top V^{-1}\mathbf{1}\right) \tag{2.11}$$

Multiplying both sides of (2.9) by $\mathbf{1}^\top$, one gets

$$\mathbf{1}^\top w = \lambda \left(\mathbf{1}^\top V^{-1}\boldsymbol{\mu}\right) + \gamma \left(\mathbf{1}^\top V^{-1}\mathbf{1}\right) \tag{2.12}$$

Then, considering (2.12) and (2.8) we have that

$$1 = \lambda \left(\mathbf{1}^\top V^{-1}\boldsymbol{\mu}\right) + \gamma \left(\mathbf{1}^\top V^{-1}\mathbf{1}\right) \tag{2.13}$$

Define now the following four coefficients:

$$A{:} = \mathbf{1}^\top V^{-1}\boldsymbol{\mu} = \boldsymbol{\mu}^\top V^{-1}\mathbf{1} \tag{2.14}$$

$$B{:} = \boldsymbol{\mu}^\top V^{-1}\boldsymbol{\mu} \tag{2.15}$$

$$C{:} = \mathbf{1}^\top V^{-1}\mathbf{1} \tag{2.16}$$

$$D{:} = BC - A^2 \tag{2.17}$$

Then (2.11) and (2.13) imply the following linear system for λ and γ:

$$\begin{cases} \lambda B + \gamma A = \mu_p \\ \lambda A + \gamma C = 1 \end{cases}$$

Solving it, one derives the expression of λ and γ the Lagrangian multipliers as a function of the portfolio expected return is given by

$$\lambda(\mu_p) = \frac{C\mu_p - A}{D} \tag{2.18}$$

$$\gamma(\mu_p) = \frac{B - A\mu_p}{D} \tag{2.19}$$

Insertion in (2.9) of the expressions of $\lambda(\mu_p)$ and $\gamma(\mu_p)$ produces the unique set of portfolio weights for the frontier portfolio having an expected rate of return of μ_p

$$w = g + h\mu_p \tag{2.20}$$

where, using the notation originally introduced by Merton

$$g := \frac{\left[B\left(V^{-1}\mathbf{1}\right) - A\left(V^{-1}\boldsymbol{\mu}\right)\right]}{D}$$

$$h := \frac{\left[C\left(V^{-1}\boldsymbol{\mu}\right) - A\left(V^{-1}\mathbf{1}\right)\right]}{D}$$

Note that, setting $\mu_p = 0 \Rightarrow w_p = g$. Hence g can be associated to the vector of portfolio weights for the frontier portfolio whose expected return equals to zero. Setting $\mu_p = 1 \Rightarrow w_p = g + h$. Then $w_p = g + h$ can be seen as the vector of portfolio weights for the frontier portfolio with expected return equal to one. Hence, if I want to build a frontier portfolio with expected return equal to μ_p, I know from the (2.20) that

$$w_p = g + h\mu_p$$

This portfolio can be built by combining g and $g + h$ with weights $(1 - \mu_p)$ and μ_p

$$(1 - \mu_p)\, g + \mu_p (g + h) = g + h\mu_p = w_p \qquad \square$$

The above proposition produces an important result. The full set of minimum variance portfolios is spanned by only two portfolios, g and h. In the traditional financial economic terminology, we have identified two mutual funds that span the full set of minimum variance portfolios. Since all rational investors following a mean–variance selection approach will invest in efficient portfolios, hence in a minimum variance one, this result shows that there is room for an intermediary offering at a fee the passive replication of these (or any other) two portfolios as a service. This will give investors the same set of efficient investment possibilities they would get by investing in any portfolio of the original N risky securities without incurring in the transaction costs and frictions that would derive from managing a larger portfolio. Having determined the minimum variance portfolio allocations, it is possible to compute the analytical expression of the efficient frontier:

Proposition 30. *The parametric expression of the efficient frontier is given by*

$$\sigma_P = \sqrt{\frac{1}{D}\left(C\mu_P^2 - 2A\mu_P + B\right)}$$

$$\mu_P \geq \frac{A}{C}$$

Proof. Let us denote with S the matrix:

$$S = \begin{bmatrix} B & A \\ A & C \end{bmatrix}$$

then λ, γ are related to the expected portfolio return by

$$\begin{pmatrix} \lambda \\ \gamma \end{pmatrix} = S^{-1}\begin{pmatrix} \mu_P \\ 1 \end{pmatrix}$$

and the optimal allocation is

$$w_P = \left[(V^{-1}\mu), (V^{-1}\mathbf{e})\right] S^{-1}\begin{pmatrix} \mu_P \\ 1 \end{pmatrix}$$

hence the variance of the optimal portfolio is given by

$$\begin{aligned}
\sigma_P^2 &= w_P^T V w_P \\
&= [\mu_P, 1]\, S^{-1}\begin{bmatrix} (\mu^T V^{-1}) \\ (\mathbb{I}^T V^{-1}) \end{bmatrix} V\left[(V^{-1}\mu), (V^{-1}\mathbf{e})\right] S^{-1}\begin{bmatrix} \mu_P \\ \mathbb{I} \end{bmatrix} \\
&= [\mu_P, 1]\, S^{-1}\begin{bmatrix} B & A \\ A & C \end{bmatrix} S^{-1}\begin{bmatrix} \mu_P \\ 1 \end{bmatrix} \\
&= [\mu_P, 1]\, S^{-1} S S^{-1}\begin{bmatrix} \mu_P \\ 1 \end{bmatrix}
\end{aligned}$$

$$= [\mu_P, 1]\, S^{-1} \begin{bmatrix} \mu_P \\ 1 \end{bmatrix}$$

$$= \frac{1}{D}\left(C\mu_P^2 - 2A\mu_P + B\right)$$

thus the volatility of the minimum variance frontier is obtained considering the square root of the last expression. The minimum variance portfolio is identified by the condition:

$$\frac{d\sigma_p^2}{d\mu_p} = \frac{1}{D}\left(2C\mu_P - 2A\right) = 0$$

hence $\mu_P = \frac{A}{C}$. □

It is now possible to illustrate the general shape of the efficient frontier determined by N securities analyzing the possible shapes that occur in the simplest market formed by two non-dominated risky securities.

2.1.7 *The general solution in the presence of a risk-free security*

We conclude reporting for completeness the vector solution of the general case with N risky assets and a riskless security. Let w be the column vector of the N weights of the risky assets and $w_f = 1 - w^\top \mathbf{1}$ the weight of the investment in the risk free security. The expected return of the portfolio can be written as

$$\begin{aligned}\mu_p &= w_f r_f + w^\top \boldsymbol{\mu} \\ &= \left(1 - w^\top \mathbf{1}\right) r_f + w^\top \boldsymbol{\mu} \\ &= r_f + w^\top \left(\boldsymbol{\mu} - r_f \mathbf{1}\right)\end{aligned}$$

We can find the optimal weights by solving the following quadratic problem:

$$\min_w \frac{1}{2} w^\top V w$$

$$\text{s.t.}\quad w^\top \left(\boldsymbol{\mu} - r_f \mathbf{1}\right) = \mu_{p^*} - r_f$$

then, we can state the following result:

Proposition 31. *The set of efficient portfolios in a market of N risky assets and a risk-free one is spanned by two funds: the risk-free fund corresponding to the allocation $(w_f, 0) \in R^{N+1}$ and the tangency portfolio $(0, w^*) \in R^{N+1}$ to the efficient frontier of risky securities only, where:*

$$w_f = \frac{B - Ar_f - \mu_{p^*}(A - Cr_f)}{H}$$

$$w^* = \lambda V^{-1}(\boldsymbol{\mu} - r_f \mathbf{1})$$

$$\lambda = \frac{\mu_{p^*} - r_f}{H}$$

The expressions of A, B, and C are given by Eqs. (2.14)–(2.16). *The efficient frontier is linear and is given by*

$$\mu_{p^*} - r_f = \sqrt{H}\sigma_{p^*}$$

$$H = B - 2Ar_f + Cr_f^2$$

Proof. The Lagrangian is

$$L = \frac{1}{2}w^\top V w + \lambda\left[\mu_p - r_f - w^\top(\boldsymbol{\mu} - r_f\mathbf{1})\right]$$

and the FOCs are

$$\frac{\partial L}{\partial w} = Vw - \lambda(\boldsymbol{\mu} - r_f\mathbf{1}) = 0$$

$$\frac{\partial L}{\partial \lambda} = \mu_p - r_f - w^\top(\boldsymbol{\mu} - r_f\mathbf{1}) = 0$$

From the first condition, we know that

$$w = \lambda V^{-1}(\boldsymbol{\mu} - r_f\mathbf{1}) \tag{2.21}$$

This condition shows that the allocation in the portfolio of risky securities is the same for any target expected return which will affect only the value of the scalar quantity λ. This fact proves the two fund separation theorem. The risky portfolio allocations will be proportional to $V^{-1}(\boldsymbol{\mu} - r_f\mathbf{1})$. If we multiply now both sides of (2.21) by $(\boldsymbol{\mu} - r_f\mathbf{1})^\top$ we get:

$$(\boldsymbol{\mu} - r_f\mathbf{1})^\top w = \lambda(\boldsymbol{\mu} - r_f\mathbf{1})^\top V^{-1}(\boldsymbol{\mu} - r_f\mathbf{1}) \tag{2.22}$$

From the last FOC, we have that

$$(\boldsymbol{\mu} - r_f\mathbf{1})^\top w = \mu_{p^*} - r_f$$

If we substitute this result in (2.22) we see that

$$\begin{aligned}
\mu_{p^*} - r_f &= \lambda\,(\boldsymbol{\mu} - r_f\mathbf{1})^\top V^{-1}(\boldsymbol{\mu} - r_f\mathbf{1}) \\
\lambda &= \frac{\mu_{p^*} - r_f}{(\boldsymbol{\mu} - r_f\mathbf{1})^\top V^{-1}(\boldsymbol{\mu} - r_f\mathbf{1})} \\
\lambda &= \frac{\mu_{p^*} - r_f}{H}
\end{aligned}$$

where H is equal to

$$H = (\boldsymbol{\mu} - r_f\mathbf{1})^\top V^{-1}(\boldsymbol{\mu} - r_f\mathbf{1}) = B - 2Ar_f + Cr_f^2 \tag{2.23}$$

and A, B, and C are determined by Eqs. (2.14)–(2.16). If we substitute the value of λ in the (2.21) we can find the value of the optimal weights for the risky assets

$$w = \underbrace{\frac{\mu_p - r_f}{H}}_{1\times 1}\underbrace{\underbrace{V^{-1}}_{N\times N}\underbrace{(\boldsymbol{\mu} - r_f\mathbf{1})}_{N\times 1}}_{N\times 1} \tag{2.24}$$

As we can see the weights of the MV portfolios are the product of a scalar (function of the desired excess return over the risk-free) times a $N\times 1$ vector. This means the proportion of the different risky assets in every portfolio will be the same (defined by $V^{-1}(\boldsymbol{\mu} - r_f\mathbf{1})$). The variance of the portfolio is

$$\begin{aligned}
\sigma^2 &= w^\top V w \\
&= \left(\frac{\mu_{p^*} - r_f}{H} V^{-1}(\boldsymbol{\mu} - r_f\mathbf{1})\right)^\top V \left(\frac{\mu_{p^*} - r_f}{H} V^{-1}(\boldsymbol{\mu} - r_f\mathbf{1})\right) \\
&= \frac{[\mu_{p^*} - r_f]^2}{H}
\end{aligned}$$

which implies that the analytical expression of the efficient frontier is given by

$$\sigma_{p^*} = \frac{\mu_{p^*} - r_0}{\sqrt{H}}$$

i.e., an additional unit of risk implies an increase in the required expected return of an amount:

$$\frac{\mu_{p^*} - r_f}{\sigma_{p^*}} = (\mu_{p^*} - r_f) \times \frac{\sqrt{H}}{\mu_{p^*} - r_f} = \sqrt{H} \tag{2.25}$$

This yields to the linear interpretation of the efficient set. The weight of the risk-free security can be determined in the following residual way:

$$\begin{aligned} w_f &= 1 - w^{\intercal}\mathbf{1} \\ &= \frac{B - Ar_f - \mu_{p^*}(A - Cr_f)}{H} \end{aligned}$$

□

These results provide a suitable analytical framework to formulate the game solution concepts that underlie the equilibrium asset pricing approach that will be discussed in the next sections.

2.1.8 *The FOC for a mean–variance investor when a risk-free asset is present*

Given a degree of risk aversion τ, the standard *mean-variance* investor allocation problem can be formulates as follows:

$$\max_{\mathbf{w}} \left(1 - \mathbf{w}'\mathbf{e}\right) r^f + \mathbf{w}'\mu - \frac{1}{2}\tau(\mathbf{w}'\Sigma\mathbf{w})$$

where $E[\mathbf{r}] = (1 - \mathbf{w}'\mathbf{e})\, r^f + \mathbf{w}'\mu = r^f + \mathbf{w}'(\mu - r^f\mathbf{e})$ and $\text{Var}[\mathbf{w}'\mathbf{r}] = \mathbf{w}'\Sigma\mathbf{w}$.

Concavity of the problem implies that FOC are necessary and sufficient and define the following system of N linear equations in N unknowns, the portfolio weights $\mathbf{w} \in \mathcal{R}^N$:

$$(\mu - r^f\mathbf{e}) - \tau\Sigma\mathbf{w} = \mathbf{0}$$

Solving the FOC yields:

$$\hat{\mathbf{w}} = \frac{1}{\tau}\Sigma^{-1}\left(\mu - r^f\mathbf{e}\right)$$

which makes clear that optimal weights depend on preferences and the first two moments of the distribution of future returns.

Consider now the special case in which $\hat{\mathbf{w}}'\mathbf{e} = 1$, that is no investment in the risk-free asset is allowed. The optimal portfolio in this case one recovers the allocation corresponding to the *tangency portfolio* which depends exclusively on the first two moments of the distribution of future returns:

$$\mathbf{e}'\hat{\mathbf{w}} = \frac{1}{\tau}\mathbf{e}'\Sigma^{-1}\left(\mu - r^f\mathbf{e}\right) = 1 \Longrightarrow \tau = \mathbf{e}'\Sigma^{-1}\left(\mu - r^f\mathbf{e}\right)$$

$$\hat{\mathbf{w}}^T = \frac{\Sigma^{-1}\left(\mu - r^f\mathbf{e}\right)}{\mathbf{e}'\Sigma^{-1}\left(\mu - r^f\mathbf{e}\right)}$$

2.2 Market-Based Asset Pricing

2.2.1 *The capital asset pricing model*

When prices are determined solely based on purely subjective preferences and beliefs, the valuation of buyers and sellers might be divergent and do not give rise to trade. To analyze the relationship between the fair price of an asset and its characteristics, it is therefore necessary to introduce a minimal strategic framework to identify the minimum set of conditions on agent beliefs and preferences and on the exchange conditions that guarantee the existence of an equilibrium where traders are willing to transact.

The capital asset pricing model, originally proposed by Sharpe Lintner and Mossin, characterizes a simple set of conditions that are sufficient to prove the existence of a single-period market equilibrium and work out the corresponding pricing equations. In the following, we list these conditions:

(1) **Preferences:** agent's subjective valuations are consistent with a mean–variance selection principle.
(2) **Beliefs:** agent's beliefs are homogeneous and all the relevant information is public.
(3) **Exchange conditions:** investors are price takers and there is no market impact, i.e., all assets can be bought/sold at the observed market price.
(4) **Markets are frictionless:**
    (a) Zero transaction costs.
    (b) Assets are divisible into any desired unit and available in any quantity.

(c) There are no institutional restrictions to trades, e.g., short-selling is allowed.
(d) Taxes are not distortionary.

(5) The market includes a risk-free security remunerated at a rate r_f and investors have the unlimited ability to borrow or to invest.

2.2.2 *The market portfolio*

We are now ready to prove:

Proposition 32. *Under Assumptions* 1–5, *all the investors demand the same portfolio of risky assets, the so called market portfolio* $\mathbf{x}^M$. *Denoting by* $x_i^{T,a}$ *the allocation to security* i *in the tangency portfolio of any investor* a, *and* x_i^M *the allocation to security* i *in the market portfolio* M

$$x_i^{T,a} = x_i^M \quad i = 1, \ldots, N \text{ for any agent } a \text{ trading in the market.}$$

This market fund is constructed as follows: it includes all risky assets with non-zero price, each one in proportion to its relative market capitalization:

$$x_i^M = \frac{P_i \times N\text{-}shares_i}{\sum_{j=1}^N P_j \times N\text{-}shares_j}$$

where P_i *is the price of a single share of asset* i *and* N-$shares_i$ *is the number of shares outstanding.*

Proof. Given Assumptions 1 and 2 and 5, every investor will face the same efficient frontier, in fact the two-fund separation theorem implies that all the investors will hold a fraction of wealth in the risk-free rate and a fraction in the tangency portfolio. Homogeneity of expectation implies that the tangency portfolios is the same for everybody $x_i^{T,a} = x_i^{T,a'}$ for any two agents a and a' and $i = 1, \ldots, N$. In light of Assumptions 3 and 4, a risky security may have a non-zero equilibrium price if and only if it has a non-zero demand. Hence it must belong to the tangency portfolio of at least one agent and thus, in light of the previous observation, of each investor. Then we can conclude $x_i^M := x_i^{T,a}$ and $i = 1, \ldots, N$. On the other hand, in equilibrium the supply of each asset must be equal to the demand. The total supply of each risky asset is given by the price of a single share P_i multiplied by the number of shares outstanding $N\text{-}shares_i$. Since the risky fund of all the investors has the same compositions, in equilibrium the share of the market portfolio supplied by asset i must be equal to the share demanded by each investor:

$$x_i^M = \frac{P_i \times N\text{-}shares_i}{\sum_{j=1}^{N} P_j \times N\text{-}shares_j}$$

and the proposition is proved. □

2.2.3 *The capital market line*

In light of the previous proposition, the efficient portfolios form a linear frontier whose equation is obtained setting the tangency portfolio equal to the market one. Then

$$\frac{\mu_T - r_f}{\sigma_T} = \frac{\mu_M - r_f}{\sigma_M}$$

and for any efficient portfolio:

$$\mu_e - r_f = \frac{\mu_M - r_f}{\sigma_M}\sigma_e \tag{2.26}$$

The capital market line (CML) states that the expected return of any efficient risky portfolio in excess of the risk-free is proportional to the asset volatility and the coefficient of proportionality, which is the maximal one that can be achieved by investing in the market. It is equal to the expected excess return-to-risk ratio for the market portfolio. This ratio is known as the name of Sharpe ratio.

2.2.4 *The security market line*

To characterize the value of any asset in equilibrium, it is necessary and possible to assess the expected return also for possibly inefficient portfolios.

Proposition 33. *The security market line (SML) describes a linear relation between the expected the excess return of a generic portfolio and the excess return of the market portfolio:*

$$\mu_i - r_f = \beta_i (\mu_M - r_f)$$

$$\beta_i = \frac{\sigma_{i,M}}{\sigma_M^2}$$

It shows that the risk premium for a generic security in the CAPM can be decomposed as the product of a firm-specific index of risk exposure, the β_i index, and of a market invariant price of risk, equal to the market risk premium $(\mu_M - r_f)$.

Proof. From the FOC conditions for a market with N risky and one risk-free asset, it is immediate to verify that for any efficient portfolio p and every other portfolio q,

$$\sigma_p^2 = \frac{(\mu_p - r_f)^2}{H} \tag{2.27}$$

$$\sigma_{pq} = \frac{(\mu_p - r_f)(\mu_q - r_f)}{H} \tag{2.28}$$

We can solve (2.28) for μ_q

$$\mu_q - r_f = \frac{H\sigma_{pq}}{\mu_p - r_f} \tag{2.29}$$

We can now solve (2.27) for H

$$H = \frac{(\mu_p - r_f)^2}{\sigma_p^2}$$

and inserting this expression in (2.29)

$$\mu_q - r_f = \frac{\sigma_{pq}}{\sigma_p^2}(\mu_p - r_f).$$

Without loss of generality, we can consider a special frontier portfolio, the tangency portfolio that, by the previous proposition, in equilibrium must be equal to the market portfolio M. Then we can conclude that

$$\mu_q = r_f + \beta_q(\mu_M - r_f)$$

□

2.2.5 *SML and CML*

The SML is not an equilibrium condition alternative to the CML: it is simply its extension to possibly non-efficient portfolios. It is useful to compare the two expressions. Recalling that $\beta_i = \frac{\sigma_i}{\sigma_M}\rho_{iM}$

$$SML \Rightarrow \mu_i = r_f + (\mu_M - r_f)\frac{\sigma_i}{\sigma_M}\rho_{iM}$$

$$CML \Rightarrow \mu_e = r_f + (\mu_M - r_f)\frac{\sigma_e}{\sigma_M}$$

The first important observation is that the two equations coincide if the correlation coefficient is equal to $\rho_{eM} = 1$. Hence, in equilibrium, *a portfolio is efficient if and only if it is perfectly correlated with the market one.*

Risk premium and diversification

For a fixed level of volatility $\sigma_i = \sigma_e$, $\mu_i - r_f \leq \mu_e - r_f$. In other words, among all the assets with the same level of volatility, those that are efficient receive the highest compensation. This fact can be rationalized by observing that in a CAPM framework, the only compensated risk is the so-called systematic one, i.e., the one perfectly correlated with the aggregate market fluctuations and thus cannot be diversified away.

It is possible to formalize this argument by introducing a regression model that correlates the fluctuations of each portfolio return with those of the market portfolio. This is the Sharpe regression model:

$$\widetilde{r}_i - r_f = \alpha_i + \beta_i \left(\widetilde{r}_M - r_f\right) + \varepsilon_i$$

which is compatible with the SML provided $\alpha_i = 0$. Then, under the conventional assumptions on the residual term ε_i, one can verify that

$$\sigma_i^2 = \beta_i^2 \sigma_M^2 + \sigma_{\varepsilon_i}^2$$

The first contribution, $\beta_i^2 \sigma_M^2$, accounts for the so-called systematic risk, while the second one, $\sigma_{\varepsilon_i}^2$, accounts for the idiosyncratic or diversifiable one.

If now we assume that residuals are uncorrelated $E\left[\varepsilon_i \varepsilon_j\right] = 0$ and compute the portfolio variance

$$\sigma_p^2 = Var^{\mathbb{P}}\left[\sum_{i=1}^{N} w_i \widetilde{r}_i\right] = \beta_p^2 \sigma_M^2 + \sigma_{\varepsilon p}^2$$

we can observe that in the limit of a large portfolio, $N \to +\infty$, by considering the equally weighted portfolio $w_i = N^{-1}$

$$\sigma_{\varepsilon p}^2 = \sum_{i=1}^{N} \frac{\sigma_{\varepsilon i}^2}{N^2} \to 0$$

showing that in a sufficiently large market, the risk component associated to the residuals can be diversified out at no cost.

2.2.6 *Market price as the present value of cash flows*

The role of CAPM as a tool to relate the market price of each security to its characteristics is best understood observing that the SML may be used to relate the market price to the expected cash flows. Consider a single period project that is funded at time t, today, and liquidated at time $t+1$. Its liquidation will produce a random cash flow $\widetilde{CF}_{t+1}$ and a simple accounting relationship, the definition of the random return $\tilde{r}$, connects it to the fair price p_t. In fact:

$$\tilde{r} = \frac{\widetilde{CF}_{t+1} - p_t}{p_t}$$

Then its $\mathbb{P}$-expectation is

$$E_t^{\mathbb{P}}[\tilde{r}] = \frac{E_t^{\mathbb{P}}\left[\widetilde{CF}_{t+1}\right] - p_t}{p_t}$$

$$1 + E_t^{\mathbb{P}}[\tilde{r}] = \frac{E_t^{\mathbb{P}}\left[\widetilde{CF}_{t+1}\right]}{p_t}$$

$$p_t = \frac{E_t^{\mathbb{P}}\left[\widetilde{CF}_{t+1}\right]}{1+\mu}$$

Since the CAPM SML states that

$$\mu = r_f + \beta\left[\mu_M - r_f\right]$$

where β is the risk exposure of a security belonging to the same asset class of the original project, i.e., a security whose payoff has a similar risk profile, we can conclude that

$$p_t = \frac{E_t^{\mathbb{P}}\left[\widetilde{CF}_{t+1}\right]}{1 + r_f + \beta\left[\mu_M - r_f\right]}$$

This present value relation shows that a variation in the market price may be driven by two independent causes: a structural change of the expected cash flows, or a change in the discount rate. The SML shows that in a CAPM equilibrium the variation of the discount rate may change for three reasons: a change in the level of the risk-free rate r_f, a change in the price of market risk $[\mu_M - r_f]$, or a change in the risk exposure β_j. A similar decomposition is testable relying on market data and is a cornerstone of modern corporate valuation approaches. A strong limitation to this formula is its static single-period nature, i.e., the above discussion offers only comparative statics and no dynamic information on price changes can be extracted from it.

Exercise 34. *There are two stocks A and B, whose market prices are given by $p_A = 50\$$ and $p_B = 75\$$. Suppose returns are described by the following single factor model without idiosyncratic risk*

$$r_i = r_0 + \beta_i (r_m - r_0)$$

and consider the following parameters: $\mu_m = 10\%$ per annum, $r_0 = 3\%$ p.a., $\beta_A = 2$, and $\beta_B = 1.5$. What prices for the two stocks do you expect one year from today?

Solution. The expected returns according to the model are

$$\mu_j = r_0 + \beta_j (\mu_m - r_0)$$

and substituting numbers

$$\mu_A = 0.03 + 2\,(0.07) = 17$$

$$\mu_B = 0.03 + 1.5\,(0.07) = 13.5$$

Therefore expected prices are

$$E_t^{\mathbb{P}}[p_{j,t+1}] = p_{j,t}(1 + \mu_j)$$

$$E_t^{\mathbb{P}}[p_{A,t+1}] = 50\,(1.17) = 58.5$$

$$E_t^{\mathbb{P}}[p_{B,t+1}] = 75\,(1.135) = 85.125$$

2.2.7 *The zero-beta CAPM (Black)*

Black (1972) developed a pricing model for risky assets that does not consider the existence of a risk-free security. In the following proposition, we derive the pricing equation corresponding to the SML within this simplified framework.

Proposition 35. *Consider an efficient portfolio p_M, as the proxy of the market portfolio different from the (absolute) minimum* *variance portfolio. Then there exists a unique minimum variance (inefficient) portfolio,* $ZC(p_M)$*, which has zero covariance with* p_M*. Then for any portfolio* q*:*

$$\mu_q = \mu_{ZC(p_M)} + \beta_q^{p_M}\left[\mu_{p_M} - \mu_{ZC(p_M)}\right]$$

Proof. The standard definition of covariance between two portfolios is

$$\mathrm{Cov}^{\mathbb{P}}(\tilde{r}_p, \tilde{r}_q) \equiv w_p^\top V w_q \tag{2.30}$$

Consider now the FOC used in the derivation of the minimum variance frontier with N risky assets. When p is efficient, we know that the optimal weights are

$$w_p = \lambda V^{-1}e + \gamma V^{-1}\mathbf{1} \tag{2.31}$$

where λ and γ are function of the expected return of the portfolio p. Let's substitute (2.30) in the (2.31)

$$\begin{aligned}\mathrm{Cov}(\tilde{r}_p, \tilde{r}_q) &= \left[\lambda V^{-1}e + \gamma V^{-1}\mathbf{1}\right]^\top V w_q \\ &= \lambda e^\top V^{-1} V w_q + \gamma \mathbf{1}^\top V^{-1} V w_q \\ &= \lambda e^\top w_q + \gamma \mathbf{1}^\top w_q\end{aligned}$$

and knowing that

$$\begin{aligned} e^\top w_q &= E_t^{\mathbb{P}}(\tilde{r}_q) \\ \mathbf{1}^\top w_q &= 1 \end{aligned}$$

we can write

$$\mathrm{Cov}(\tilde{r}_p, \tilde{r}_q) = \lambda E_t^{\mathbb{P}}[\tilde{r}_q] + \gamma \tag{2.32}$$

Let's now set $q = ZC(p)$. Then

$$\begin{aligned}\mathrm{Cov}\left(\tilde{r}_p, \tilde{r}_{ZC(p)}\right) = \lambda E^{\mathbb{P}}\left[\tilde{r}_{ZC(p)}\right] + \gamma = 0 \\ \gamma = -\lambda E_t^{\mathbb{P}}\left[\tilde{r}_{ZC(p)}\right]\end{aligned}$$

and we can substitute this in the (2.32)

$$\mathrm{Cov}(\tilde{r}_p, \tilde{r}_q) = \lambda\left[E^{\mathbb{P}}[\tilde{r}_q] - E^{\mathbb{P}}\left[\tilde{r}_{ZC(p)}\right]\right] \tag{2.33}$$

Let apply this last result to the special case where $q = p$

$$\mathrm{Cov}\left(\tilde{r}_p, \tilde{r}_p\right) = \sigma_p^2 = \lambda \left[E^{\mathbb{P}}\left[\tilde{r}_p\right] - E^{\mathbb{P}}\left[\tilde{r}_{ZC(p)}\right]\right] \tag{2.34}$$

We can now divide the (2.33) by the (2.34)

$$\frac{\mathrm{Cov}\left(\tilde{r}_p, \tilde{r}_q\right)}{\sigma_p^2} = \frac{\lambda \left[E^{\mathbb{P}}\left[\tilde{r}_q\right] - E^{\mathbb{P}}\left[\tilde{r}_{ZC(p)}\right]\right]}{\lambda \left[E^{\mathbb{P}}\left[\tilde{r}_p\right] - E^{\mathbb{P}}\left[\tilde{r}_{ZC(p)}\right]\right]}$$

$$\beta_q^p = \frac{\left[E^{\mathbb{P}}\left[\tilde{r}_q\right] - E^{\mathbb{P}}\left[\tilde{r}_{ZC(p)}\right]\right]}{\left[E^{\mathbb{P}}\left[\tilde{r}_p\right] - E^{\mathbb{P}}\left[\tilde{r}_{ZC(p)}\right]\right]}$$

We can solve this equation for $E\left(\tilde{r}_q\right)$ and selecting p as an efficient proxy of the market portfolio p_M we can conclude that:

$$\left[E^{\mathbb{P}}\left[\tilde{r}_q\right] - E^{\mathbb{P}}\left[\tilde{r}_{ZC(p_M)}\right]\right] = \beta_q^p \left[E^{\mathbb{P}}\left[\tilde{r}_{p_M}\right] - E^{\mathbb{P}}\left[\tilde{r}_{ZC(p_M)}\right]\right] \quad \square$$

Remark 36. The existence of a linear relationship between the risk measure $\beta_q^{p_M}$ and the compensation for the risk-taking $\mu_q - \mu_{ZC(p_M)}$ requires only on the efficiency of the market proxy p_M. In addition, note that in light of this Proposition, the selection of the 'zero beta' fund, $ZC\left(p_M\right)$, the proxy for the risk-free asset, will have some degree of arbitrariness depending on the selection of p_M.

2.2.8 *The Roll's critique*

Directly related to Black's result is Roll's critique of CAPM asset pricing tests. It states that the existence of the CAPM equilibrium hypothesis cannot be tested unless the exact composition of the market portfolio is known. This is due to the combination of the following two facts:

- As highlighted in Remark 36, testing linearity of the risk-return trade-off relationship corresponding to the SML is fully equivalent to testing the mean-variance efficiency of the proxy of the selected market portfolio p_M.
- Because of the previous observation, in order to create a test for the CAPM equilibrium, it is then necessary to identify the exact composition of the market portfolio, but such a portfolio is unobservable. In fact, there is a conflict between two properties of the

market portfolio: on one side the portfolio must be tradeable for all the investors willing to allocate their wealth optimally. On the other hand, a large share of valuable assets like human capital or real estate that cannot be freely exchanged should be included in the market portfolio.

2.3 A Structural Interpretation

The paper "Betting Against Beta" by Frazzini and Pedersen (2014) proposes a structural explanation of the positive wedge between the expected return of the empirically determined zero market beta realized return μ_{ZC_M} and a r_f, as stable outcome in the empirical tests of CAPM since the earliest test carried out in Black *et al.* (1972) identifies a precise portfolio that exploits an anomalous return that the classical CAPM equilibrium is unable to capture.

The model proposed by Frazzini and Pedersen (2014), considers two kinds of agents. The first group of them faces leverage constraints and, therefore, over-weights high-beta assets in order to achieve the required return. The remaining agents can use leverage, but face margin constraints. Unconstrained agents underweight (i.e., short-sell) high-beta assets and buy low-beta assets that they can lever up. Hence in this model, the zero-beta extra-return originates compensates leverage-unconstrained investors and is paid by leverage-constrained investors that, trying to optimize their risk-return trade-off generate an anomalous price pressure on high-beta securities securities while reducing that on low-beta ones.

These findings rationalize a flatter security market line relative to the CAPM, that is better explained by the CAPM with restricted borrowing (as in Black (1972) and Brennan (1971)), and predicts that the slope depends on the tightness of the funding constraints across agents. Frazzini and Pedersen (2014) prove the following:

Proposition 37. *The equilibrium required return for any security i is*

$$\mu_i := \mathrm{E}_t(r^i_{t+1}) = r^f + \psi + \beta_i \lambda$$

$$\beta_i = \mathrm{Cov}_t\left(r^M_{t+1}, r^i_{t+1}\right)$$

$$\lambda = \mu_M - r^f - \psi$$

where ψ is the Lagrange multiplier, the shadow cost, of the funding constraint.

Remark 38. The result can be restated as follows: the resulting security market line is equivalent to the one of a Black CAPM with $\mu_{ZC(M)} - r_f = \psi$.

Proof. Consider an overlapping-generations (OLGs) economy, with agents $i = 1, \ldots, I$ born in each time period t with wealth W_t^i, and living for two periods. Securities $s = 1, \ldots, S$ are traded by investors, in a way such that each security s pays dividends δ_t^s and has x^{*s} shares outstanding. Each time period t, young agents then choose a portfolio of shares $x = (x^1, \ldots, x^S)'$, investing the rest of their wealth in a risk-free asset, with return r^f. The utility maximization problem is then

$$\max x'(\mathrm{E}_t(P_{t+1} + \delta_{t+1}) - (1 + r^f)P_t) - \frac{\gamma^i}{2} x'\Omega x \tag{2.35}$$

where P_t is the vector of prices at time t, Ω is the variance–covariance matrix of $(P_{t+1} + \delta_{t+1})$, γ^i denotes individual i's risk aversion. Agent i is subject to the portfolio constraint

$$m^i \sum_s x^s P_t^s \leq W_t^i \tag{2.36}$$

requiring that some multiple m^i of the total investment, i.e., of the sum over s of the shares in each security multiplied by their respective prices must be less than the total agent's wealth. The investment constraint depends then on the agent i: for example, some investors might not be allowed to use leverage, i.e., might have $m^i = 1$, others might not only not be allowed to use leverage, but might also be obliged to have reserves in cash (so that $m^i > 1$). Assuming a competitive equilibrium where demand equals supply. i.e., $\sum_i x^i = x^*$, and deriving hence the FOC and solving for agent i the condition

$$0 = \mathrm{E}_t(P_{t+1} + \delta_{t+1}) - (1 + r^f)P_t - \gamma^i \Omega x^i - \psi^i P_t \tag{2.37}$$

where ψ^i is the Lagrangian multiplier of the portfolio constraint, we get for each investor i that the corresponding optimal portfolio x^i which is given by

$$x^i = \frac{1}{\gamma^i} \Omega^{-1}(\mathrm{E}_t(P_{t+1} + \delta_{t+1}) - (1 + r^f + \psi^i)P_t). \tag{2.38}$$

Then, the equilibrium condition will imply that

$$x^* = \frac{1}{\gamma}\Omega^{-1}(\mathrm{E}_t(P_{t+1} + \delta_{t+1}) - (1 + r^f + \psi)P_t) \tag{2.39}$$

where the aggregate risk aversion γ is defined as $1/\gamma = \sum_i 1/\gamma^i$ and $\psi = \sum_i(\gamma/\gamma^i)\psi^i$ is the weighted average Lagrange multiplier. Recalling that the return of any security s is always defined as $r^i_{t+1} = (P^i_{t+1} + \delta^i_{t+1})/P^i_t - 1$, that the expression for beta of a stock is $\beta_s = \mathrm{Cov}_t(r^s_{t+1}, r^M_{t+1})/\mathrm{Var}_t(r^M_{t+1})$, and defining the return of the market index as r^M_{t+1}, the results follow. □

Explicitly, then, risk premia are affected by the tightness of agents' portfolio constraints, as measured by the Lagrangian multiplier ψ. Then, tighter portfolio constraints, i.e. higher ψ, flatten the security market line by increasing the intercept and decreasing the slope λ.

Betting against beta factor

As a second constructive result, they suggest the introduction of a tradeable factor, i.e., a zero beta portfolio is named Betting Against Beta (BAB), that goes long under-priced low-beta assets and shorts overpriced high-beta ones. The main properties of the BAB portfolio are stated in the following:

Proposition 39 (Positive expected return of BAB). *Let the BAB portfolio be defined as a self-financing portfolio ($1'_n w_H = 1$ and $1'_n w_L = 1$) observed at time t that is long the low-beta portfolio and short the high-beta portfolio, with return given by:*

$$r^{BAB}_{t+1} = \frac{1}{\beta^L}(r^L_{t+1} - r^f) - \frac{1}{\beta^H}(r^H_{t+1} - r^f) \tag{2.40}$$

where $r^L = r'_{t+1}w_L$, $r^H = r'_{t+1}w_H$, $\beta^L = \beta' w_L$ and $\beta^H = \beta' w_H$ denote respectively the betas of the high- and low-beta assets portfolios, with $\beta^H > \beta^L$. The resulting portfolio is market neutral, $\beta_{BAB} = 0$: the long side has been leveraged to a unit beta, and the short side has been de-leveraged to a beta of 1. The expected excess return of the self-financing BAB factor is positive and is given by

$$\mathrm{E}_t(r^{BAB}_{t+1} - r_f) = \left(\frac{1}{\beta^L} - \frac{1}{\beta^H}\right)\psi > 0 \tag{2.41}$$

It is increasing in the ex-ante beta spread $(\beta^H - \beta^L)/\left(\beta^L\beta^H\right)$ *and in the funding tightness as measured by* ψ.

Proof. It is sufficient to work out the expected return using the modified SML and the result follows from simple linear algebra. □

In summary, a BAB portfolio earns a positive expected return on average: the size of the expected return depends on the spread in the betas and on the intensity of portfolio constraints in the market, as captured by the average of the Lagrange multipliers ψ.

2.4 Arbitrage-Based Pricing Theory

To overcome the empirical limitation of the CAPM theory highlighted by the empirical tests and by the Roll's critique, it is necessary to introduce a novel solution concept that gives rise to the so-called Arbitrage Pricing Theory (APT). In this new approach, the demand and supply of securities are not explicitly modeled while anticipate subject and verb it is retained the basic assumption that individual traders in the market will compete to exploit the speculative opportunities. Then the resulting price pressure will act reducing the size of these opportunities and driving asset prices to "efficiency", a condition which is formalized requiring that profitable investment opportunities at zero cost and zero risk are absent from the market.

Ross (1973) proves that this condition is sufficient to characterize the emergent risk-return trade-off. We formalize this argument in a static, single-period market where a linear multi-factor regression model describes asset returns fluctuations.

2.4.1 *The linear factor model*

As far as the return-generating process is concerned, the framework can accommodate both single-factor and multi-factor models

$$r_i = b_{i0} + b_{i1}F_1 + \varepsilon_i$$
$$r_i = b_{i0} + b_{i1}F_1 + b_{i2}F_2 + \cdots + b_{ik}F_k + \varepsilon_i$$

where F_{1t} is the return of the first risk factor in time t and b_{i1} is the sensitivity (exposure) of security i to the first risk factor. The most general factor model can be described as follows: the return generating process can be represented as follows:

$$\mathbf{r} = \mathbf{b}_0 + \mathbf{BF} + \varepsilon$$

Where

$$\mathbf{r}_t = \begin{bmatrix} r_{1t} \\ r_{2t} \\ \vdots \\ r_{nt} \end{bmatrix} \qquad \mathbf{b}_0 = \begin{bmatrix} b_{10} \\ b_{20} \\ \vdots \\ b_{n0} \end{bmatrix} \qquad \mathbf{B} = \begin{bmatrix} b_{11} & b_{12} & \cdots & b_{1k} \\ b_{21} & b_{22} & \cdots & b_{2k} \\ \vdots & \vdots & \ddots & \vdots \\ b_{n1} & b_{n2} & \cdots & b_{nk} \end{bmatrix}$$

$$\mathbf{F}_t = \begin{bmatrix} F_{1t} \\ F_{2t} \\ \vdots \\ F_{kt} \end{bmatrix} \qquad \varepsilon_t = \begin{bmatrix} \varepsilon_{1t} \\ \varepsilon_{2t} \\ \vdots \\ \varepsilon_{kt} \end{bmatrix}$$

where the driving uncertainty satisfies the following hypotheses:

$$E^{\mathbb{P}}\left(\varepsilon_{i,t}\varepsilon_{j,t}\right) = E^{\mathbb{P}}\left(F_{i,t}\varepsilon_{j,t}\right) = E^{\mathbb{P}}\left(F_{i,t}F_{j,t}\right) = 0,\ i \neq j$$
$$E^{\mathbb{P}}\left(\varepsilon_{i,t}^2\right) = s_i^2 < +\infty,$$

The formulation of the APT does not provide any prescription on the selection of the risk factors driving the return-generating process. The final characterization of the emerging risk-return trade-off will produce a testable hypothesis useful to discriminate the statistical accuracy implied by the selection of a specific set of factors. This makes the model flexible but hard to assess empirically.

The APT is a static model that makes predictions on unconditional expectations, thus no assumption on temporal correlations is necessary. The vector of expected return is given by:

$$\mu = E^{\mathbb{P}}(\mathbf{r}) = \mathbf{b}_0 + BE^{\mathbb{P}}(\mathbf{F}) \tag{2.42}$$

In statistical applications, it is sometimes useful to consider the specific normalization $E(\mathbf{F}) = 0$, $E(\mathbf{r}) = b_0$.[2] The main advantage of

---

[2]Note that this condition is not really restrictive since any model with $E(\mathbf{F}_t) \neq 0$ can be translated into an equivalent model with zero mean factors. This can be simply obtained defining the new factors as $\mathbf{F}' = \mathbf{F} - E(\mathbf{F})$, $b_0' = b_0 + E(\mathbf{F})$ and $\mathbf{B}' = \mathbf{B}$.

the linear factor assumption computation of the variance–covariance matrix:

$$E^{\mathbb{P}}\left[(\mathbf{r}-E(\mathbf{r}))^2\right]=\mathbf{B}E^{\mathbb{P}}\left[\mathbf{F}\mathbf{F}'\right]\mathbf{B}'+\mathbf{s}^2$$

which is equivalent, in a different notation to

$$\mathrm{Var}^{\mathbb{P}}(r_i)=\sum_k b_{i,k}^2\mathrm{Var}^{\mathbb{P}}(F_k)+s_i^2 \tag{2.43}$$

$$\mathrm{Cov}^{\mathbb{P}}(r_i,r_j)=\sum_k b_{i,k}b_{j,k}\mathrm{Var}^{\mathbb{P}}(F_k) \tag{2.44}$$

where the idiosyncratic components s_i^2 are expected to be small and vanishing in the limit of $N\to+\infty$.

2.4.2 *Arbitrage portfolios*

Consider a market with $N+1$ securities where the allocation w_0 on the risk-free security is determined by the budget constraint: $w_0 = 1-\sum_{i=1}^N w_i$ where $i=1,\dots,N$ are risky securities. Then we can define:

Definition 40. An arbitrage portfolio P_N with risky allocations $\mathbf{w}_P$ is a portfolio of N assets which fulfills the following properties.

Condition 41 (Zero initial investment). *The sum of the values invested in the n securities has to be equal to zero*

$$\sum_{i=1}^N w_i = 0 = \mathbf{w}_P^\top\mathbf{1}$$

Condition 42 (No systematic risk). *The weighted average sensitivity coefficient of the portfolio with respect to every risk factor has to be equal to zero*

$$\sum_{i=1}^N w_i b_{ij} = 0 = \mathbf{w}_P^\top\mathbf{b}_j \quad \forall j$$

or in vector notation:

$$\underbrace{\mathbf{w}_P^\top}_{1\times N}\underbrace{\mathbf{B}}_{N\times K}=\underbrace{\mathbf{0}}_{1\times K}$$

Condition 43 (Positive return). *The portfolio P has a strictly positive expected return:*

$$\mathbf{w}_P^\top \mathbf{1} = \mathbf{0}, \quad \mathbf{w}_P^\top \mathbf{B} = 0, \quad \mu_P = \mathbf{w}_P^\top \mu > 0$$

To avoid overly complicated statistical estimates of the idiosyncratic risk components, the main result will be stated assuming that the number of securities in the market is divergent $N \to +\infty$. In fact, since the idiosyncratic volatility components are uncorrelated among stocks hence, in the limit $N \to +\infty$, these contributions can be completely diversified out. Hence we introduce the following:

Definition 44. An asymptotic arbitrage opportunity is a sequence of portfolios $\{P_N\}_{N>\overline{N}}$, each one investing in N securities $N > \overline{N}$, satisfying these properties: (i) each portfolio of the sequence is an arbitrage portfolio and (ii) the limiting expected return remains positive while (iii) the idiosyncratic variance of the portfolio returns is completely diversified out as $N \to +\infty$:

$$\lim_{N\to+\infty} \mu_{P_N} = \mu_\infty > 0$$

$$\lim_{N\to+\infty} \mathrm{Var}^{\mathbb{P}}\left(\mathbf{w}_{P_N}^\top \varepsilon\right) = 0$$

From a practical point of view, we can interpret this limiting procedure as the requirement that the market is large enough that candidate arbitrage portfolios have an idiosyncratic risk with a variance lower than an arbitrary "confidence level" that is set up by the investor/econometrician.

The standard hypothesis of the APT model is that arbitrage opportunities are not present in the financial market. Hence in the following, we will assume the following:

Condition 45 (Zero expected return). *In the market there are no asymptotic arbitrage opportunities.*

In other words, any portfolio that does not require capital does not yield systematic risk, and has a small enough idiosyncratic variance, must have a negligible expected return. It is a weaker requirement than the existence of an equilibrium: it is possible to show that it is implied by the existence of an equilibrium (e.g., CAPM equilibrium is free from arbitrage opportunities) but the opposite implication is invalid.

2.4.3 *The Ross (1973) arbitrage pricing argument*

Suppose there are N stocks listed in the market and the number of relevant risk factors is K. The main result to value stocks within the APT framework proved by Ross is:

Theorem 46. *If no asymptotic arbitrage opportunities exist in the market, then the expected return of asset i, μ_i, is a linear combination of a constant component λ_0, a systematic component obtained by multiplication of the risk exposure b_{ij} of the security with respect to the jth factor price of risk λ_j, plus a non-systematic component*

$$\mu_i = \lambda_0 + \sum_{j=1}^{K} b_{ij}\lambda_j + v_i$$

The limit as $N \to \infty$ of the mean square non-systematic contribution, $N \to +\infty$

$$\lim_{N\to\infty} \frac{1}{N}\sum_{i=1}^{N} v_i^2 = 0$$

is zero.

Proof. Let's assume that we perform a cross-sectional regression of the expected returns of the stocks μ on a vector of ones $\mathbf{1}$ and the matrix of the risk exposures, $\mathbf{B}$, that is on the columns of the matrix $[\mathbf{1}, \mathbf{B}]$. Then each expected return can be represented as follows

$$\mu_i = \lambda_0 + \sum_{j=1}^{K} b_{ij}\lambda_j + v_i$$

and we may produce get OLS estimates for λ_0, λ_j $j = 1, \ldots, K$. Consider now a portfolio P invested in each stock with a weight w_i^ν proportional to the residual ν_i of the regression relative to that precise security. Specifically we will assume that the allocation on asset i is given by $w_i^\nu = \frac{\nu_i}{\sqrt{N}\|v\|_N}$, $\|v\|_N = \left(\sum_{i=1}^{N}\nu_i^2\right)^{1/2}$. By construction, in an OLS regression the error terms have zero mean and are uncorrelated with the independent variables so we have that

$$\sum_{i=1}^{N} w_i^\nu = \frac{1}{\sqrt{n}\,\|v\|_N}\sum_{i=1}^{N}\nu_i = 0$$

an

$$\sum_{i=1}^{N} w_i^{\nu} b_{ij} = \frac{1}{\sqrt{N}\,\|v\|_N} \sum_{i=1}^{N} b_{ij} v_i = 0 \quad j = 1, \ldots, K$$

From the portfolio perspective, these two statistical regularities generate a portfolio P with zero initial investment and zero exposure to each one of the K risk factors. Hence this portfolio satisfies two out of the three properties that define an arbitrage portfolio. We can compute the expected return of the portfolio P_N^{ν} set up of

$$E\left[r_{P_N^{\nu}}\right] = (\mathbf{w}^{\nu})^T \cdot \mu = \sum_{i=1}^{N} w_i^{\nu} \mu_i = \sum_{i=1}^{N} w_i^{\nu} \left(\lambda_0 + \sum_{j=1}^{K} b_{ij} \lambda_j + v_i \right)$$

We can see that this is the sum of three components but only the last one is different from zero. In fact

$$\sum_{i=1}^{N} w_i \lambda_0 = \sum_{i=1}^{N} \frac{\nu_i}{\|v\|_N \sqrt{N}} \lambda_0 = \frac{\lambda_0}{\sqrt{N}} \sum_{i=1}^{N} \nu_i = 0$$

The second component of the expected return is related to the exposure to the systematic risk factors, and also in this case we can show that, given the nature of our portfolio, this component has a zero value

$$\sum_{i=1}^{N} w_i^{\nu} \sum_{j=1}^{K} b_{ij} \lambda_j = \sum_{i=1}^{N} \frac{\nu_i}{\sqrt{N}} \sum_{j=1}^{K} b_{ij} \lambda_j = \sum_{j=1}^{K} \frac{\lambda_j}{\sqrt{N}} \sum_{i=1}^{N} b_{ij} \nu_i = 0.$$

The resulting expression of the expected return of

$$E^{\mathbb{P}}\left[r_{P_N^{\nu}}\right] = \mu_{P_N^{\nu}} = \sum_{i=1}^{N} w_i v_i$$

If $\mu_{P_N^{\nu}} > 0$ the corresponding portfolio would be an arbitrage. The absence of asymptotic arbitrage opportunities implies that a well-diversified portfolio in the limit $N \to \infty$ must have a limiting expected return $\mu_{P_\infty^{\nu}} = 0$, hence:

$$\lim_{N \to \infty} \mu_{P_N^{\nu}} = \mu_{P_\infty^{\nu}} = 0$$

$$\lim_{N \to \infty} \sum_{i=1}^{N} \frac{\nu_i}{\sqrt{N}\,\|v\|_N} v_i = \lim_{N \to \infty} \frac{1}{\sqrt{N}\,\|v\|_N} \sum_{i=1}^{N} \nu_i^2 = \lim_{N \to \infty} \frac{\|v\|_N}{\sqrt{N}} = 0$$

This last result concludes our demonstration because we can easily see that

$$\lim_{N\to\infty}\frac{1}{N}\sum_{i=1}^{N}\nu_i^2=\lim_{N\to\infty}\left(\frac{\|v\|_N}{\sqrt{N}}\right)^2=0$$

And the absence of arbitrage implies that in this market, in the limit of vanishing idiosyncratic volatility emerges a linear risk-return trade-off. □

2.4.4 *Economic interpretation of the λ coefficients*

In the previous section, we demonstrated that we can find a vector of $K+1$ coefficients $[\lambda_0,\lambda]=[\lambda_0,\lambda_1,\ldots,\lambda_K]$.

To identify the proper economic interpretation of these coefficients, consider first the portfolio with zero risk exposures $b_{0,j}=0$. Then $\mu_0=\lambda_0$ and absence of arbitrage opportunities jointly with the availability of the risk-free security impose also $\mu_0=r_f$. Then a proper APT, where relevant factors have been included, must verify the empirically testable condition:

$$H_0:\lambda_0=r_f$$

Consider now the so-called factor mimicking portfolios (FMPs) P_{F_k} for each relevant factor F_k $k=1,\ldots,K$. They are defined as traded replication portfolios for the factor F_k with risk exposures that are given by $b_{F_{P_k},m}=1$ is $m=k$, while $b_{P_{F_k},m}=0$ is $m\neq k$. Then, for each FMP security, we have that:

$$\mu_{P_{F_k}}-r_f=\lambda_k$$

λ_k, which is the price of the risk factor k, equals the excess return over the risk-free of a portfolio with a unit exposure to risk factor k and zero exposure to all other factors $m\neq k$. It can thus be interpreted as the risk premium that the investor gets for assuming a non zero exposure to this particular risk factor.

2.4.5 *APT when the risk factors are portfolio excess returns*

The identification of the factors is the crucial step in the definition of the APT. A method that turns out to be important in the application consists of choosing as factors excess returns for portfolios of stocks which are maximally correlated with some relevant economic variables. Let's assume that A and B are two portfolios and $K = 2$. The return-generating process in the market is

$$r_i - r_f = b_{i0} + b_{i1}F_1 + b_{i2}F_2 + \varepsilon_i$$

$$F_1 = r_A - r_f \quad \text{and} \quad F_2 = r_B - r_f$$

Now, from the APT

$$\mu_i - r_f = b_{i1}\lambda_1 + b_{i2}\lambda_2$$

and the previous equation must hold for every stock and for every portfolio, and in particular it must hold also for A and B. Thus by definition and without error it holds that for replicating portfolios:

$$b_{A1} = 1, \quad b_{A2} = 0 \quad \text{and} \quad \varepsilon_A = 0$$

$$b_{B1} = 0, \quad b_{B2} = 1 \quad \text{and} \quad \varepsilon_B = 0$$

Hence in this setting:

$$\lambda_1 = [\mu_A - r_f] = E^{\mathbb{P}}[F_1]$$

$$\lambda_2 = [\mu_B - r_f] = E^{\mathbb{P}}[F_2]$$

2.4.6 *APT and CAPM*

Suppose that

(1) The APT holds in a single-factor environment.
(2) The risk factor is the excess return of the market portfolio over the risk free rate: $r_M - r_f$.

From the return-generating process we have that

$$r_i - r_f = b_{i0} + b_{i1}(r_M - r_f) + \varepsilon_i$$

Since we assume that the market portfolio is the unique relevant factor in the APT model $b_{i0} = 0$

$$r_i - r_f = b_{i1}(r_M - r_f) + \varepsilon_i$$

Since the market portfolio is traded:

$$\mu_i - r_f = b_{i1}(\mu_M - r_f)$$

and we can conclude that $\beta_i = b_{i1}$ and the CAPM SML is consistent with the APT single-factor model. Which one of the two provides the most accurate description of a market can only be verified on an empirical basis.

2.4.7 *APT tests and factor-mimicking portfolios*

The methodology developed by Fama and MacBeth (1973) to estimate CAPM can be easily extended to the APT multifactor models. The general procedure can be summarized using vector notation as follows:

- Assume that the vector of excess expected returns $\widehat{\mu}_t - \widehat{\mu}_f \mathbf{I} \in \mathbb{R}^N$ and the risk exposures $\widehat{\mathbf{B}}$ are estimated using the a window of S observations between time $t-1$ and time $t-S$ and run the cross-sectional estimation:

$$\widehat{\mu}_t - \widehat{\mu}_f \mathbf{I} = \widehat{\mathbf{B}}\lambda + e_t$$

- Then:

$$\widehat{\lambda}_t = \left[(\widehat{\mathbf{B}})'\widehat{\mathbf{B}}\right]^{-1} \left[(\widehat{\mathbf{B}})' \left(\widehat{\mu}_t - \widehat{\mu}_f \mathbf{I}\right)\right]$$

and the final estimate is determined by the time series mean of the estimators:

$$\widehat{\lambda} = \frac{1}{T-S} \sum_{t=S+1}^{T} \widehat{\lambda}_t \quad \widehat{\mathbf{e}} = \frac{1}{T-S} \sum_{t=S+1}^{T} \widehat{\mathbf{e}}_t$$

As in the classical CAPM specification, it is possible to associate a portfolio return to each estimated coefficient, similarly, regression coefficients in the cross-sectional regression test of APT can be interpreted as expected excess returns for factor-mimicking portfolios. Fama (1970) proved the more general result that applies to any firm-specific characteristic. We can state the following:

Proposition 47. *Let the $N \times K$ matrix $(\widetilde{X}_t)_{i,k}$ include as regressors K arbitrary firm characteristics. Then the coefficients $\lambda_1, \ldots, \lambda_K$ in the cross-sectional regression:*

$$\underset{N\times 1}{R^e_{t+1}} = \underset{N\times(K+1)}{X_t} \cdot \underset{(K+1)\times 1}{\Lambda} + \underset{N\times 1}{\eta_{t+1}}$$

$$X_t := \begin{bmatrix} \mathbf{1}'_N \\ \widetilde{X}_t \end{bmatrix}, \Lambda := [\lambda_0, \lambda]$$

are the returns on K zero investment portfolios $p^{(k)} = (X_t'X_t)^{-1} X_t'e_k$. Portfolio $p^{(k)}$ has unit exposure on characteristics (k) and zero on the others. In addition, it minimizes the sum of squared allocations:

$$\min Tr\left[w'w\right]$$

$$\text{s.t. } : X_t'w = e_k$$

where $(e_k)_l = \delta_{k,l}$.

Proof. Introduce the following notation: $\left(R_{t+1}^e\right)_i$ excess return on security i, $(\widetilde{X}_t)_{i,k}$ characteristics k of security i at time t and define:

$$X_t := \left[\mathbf{1}_N, \widetilde{X}_t\right]$$

$$\underset{N\times(K+1)}{P_t} := \underset{N\times(K+1)}{(X_t)} \underset{(K+1)\times(K+1)}{\left(X_t X_t'\right)^{-1}}$$

denoting by $p_t^{(k)}$, $k = 0, \ldots, K$ the column vectors of P_t

$$P_t = \left[p_t^{(0)}, p_t^{(1)}, \ldots, p_t^{(K)}\right]$$

Each column vector $p_t^{(k)} \in \mathbb{R}^N$ identifies a portfolio. In fact by definition the following property holds:

$$P_t'X_t = \left(X_t'X_t\right)^{-1}\left(X_t'X_t\right) = \mathbb{I}_{(K\times 1)\times(K\times 1)} \tag{2.45}$$

and recalling that the first column of X_t is the vector $\mathbf{1}_N$, one gets:

$$\left(p^{(0)}\right)' \cdot \mathbf{1}_N = 1$$

$$\left(p^{(k)}\right)' \cdot \mathbf{1}_N = 0 \quad k > 1$$

The first portfolio $p^{(0)}$ invests a unit of capital, while the characteristics portfolios $p^{(k)}$, $k > 1$, are zero investment capital. The total allocations in the risk-free security will not sum to one. The cross-sectional regression on the vector of characteristics can be written in vector notation as

$$\underset{N\times 1}{R_{t+1}^e} = \underset{N\times(K+1)}{X_t} \cdot \underset{(K+1)\times 1}{\Lambda} + \underset{N\times 1}{\eta_{t+1}}$$

$$X_t := [\mathbf{1}_N, \widetilde{X}_t] \quad \Lambda := [\lambda_0, \lambda].$$

Then the OLS estimator for Λ will be:

$$\begin{aligned}\underset{(K+1)\times 1}{\widehat{\Lambda}} &= \underset{(K+1)\times(K+1)}{\left(X_t' X_t\right)^{-1}} \underset{(K+1)\times 1}{\left(X_t' R_{t+1}^e\right)} \\ &= \underset{(K+1)\times 1}{\left(P_t' R_{t+1}^e\right)}\end{aligned}$$

confirming that the coefficient $\widehat{\lambda}_k$ will correspond to the return of portfolio $p_t^{(k)}$. Let $(e_k)_l = \delta_{k,l}$, then the portfolio $p^{(k)}$ is by construction

$$\left(X_t' X_t\right)^{-1} X_t' e_k = p^{(k)}$$

Portfolio $p_k^{(k)}$ is then characterized by a unit value of characteristics k while 0 for all other characteristics. Equation (2.45) implies:

$$\sum_{n=1}^{N} \left(p_n^{(k)}\right)' (\widetilde{X}_t)_{n,k'} = \delta_{k,k'}, \quad k, k' > 1$$

Writing the first order condition of the corresponding constrained optimization problem, it is straightforward to prove that portfolio $p^{(k)}$ minimizes the sum of squared allocations:

$$\begin{aligned}&\min Tr\left[w'w\right] \\ s.t. \ &: X_t' w = e_k\end{aligned}$$

and the result is proved. □

2.5 APT and Risk-Neutral Valuation

In light of the above considerations, when a market is free from asymptotic arbitrage opportunities, it is possible to determine the risk premium of a generic asset as a linear function of the risk exposure. This implies that APT produces the following asset pricing formula:

$$\begin{aligned}p &= \frac{E^{\mathbb{P}}\left[\widetilde{CF}\right]}{1+\mu} \qquad (2.46) \\ &= \frac{E^{\mathbb{P}}\left[\widetilde{CF}\right]}{1 + r_f + \sum_{j=1}^{K} b_{ij}\lambda_j}\end{aligned}$$

where the individual risk exposures b_{ij} must be determined considering other securities with a similar risk profile. Hence linear APT predicts the risk adjustment which has to be applied in order to evaluate risky projects.

A key advantage of arbitrage pricing theory where the selection of factors is statistically validated, is that this valuation is common knowledge and shared among market participants. Now we show that it can be used to define a pricing kernel and a risk-neutral measure. In such a way that linear beta pricing in the multi-factor model and risk-neutral valuation produce the same price. This is done in the following:

Proposition 48. *Assume that in the market there are no arbitrage opportunities and the linear beta pricing model applies:*

$$E^{\mathbb{P}}[\mathbf{R} - r_f\mathbf{1}] = [B][\lambda]$$

then we can define

$$m^{APT}(\omega) := \left(1 - (\mathbf{F} - \mu)' \mathbf{V}^{-1}\lambda\right)$$

and

$$\mathbb{Q}^{APT}(\omega) := \mathbb{P}(\omega)\, m^{APT}(\omega)$$

Then, for any security with cash flow $\widetilde{CF}(\omega)$, the fair price is

$$p^{APT} = \frac{E^{\mathbb{P}}\left[\widetilde{CF}\right]}{1 + r_f + \sum_{j=1}^{K} b_{ij}\lambda_j} = \frac{E^{\mathbb{Q}^{APT}}\left[\widetilde{CF}\right]}{1 + r_f}$$

Proof. A linear beta pricing model is equivalent to

$$\underbrace{E^{\mathbb{P}}[\mathbf{R} - r_f\mathbf{1}]}_{N\times 1} = \underbrace{[B]}_{N\times K}\underbrace{[\lambda]}_{K\times 1} \tag{2.47}$$

where $\mathbf{R} = (R_1, \ldots, R_N)^T$ is the vector of N traded securities, $\lambda = (\lambda_1, \ldots, \lambda_K)^T$, $B = [b_1, \ldots, b_N]^T$

$$B = E^{\mathbb{P}}\left[(\mathbf{R} - r_f\mathbf{1})(\mathbf{F} - \mu)'\right]\mathbf{V}^{-1}$$

where

$$\mathbf{V} = E^{\mathbb{P}}\left[(\mathbf{F} - \mu)(\mathbf{F} - \mu)'\right].$$

Inserting the definition of the sensitivity matrix in (2.47), one gets

$$E^{\mathbb{P}}[\mathbf{R}-r_f\mathbf{1}]-E^{\mathbb{P}}\left[(\mathbf{R}-r_f\mathbf{1})(\mathbf{F}-\mu)'\right]\mathbf{V}^{-1}[\lambda]=\mathbf{0}$$
$$E^{\mathbb{P}}\left[(\mathbf{R}-r_f\mathbf{1})\left(1-(\mathbf{F}-\mu)'\mathbf{V}^{-1}\lambda\right)\right]=\mathbf{0}$$

hence, if one defines a pricing kernel:

$$m^{\text{APT}}:=\left(1-(\mathbf{F}-\mu)'\mathbf{V}^{-1}\lambda\right) \tag{2.48}$$

then one can conclude that the APT equation can be restated as

$$E^{\mathbb{P}}\left[m^{\text{APT}}(\mathbf{R}-r_f\mathbf{1})\right]=\mathbf{0}$$

and, assuming $m^{\text{APT}}(\omega)>0, \forall\omega\in\Omega$, one can define a risk-neutral measure:

$$\mathbb{Q}(\omega)=m^{\text{APT}}(\omega)\,\mathbb{P}(\omega)$$

that prices securities in the same way as a multi-factor APT does. Observe that $\widetilde{r}=(\widetilde{CF}-p)/p$ where p is given by Eq. (2.46) and the return of any portfolio must satisfy the FOC condition:

$$E^{\mathbb{Q}}[(\widetilde{r}-r_f)]=E^{\mathbb{P}}\left[m^{\text{APT}}(\widetilde{r}-r_f)\right]=\mathbf{0}$$

hence:

$$\frac{E^{\mathbb{Q}}\left[\widetilde{CF}\right]}{p}=1+r_f$$

and the theorem is proved. □

As an example, setting $F=r_M-r_f$ where r_M is the market factor, one can determine the pricing kernel corresponding to the CAPM. It will be:

$$m^{\text{CAPM}}(\omega):=\left(1-\frac{\mu_M-r_f}{\sigma_M^2}\left(r_M(\omega)-\mu_M\right)\right)$$

The following one-factor model example clarifies the relationship between the two approaches.

2.5.1 *CAPM and SDF*

To illustrate the above argument in the simplest framework, it is interesting to reconsider the "toy economy" considered in the past chapter where the number of states of nature is 2, $\omega = up, down$ and $\mathbb{P}(up) = \mathbb{P}(down) = 0.5$ and there are two traded securities in this economy, a risk-free and a risky asset. The risk-free rate of return R_f is equal to 2%. The payoff of the traded risky security, TR, is given by

TR	$
up	3
down	2

and the current price is 2.3$. A corporation is considering the opportunity to run a New Business whose cash flows are expected to be

NB	$
up	2.8
down	2.4

and its expected return $\mu_{NB} = 4.4753 \times 10^{-2}$.

In light of the above information, one can also compute the expected return μ_{TR} and the volatility σ_{TR} for TR that are given by

$$\mu_{TR} = 8.6957 \times 10^{-2}$$

$$\sigma_{TR} = \left(4.7259 \times 10^{-2}\right)^{1/2} = 0.21739$$

and the fair price of the opportunity NB is given by

$$P_{NB} = \frac{E^{\mathbb{P}}\left[S_1(\omega)\right]}{1 + \mu_{NB}} \tag{2.49}$$

$$P_{NB} = \frac{0.5 \times 2.8 + 0.5 \times 2.4}{1 + 4.4753 \times 10^{-2}} = 2.4886$$

Assuming that a CAPM equilibrium holds in the market and that TR is the market portfolio, one can verify that NB is in the set of efficient opportunities verifying that it is perfectly correlated with the market portfolio, in fact[3]:

$$\sigma_{NB} = 8.0367 \times 10^{-2}$$

$$\mathrm{Cov}\left(R_{NB}(\omega), R_{TR}(\omega)\right) = 1.7471 \times 10^{-2}$$

$$\rho_{NB;TR} = \frac{1.7471 \times 10^{-2}}{8.0367 \times 10^{-2} \times 0.21739} = 1.0$$

[3]This market is rather special, in fact, the number of independent final states equals the number of tradeable securities. This property is conventionally named market completeness.

Note that the new business is expected to belong to a risk class described by a risk exposure $\beta_{NB} = 0.369\,69$ hence its expected return is determined by the SML equation and is given by:

$$\mu_{NB} = 0.369\,69\left(8.695\,7 \times 10^{-2} - 0.02\right) + 0.02 = 4.475\,3 \times 10^{-2}$$

Now it is possible to verify that the same valuation can be obtained by introducing a risk-neutral measure using Eq. (2.48). If one sets:

$$m_{\text{CAPM}}(\omega) = 1 - \Psi\left(R_{TR}(\omega) - \mu_{TR}\right)$$
$$\Psi = \frac{\mu_{TR} - \mu_f}{\sigma_{TR}^2}$$

then the corresponding risk-neutral measure $\mathbb{Q}$ can be computed and is given by

$$\begin{aligned}
m(up) &= 1 - \Psi\left(R_{TR}(up) - \mu_{TR}\right) \\
&= 1 - 1.417\,7\left(\frac{3}{2.3} - \frac{0.5 \times 2 + 0.5 \times 3}{2.3}\right) = 0.691\,8 \\
\mathbb{Q}(up) &= m(up)\,\mathbb{P}(up) \\
&= 0.5 \times 0.691\,8 = 0.345\,9 \\
m(down) &= 1 - \Psi\left(R_{TR}(down) - \mu_{TR}\right) \\
&= 1 - 1.417\,7\left(\frac{2}{2.3} - \frac{0.5 \times 2 + 0.5 \times 3}{2.3}\right) = 1.308\,2 \\
\mathbb{Q}(down) &= m(down)\,\mathbb{P}(down) \\
&= 0.5 \times 1.308\,2 = 0.654\,1
\end{aligned}$$

and the verification that the fair price P_{NB} is also obtained as the risk-neutral discounted expectation of the cash flows is given by

$$S_0 = \frac{E^{\mathbb{Q}}\left[S_1(\omega)\right]}{1 + R_f} = \frac{0.345\,9 \times 2.8 + 0.654\,1 \times 2.4}{1.02} = 2.488\,6$$

which, as expected, is equal to the value computed in (2.49) using the CAPM equation to compute the discount rate adjustment for risk. As a last comment, note that in this example the number of tradable securities equals the number of independent states of nature. In this case, the market is said to be complete and there is only one possible risk-neutral valuation measure that a fortiori will be consistent with the CAPM-implied one.

Chapter 3

Empirical Tests of Asset Pricing Models

There has been a remarkable evolution in the understanding and empirical modelling of asset prices and financial returns from the 1960s onwards. The view from the sixties was based on the Constant Expected Returns (CER) model and the CAPM. In this framework, a simple econometric model serves the purpose of modelling returns at all horizons and a one-factor model determines the cross-section of asset returns.

3.1 The View from the 1960s: Efficient Markets and Constant Expected Returns

The history of empirical finance starts with the "efficient market hypothesis" Fama (1970). This view, that dominated the field in the 1960s and 1970s, can be summarized as follows (see also the discussion in Cochrane (1999)):

- expected returns are constant and normally independently distributed;
- the CAPM is a good measure of risk and thus a good explanation of why some stocks earn higher average returns than others;

- excess returns are close to being unpredictable: any predictability is a statistical artefact or cannot be exploited after transaction costs are taken into account;
- the volatility of returns is constant.

Fama (1970) clearly stated:

> ... For data on common stocks, tests of 'fair game' (and random walk) properties seem to go well when conditional expected returns are estimated as the average return for the sample of data at hand. Apparently, the variation in common stock returns about their expected values is so large relative to any changes in expected values that the latter can be safely ignored....

In the following, we describe some basic empirical tests useful to identify deviations from the benchmark and pose the basis for a new generation of asset pricing models.

3.2 The Cross-Sectional Evidence: CAPM Verification

The design of cross-sectional tests is particularly relevant both from a theoretical and a practical point of view. They have been introduced to verify the empirical reliability of CAPM and APT theories. Later on, the econometric approaches developed in this context contributed to the development of the passive investing industry.

To fix the ideas, consider the empirical test of the standard CAPM or the zero beta (two-factor) form of the CAPM. The basic Sharpe–Lintner–Mossin CAPM security market line (SML hereafter) can be written as

$$\mu_i - r_f = \beta_i[\mu_M - r_f] \tag{3.1}$$

while the corresponding zero-beta or Black version of the CAPM SML can be written as

$$\mu_i - \mu_{ZC_M} = \beta_i[\mu_M - \mu_{ZC_M}] \tag{3.2}$$

where μ_{ZC_M} is the expected return on the minimum variance portfolio that is uncorrelated with the efficient proxy of the market portfolio. These models produce predictions about investor expectations.

The only way to test directly their ability to reproduce revealed expectations is to compare them with survey data. For a review of these approaches, see Kothari *et al.* (2016).

Traditional tests of the CAPM have been performed using ex-post observed values for the securities' returns as proxies of *ex-ante* expectations. This approach will provide reliable information only if the relationship between return expectations and effective realizations satisfies precise statistical conditions. First of all, it is necessary to argue and possibly empirically verify that *expectations are on average unbiased estimates of realizations.*

In the following, we will assume that security excess returns are linearly related to the excess return on a market portfolio. Then:

$$r_t^i - r_{ft} = \alpha_i + \beta_i \left(r_t^M - r_{ft}\right) + \varepsilon_t^i \tag{3.3}$$

The statistical model that determines all returns r_t^i and the market return r_t^m, can be described as follows:

$$\left(r_t^i - r_{ft}\right) = \mu_i - r_f + \beta_i u_{m,t} + u_{i,t}$$

$$\left(r_t^M - r_{ft}\right) = \mu_m - r_f + u_{m,t}$$

$$\begin{pmatrix} u_{i,t} \\ u_{m,t} \end{pmatrix} \sim n.i.d. \left[\begin{pmatrix} 0 \\ 0 \end{pmatrix}, \begin{pmatrix} \sigma_{ii} & \sigma_{im} \\ \sigma_{im} & \sigma_{mm} \end{pmatrix}\right]$$

where r_{ft} is the return on the risk-free asset and r_f its time series mean. $\sigma_{im} = 0$ is a crucial assumption for the valid estimation of the CAPM betas, and that assumption that risk-adjusted excess returns are zero (usually known as zero alpha assumption) requires that $\mu_i - r_f = \beta_i(\mu_m - r_f)$. Comparing Eqs. (3.1) and (3.2) with the expectation of (3.3), it is immediate to verify that the two versions of CAPM imply:

$$\text{Classical-CAPM H}_0\text{:}\ \ \alpha_i = 0$$

$$\text{Zero-Covariance-CAPM H}_0\text{:}\ \ \alpha_i = \left(\mu_{ZC(M)} - r_f\right)(1 - \beta_i)$$

In order to test these hypotheses, it is desirable to use a large number of securities $N \to +\infty$ and a long time series $T \to +\infty$. The obvious method is to estimate in time series the linear regression for each asset and then examine the joint distribution of α_i. This approach does not go a long way. In fact, it is problematic to assume that the residuals ε_{it} are cross-sectionally and dynamically uncorrelated. In addition, the statistical power of this test is rather low because of the low coefficient of determination obtained in the linear regressions. This might depend on different reasons: most of the risk is non-systematic, i.e., the regressor is unable to capture the variability of the regressand, or time-variation in the risk exposures $\beta_{i,t}$.

In fact, the precise estimation of the risk exposure β_i is a key difficulty to be overcome to test a central implication of CAPM, i.e., the existence of a cross-sectional linear relationship between the compensation $\mu_i - r_f$ (or $\mu_i - \mu_{ZC(M)}$) and the risk index β_i for all the trade securities $i = 1, \ldots, N$. Replacing the risk exposure with its time-series estimate $\widehat{\beta}_i$ may generate an error-in-variables problem. In fact, the error term in the cross-sectional regression would correlate with the error in the time-series estimation. In the following, we illustrate a number of interesting techniques that have been introduced to overcome these difficulties.

3.2.1 *Black, Jensen, and Scholes (1972) and portfolio aggregation*

Black *et al.* (1972) (BJS hereafter) reorganize the N securities into a fixed number of portfolios, I. In particular, BJS select $I = 10$ and create ten decile equally weighted portfolios obtained ordering securities with respect an instrumental variable, in BJS they select the so-called pre-ranking beta, which is the five-year time-series estimate of individual beta that is re-estimated on a yearly basis. As $N \to +\infty$ the number of securities in each portfolio is diverging $I/N \to +\infty$ and, by the law of large numbers, diversification will reduce the variance of the portfolio returns not correlated with the instrumental variable and mitigate the error-in-variables problem.

Notice that the composition of the resulting decile portfolios will change dynamically due to the asset reallocation that will follow every re-estimation and stabilize the relationship between the resulting portfolio and the instrumental variable. Portfolios are created sorting securities with respect to firm-specific information can be considered the precursor of the passive investment products that are now of widespread use in the asset management industry.

Table 3.1. Estimated intercept, slope coefficients for each decile portfolio obtained in the replication of Black *et al.* (1972).

Decile portfolio	Excess return	$\widehat{\beta}_i$	$\widehat{\alpha}_i$	R^2
1	0.0213	1.561	−0.0829	0.927
2	0.0177	1.384	−0.1938	0.976
3	0.0171	1.248	−0.0649	0.976
4	0.0163	1.163	−0.0167	0.982
5	0.0145	1.057	−0.0543	0.984
6	0.0137	0.923	0.0593	0.966
7	0.0126	0.853	0.0462	0.970
8	0.0115	0.753	0.0812	0.958
9	0.0109	0.629	0.1968	0.913
10	0.0091	0.490	0.2012	0.806
Market	0.0142	1.000		

The exact procedure BJS is then the following:

(1) Each year, the rolling window of the prior five years of monthly data is used to estimate pre-ranking betas and rank stocks into deciles (from highest to lowest). This estimation procedure is repeated on a yearly basis for the entire sample length.
(2) Stocks sorted in deciles are included in ten equally weighted portfolio and yearly reallocated after each re-estimation.
(3) For each of the ten portfolios BJS estimate the regression (3.3) and produce the time-series estimates $(\widehat{\alpha}_p,\widehat{\beta}_p)$, $p = 1, \ldots, 10$ that are reported in Table 3.1.

Once the portfolios are formed, the pre-ranking betas are thrown out, and a post-ranking beta is assigned to each security to be used for asset-pricing tests and estimation. The post-ranking beta for security i at time t, $\beta_{i,t}$, is set equal to the beta of the decile portfolio β_p, if i belongs to decile p at time t.

The test produces the following conclusions:

- The cross-sectional regression

$$\widehat{\mu}_p - r_f = \lambda_0 + \lambda\widehat{\beta}_p + \nu_p$$

has a high coefficient of determination, thus supporting the existence of a linear risk-return tradeoff.

- The estimated slope $\widehat{\lambda}$ of the empirical SML is lower than the one predicted by the classical CAPM, $\mu_M - r_f$: $\widehat{\lambda} < \mu_M - r_f$, see the graphical illustration in Fig. 3.1(a).
- The zero beta portfolio $\widehat{\lambda}_0$ has an expected return singificantly larger than the risk free rate r_f: $\widehat{\lambda}_0 > r_f$.
- There exists a positive approximately linear relationship between $\widehat{\alpha}_p$ and $1-\widehat{\beta}_p$. The slope of the corresponding linear regression produces an estimate of the excess return $\mu_{ZC(M)} - r_f$, see Fig. 3.1(b).

In summary, while the validity of the Classical CAPM is rejected, data offer support to the existence of a linear risk-return relationship as predicted by the zero-covariance CAPM.

3.2.2 *Capital market efficiency and the two-step Fama–McBeth (1973) procedure*

Fama and MacBeth (1973) (*FMB*), introduce a two-step procedure that has become a common tool for performing simple and reliable asset pricing tests. The first-pass regression follows a procedure and a logic similar to *BJS*. They form 20 portfolios of securities using rolling windows to create estimates of the independent variables to be used in the second pass. In the second pass, *FMB* deviates from *BJS* and runs a sequence of cross-sectional regressions, one for each month over the full-time span period 1935–1968. The specification of these regressions in their analysis is

$$r_{i,t} = \gamma_{0,t} + \gamma_{1,t}\beta_i + \gamma_{2,t}\beta_i^2 + \gamma_{3,t}S_{e,i} + \eta_{i,t}$$

where $S_{e,i}$ is the standard deviation of the residuals of the first-pass time-series regression for security i. The null hypotheses to be tested are:

(1) $E(\hat{\gamma}_{3,t}) = 0$, firm-specific residual risk does not affect returns.
(2) $E(\hat{\gamma}_{2,t}) = 0$, the risk-return relationship is linear.
(3) $E(\hat{\gamma}_{1,t}) - (\mu_M - r_f) = 0$, the price of market risk and equal to the market risk premium.
(4) $E(\hat{\gamma}_{0,t}) - r_f = 0$.

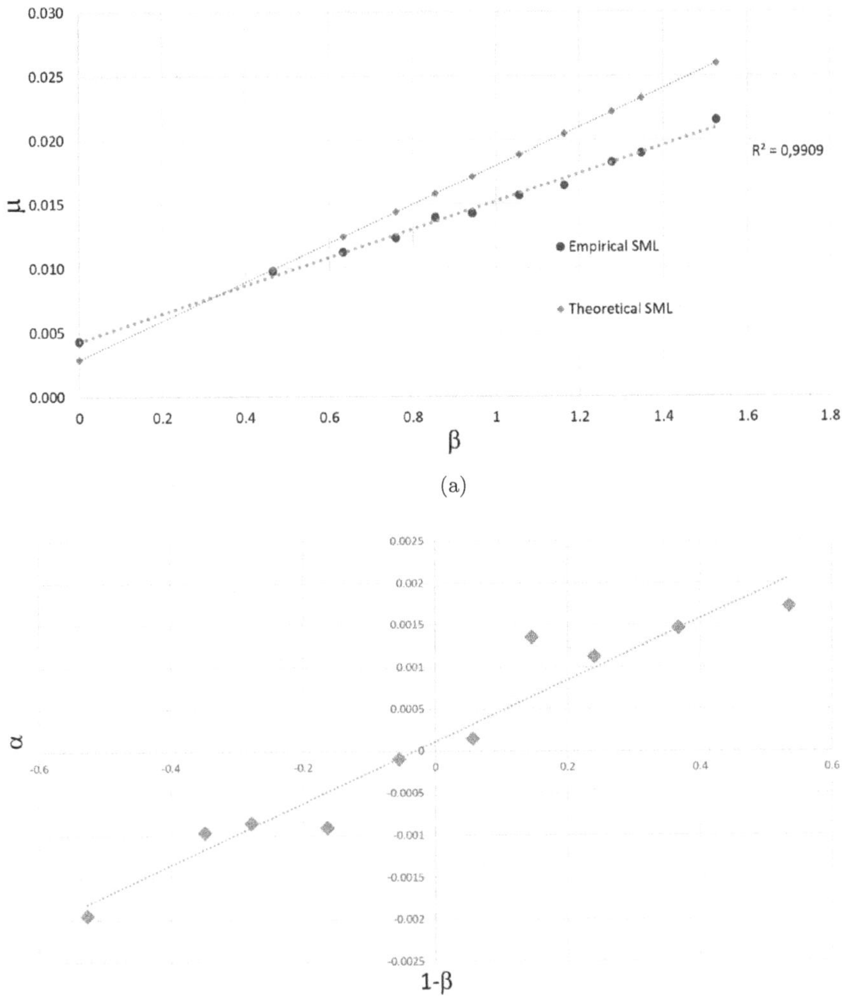

Figure 3.1. (a) Illustration of the empirical and theoretical security market lines and (b) the relationship between α and $1-\beta$. The data sample is the same as originally used in BJS.

If (1) and (2) are not rejected, $E(\hat{\gamma}_{0,t})$ and $E(\hat{\gamma}_{1,t})$ determine whether classical CAPM or zero-beta model will produce a better description of market returns.

A key observation of Fama and MacBeth (1973) is that their approach produces an additional testable implication. In fact, the time series of cross-sectional estimates $\hat{\gamma}_t := [\hat{\gamma}_{0,t}, \ldots, \hat{\gamma}_{3,t}]$, $t = S, S+1, \ldots, T$ (S is assumed to be the size of the window that used to estimate the parameters) of the vector of parameters $\gamma := [0, 0, \mu_M - r_f, r_f]$. They observe that, if the market is efficient and returns fluctuations are close to the outcomes of a fair game and are uninformative about future prices, then the deviations of these parameters from their true values $\hat{\gamma}_t - \gamma$ should be also be distributed as random outcomes in a fair game, a martingale sequence in modern language. Hence, a test on the dynamic correlations in the time series of $\hat{\gamma}_t - \gamma$ rejecting predictability can be interpreted as supporting capital market efficiency. In addition, under this assumption, the best estimate of the vector of parameters, denoted by $\bar{\gamma}$, is simply obtained by considering the sample mean and standard deviations:

$$\bar{\gamma} = \frac{1}{T-S}\sum_{t=S}^{T} \hat{\gamma}_t, \quad s(\bar{\gamma}) = \sqrt{\frac{\sum_{t=S}^{T} \hat{\gamma}_t^2}{T-S-1}}$$

and a *t-statistics* given by

$$t(\bar{\gamma}) = \frac{\bar{\gamma}}{s(\bar{\gamma})/\sqrt{T-S}}$$

FMB present the results of estimation over the full-time period as well as for several sub-periods. Here, we report only results for the full model and the entire estimation period.

Coefficient	Mean value	t-stat	Serial correlation
$\hat{\gamma}_{3,t}$	0.0516	1.11	−0.12
$\hat{\gamma}_{2,t}$	−0.0026	−0.86	−0.09
$\hat{\gamma}_{1,t}$	0.0085	2.57	0.02
$\hat{\gamma}_{0,t} - r_{f,t}$	0.0048	2.55	0.15

Empirical results reveal that $\bar{\gamma}_{2,t}$ and $\bar{\gamma}_{3,t}$ are small and not statistically different from zero. Furthermore, when examined over several sub-periods, they remain small in each sub-period, not significantly different from zero, and, in fact, exhibit different signs in different sub-periods. Hence, one can safely conclude that residual risk has no effect on the expected return of a security. Thus, both the squared residuals and the nonlinear terms do not affect the expected return on securities.

In summary, the linear risk-return tradeoff is not rejected and further tests can be run relying on the following reduced form:

$$r_{it} = \gamma_{0,t} + \gamma_{1,t}\beta_i + \eta_{it}$$

As BJS, FMB find that $\hat{\gamma}_{0t}$ is significantly greater than any reasonable proxy of the risk free rate $(r_{f,t})$ and that $\hat{\gamma}_{1,t}$ is generally lower than $r_{M,t} - r_{f,t}$. In summary, they confirm that the empirical test supports a zero-beta CAPM and produces a more reliable description of the risk-return trade-off than the classical CAPM.

3.3 The Frazzini and Pedersen (2014) BAB Factor Construction

To construct the BAB portfolio, Frazzini and Pedersen (2014) compute the pre-ranking betas with respect to the monthly returns on the CRSP value-weighted market index, exploiting monthly return data on stocks from the CRSP tape. The estimated betas for security i are given by

$$\hat{\beta}_t^{TS} = \hat{\rho}\frac{\hat{\sigma}_i}{\hat{\sigma}_m} \tag{3.4}$$

where $\hat{\sigma}_i$ and $\hat{\sigma}_m$ are the estimated volatilities for the stock and the market, and $\hat{\rho}$ is their estimated correlation. To reduce the presence of outliers, following Vasicek (1973) and Elton *et al.* (2009), the time series estimates of beta are shrinked $(\hat{\beta}_i^{TS})$ towards the cross-sectional mean $(\hat{\beta}^{XS})$:

$$\hat{\beta}_i = w_i\hat{\beta}_i^{TS} + (1 - w_i)\hat{\beta}^{XS} \tag{3.5}$$

where for simplicity $w_i = w = 0.6$ and $\beta^{XS} = 1$ for all periods and across all assets. Notice that this shrinkage procedure does not change the ranking across stocks' betas. The BAB factor by construction is long low-beta stocks and short high-beta stocks. Stocks are indeed ranked in ascending order on the basis of their estimated betas. The ranked securities are assigned to one of two portfolios, i.e., low-beta and high-beta, rebalanced every calendar month. In each portfolio, stocks are weighted by the ranked betas (i.e., lower-beta securities have larger weights in the low-beta portfolio and higher-beta securities have larger weights in the high-beta portfolio). This is done relying on the following procedure: let z denote the $n \times 1$ vector of beta ranks $z_i = rank(\beta_{it})$ in each calendar month, and let $\bar{z} = 1_n' z/n$ be the average rank, with n number of securities in each period and 1_n an $n \times 1$ vector of ones. The portfolio weights are thus given by a vector w such that, for the low-beta and high-beta portfolios it holds that in each period:

$$\begin{aligned} w_H &= k(z - \bar{z})^+ \\ w_L &= k(z - \bar{z})^- \end{aligned} \tag{3.6}$$

where $k = 2/1_n'|z - \bar{z}|$ is a normalizing constant and x^+ and x^- denote the positive and negative elements of a vector x. Hence, by construction, in each period $1_n' w_H = 1$ and $1_n' w_L = 1$. The BAB portfolio is thus a self-financing portfolio that is long the low-beta portfolio and long the high-beta portfolio, with returns given by

$$r_{t+1}^{BAB} = \frac{1}{\beta_t^L}(r_{t+1}^L - r^f) - \frac{1}{\beta_t^H}(r_{t+1}^H - r^f) \tag{3.7}$$

where $r_{t+1}^L = r'_{t+1} w_L$, $r_{t+1}^H = r'_{t+1} w_H$, $\beta_t^L = \beta_t' w_L$ and $\beta_t^H = \beta_t' w_H$. The expected return of this BAB portfolio is thus given by Proposition II. Note that the two final legs have unit beta, but the total allocation in these portfolios does not sum to one, hence the portfolio is not self-financing. The final portfolio can be decomposed as

$$\begin{aligned} r_{t+1}^{BAB} = &\underbrace{r_{t+1}^L - r_{t+1}^H}_{\text{Dollar Neutral}} \\ &+ \underbrace{\left(\frac{1}{\beta_t^L} - 1\right) r_{t+1}^L - \left(\frac{1}{\beta_t^H} - 1\right) r_{t+1}^H}_{\text{Long-position to hedge the BAB strategy}} \\ &- \underbrace{\left(\frac{1}{\beta_t^L} - \frac{1}{\beta_t^H}\right)}_{\text{Borrowing to finance the hedge}} r^f \end{aligned}$$

Novy-Marx and Velikov (2022) observe that the construction of this portfolio is anomalous with respect to the classical one. Its performance, roughly 1% per month, is driven by non-standard procedures

Table 3.2. The zero-beta rate.

	$\widehat{\gamma}_{(1)}$ GMM	$\widehat{\gamma}_{(2)}$ OLS
RF	2.747	2.747
	[3.890]	[4.004]
UMP	0.0629	0.0629
	[0.767]	[0.769]
EBP	−0.993	−0.993
	[3.879]	[4.172]
TSP	0.297	0.297
	[3.075]	[3.100]
$\text{CPI}_{\text{Rolling}}$	−2.196	−2.196
	[2.416]	[2.510]
Constant	1.002	1.002
	[8.946]	[9.027]
Wald/F	35.74	8.125
p-value	1.1e − 06	2.0e − 07
RMSE		2.671
Observations	574	574

Notes: Predictive regression $R_{t+1}^{\text{Zero\_Beta}} = \gamma Z_t + u_{t+1}$ Regressors: RF is the Treasury bill yield, UMP the unemployment rate, EBP the excess bond premium (EBP) of Gilchrist and Zakrajsek (2012), TSP the term spread (10 yr less 3 m Treasury yields), CPI a rolling average of the previous twelve months of inflation. All variables are standardized, hence the constant is the mean monthly return of the zero-beta portfolio. *t*-stats are reported in square brackets.

used in its construction that effectively, but non-transparently, equal weight stock returns. For each dollar invested in BAB, the strategy commits on average \$1.05 to stocks in the bottom 1% of total market capitalization making the full factor construction fragile and strongly reduced by transaction costs. More recently, Di Tella *et al.* (2023) provide an estimate of the zero-beta portfolio expected return that takes into account all the remarks of Novy-Marx and Velikov (2022) and produce evidence of an excess return over the risk-free rate of 7.6%. Their analysis shows that the return on this portfolio can be tracked relying on the predictors that are reported in Table 3.2.

They do not attribute this difference to a new asset pricing factor uncorrelated with all other factors, but rather they attribute the spread between the zero-beta rate and the Treasury bill yield to a convenience yield that investors accept of pay to hold Treasury bills and other safe assets.

3.4 Empirical Tests of APT, Anomalies and Fama and French (1993)

Fama and French (1993) (FF) analyze the cross-section of equity returns in order to explore the potential significance of other informational variables above and beyond the exposure to market risk exposures. The starting point of their work is the consideration of the main prediction of the Sharpe–Lintner–Black (SLB) CAPM model: the variation of expected returns driven by the change in risk exposures is fully accounted by level changes of market β.

The empirical analysis highlighted several empirical variables that generate variation in expected returns. The most prominent is the *size effect* of Banz (1981). He finds that market equity, ME (a stock's price times shares outstanding), adds to the explanation of the cross-section of average returns provided by market βs. Average returns on small (low capitalization) stocks are too high given their β estimates, and average returns on large stocks are too low. Another contradiction of the CAPM is the positive relation between *leverage* and average return documented by Bhandari (1988). It is plausible that leverage is associated with risk and expected return, but in the CAPM leverage risk should be fully captured by market β. Bhandari (1988) finds, however, that leverage helps explain the cross-section of average stock returns in tests that include size as well as β. Finally, Rosenberg *et al.* (1985) find that average returns on US stocks are positively related to the ratio of a firm's book value of common equity, BE, to its market value, ME. Chan *et al.* (1991) find that also *book-to-market* equity, BE/ME, has a strong role in explaining the cross-section of average returns on Japanese stocks. Finally, Basu (1983) shows that *earnings-price ratios* (E/P) help explain the cross-section of average returns on US stocks in tests that also include size and market β. FF combined these findings and produced a single cross-sectional experiment using data on all non-financial firms listed on the NYSE, AMEX, and NASDAQ from 1962 to 1989. They replicate on this new sample the cross-sectional regression approach of Fama and MacBeth (1973): each month the cross-section of returns on stocks is regressed on variables hypothesized to explain expected returns. The time-series means of the monthly regression coefficients then provide standard tests of whether different explanatory variables are on average priced. Since size, E/P, leverage, and BE/ME are measured precisely for individual stocks, the experiment is at the equity level instead of using portfolios as in previous research. FF compare variation of returns at single stock level driven by the post-ranking beta and by the size and book-to-market characteristics. The main results of the estimation of the following cross-sectional model

$$r_{i,t} = a_t + b_{1,t}\beta_i + b_{2,t}\ln(ME_i) + b_{3,t}\ln\left(\frac{BE_i}{ME_i}\right) + e_{it}$$

are reported in the following table:

	Jul 63–Dec 90		Jul 63–Dec 76		Jan 77–Dec 90	
Variable	Mean	t-stat	Mean	t-stat	Mean	t-stat
a	2.07	6.55	1.73	3.54	2.4	5.92
b_1	−0.17	−062	0.10	0.25	−0.44	−1.17
b_2	−0.12	−2.52	−0.15	−1.91	−0.09	−1.64
b_3	0.33	4.8	0.34	3.17	0.31	3.67

The authors conclude that both the (natural logarithm of) equity market capitalization (ME) and the (natural logarithm of) book-to-market ratio (BE/ME) capture the cross-sectional variation of realized returns and dominates the variation driven by the beta measure of risk exposure that is not significant.

These two characteristics produce pricing anomalies for the CAPM theory. An anomaly for an asset pricing theory is firm-specific information that can be used to sort securities in such a way that: (i) portfolios determined by the sort (e.g., quintile or tercile portfolios) have increasing expected excess returns and (ii) portfolio sorts generate a significant alpha that the asset pricing theory under investigation cannot explain.

3.5 Direct Construction of Traded Portfolios

APT tests can be cosiderably simplified when risk factors are selected to be tradable portfolios. Fama and French (1993) have proposed a simple approach to construct characteristics mimicking traded portfolios. We illustrate their construction in the benchmark example of the size SMB, and value HML factors. In order to create the SMB and HML portfolios, Fama and French sorted securities in two groups w.r.t. the size factor (i.e., sorting variable $\ln(ME)$) and three groups w.r.t. the value factor (i.e., sorting variable $\ln(BE/ME)$) creating six groups:

(S, H)	(S, M)	(S, L)
(B, H)	(B, M)	(B, L)

where $S(B)$ denotes the group of securities that have a size lower (bigger) than the median while $H(L)$ denotes the group of securities whose book to market is in the top (bottom) tercile of the distribution.

The SMB factor is a long-short portfolio such that:

$$r_S = \frac{1}{2}\left[r_{(S_{\text{SMB}}, H_{\text{HML}})} + r_{(S_{\text{SMB}}, L_{\text{HML}})}\right]$$

$$r_B = \frac{1}{2}\left[r_{(B_{\text{SMB}}, H_{\text{HML}})} + r_{(B_{\text{SMB}}, L_{\text{HML}})}\right]$$

being the difference between the performance of small and large caps, captures the idea of a risk premium based on size, while the HML factor captures the idea of a risk premium based on the book-to-market ratio and its return is given by

$$r_H = \frac{1}{2}\left[r_{(S_{\text{SMB}}, H_{\text{HML}})} + r_{(B_{\text{SMB}}, H_{\text{HML}})}\right]$$

$$r_L = \frac{1}{3}\left[r_{(S_{\text{SMB}}, L_{\text{HML}})} + r_{(B_{\text{SMB}}, L_{\text{HML}})}\right]$$

These two factors, being defined by portfolios sorted with respect to the value and size characteristics, have a low correlation with the market factor. In summary, the return-generating process is then defined as follows:

$$r_{i,t} - r_{f,t} = \alpha_i + \beta_{i,M}(r_{M,t} - r_{0t}) + \beta_{i,smb}SMB + \beta_{i,hml}HML + \varepsilon_{it}$$
$$SMB = (r_{S,t} - r_{B,t})$$
$$HML = (r_{H,t} - r_{L,t})$$

where

- $r_{M,t}$ is the return of a proxy for the market portfolio,
- $r_{S,t}$ is the return of a portfolio of stocks with low market capitalization (small caps),
- $r_{B,t}$ is the return of a portfolio of stocks with high market capitalization (large, or big, caps),
- $r_{H,t}$ is the return of a portfolio of stocks with high book-to-market ratio (value stocks),
- $r_{L,t}$ is the return of a portfolio of stocks with low book-to-market ratio (growth stocks).

More recently, Fama and French (2015) have extended the standard factor model including Market, SMB, HML and MOM, adding two more factors: RMW and CMA. Robust minus weak (RMW) is the return on a portfolio long on robust operating profitability stocks and short on weak operating profitability stocks, while conservative minus aggressive (CMA) is the average return on a position long on conservative investment portfolios and short on aggressive investment. It is interesting to note that augmenting the CAPM with SMB and HML and the other factors does not challenge per se the CER model, which still holds as valid if the constant expected return model can be applied to the two additional factors. On the contrary, an additional factor called momentum, MOM, Jegadeesh and Titman (2011) provides direct evidence against the CER model. This investment strategy buys stocks that have performed well while selling stocks that have performed poorly over the past 3- to 12-month period. It generates significant excess returns over the following year. This evidence supports the hypothesis that conditional expectations of future returns are not constant.

3.6 Time-Series Analysis of Returns

In the previous section, we focused on the cross-sectional analysis of returns. In this section, we analyze the time series dimension and illustrate some empirical facts that are hard to accommodate within a CER modeling approach.

In particular, it has been observed that:

- High-frequency returns are non-normal and heteroscedastic, therefore the risk is not constant over time and and high frequency risk dynamics is predictable.
- There are anomalies that make returns predictable on the occasion of special events.
- There is statistical evidence of return predictability that increases with the horizon at which returns are observed.

3.6.1 *The behavior of returns at high-frequency*

The CER model can be recast in terms of the simplest possible specification for the predictive models for returns, i.e.,

$$r^i_{t,t+1} = \mu^i + \sigma^i \epsilon_{it} \qquad \epsilon_{it} \sim NID(0,1)$$

$$\mathrm{Cov}(\epsilon_{it}, \epsilon_{js}) = \begin{cases} \sigma_{ij} & t = s \\ 0 & t \neq s \end{cases}$$

Note that the absence of predictability of excess returns is not a a consequence of market efficiency per se but it instead results from a joint hypothesis: market efficiency plus some assumptions on the process generating returns. CER model assumes constant volatility of returns. Hence it is unable to capture time variation of risk and market regime changes.

When the data are generated by CER, the optimal asset allocation achieved by utility maximization is horizion independent. The optimal portfolio is always a combination between the market portfolio and the risk-free asset. The risk associated to any given asset or portfolio of assets is constant over time. Think of measuring the risk of a portfolio with its value-at-risk (VaR). The Value at Risk (VaR) represents the percentage loss that is exceeded with a probability of at most α percent:

$$\Pr(R^p < -\mathrm{VaR}_\alpha) = \alpha$$

where R^p are the returns on the portfolio. If the distribution of returns is normal, then α-percent VaR_α is obtained as follows (assume $\alpha \in (0,1)$):

$$\begin{aligned}\Pr(R^p < -\mathrm{VaR}_\alpha) &= \alpha \Longleftrightarrow \Pr\left(\frac{R^p - \mu_p}{\sigma_p} < -\frac{\mathrm{VaR}_\alpha + \mu_p}{\sigma_p}\right) = \alpha \\ &\Longleftrightarrow \Phi\left(-\frac{\mathrm{VaR}_\alpha + \mu_p}{\sigma_p}\right) = \alpha\end{aligned}$$

where $\Phi(\cdot)$ is the cumulative density of a standard normal. At this point, defining $\Phi^{-1}(\cdot)$ as the inverse CDF function of a standard normal, we have that

$$-\frac{\mathrm{VaR}_\alpha + \mu_p}{\sigma_p} = \Phi^{-1}(\alpha) \Longleftrightarrow \mathrm{VaR}_\alpha = -\mu_p - \sigma_p\Phi^{-1}(\alpha)$$

and, given that μ_p and σ_p are constant over time, VaR_α is also constant over-time. Consider the case of a researcher interested in the one per cent value at risk. Because $\Phi^{-1}(0.01) = -2.33$ under the normal distribution, we can easily obtain an estimate VaR if we have available estimates of the first and second moments of the distribution of *portfolio returns*:

$$\widehat{VaR}_{0.01} = -\hat{\mu}_p - 2.33\hat{\sigma}_p$$

which are assumed to be constant across the full sample.

3.6.2 *A more realistic description*

At small horizon (i.e., when k is small: infra-daily, daily, weekly or at most monthly returns) a more appropriate modeling framework can be specified as follows:

$$\begin{aligned}R_{t,t+k} &= \sigma_{k,t}u_{t+k} \\ \sigma^2_{k,t} &= f(\mathcal{I}_t) \qquad u_{t+k} \sim IID\ \mathcal{D}(0,1)\end{aligned}$$

A number of features of this model at high frequency is noteworthy:

(1) The distribution of returns is centered around a mean of zero, and the zero mean model dominates any alternative model based on predictors.
(2) The variance is time-varying and predictable, given the information set, $\mathcal{I}_t$, available at time t.
(3) The distribution of returns at high frequency is not normal, i.e., $\mathcal{D}(0,1)$ may often differ from $\mathcal{N}(0,1)$.

3.7 Time Series Anomalies

The evidence of predictability of returns is strengthened by the presence of episodes of a non-homogeneous behavior of return predictability along the time-series dimension. An interesting illustration of this type of evidence is the one reported in Lucca and Moench (2015), who document large average excess returns on US equities in anticipation of monetary policy decisions made at scheduled meetings of the Federal Open Market Committee (FOMC) in the past few decades. Following up on this evidence, Cieslak *et al.* (2019) document that since 1994 the US equity premium has followed an alternating weekly pattern measured in FOMC cycle time, i.e., in time since the last FOMC meeting.

3.8 Returns at Different Horizons and the Dynamic Dividend Growth Model of Shiller (1981)

In a CER world, the horizon n does not matter for the prediction of returns because once μ_i and σ_i are estimated, expected returns at all horizons and the variance of returns is constant at all horizons.

$$E(r^i_{t,t+n}) = E\left(\sum_{k=1}^{n} r^i_{t+k,t+k-1}\right) = \sum_{k=1}^{n} E(r^i_{t+k,t+k-1}) = n\mu$$

$$\mathrm{Var}(r^i_{t,t+n}) = \mathrm{Var}\left(\sum_{i=1}^{n} r^i_{t+k,t+k-1}\right) = \sum_{i=1}^{n} \mathrm{Var}(r^i_{t+k,t+k-1}) = n\sigma^2$$

The work of Robert Shiller and co-authors led the profession to go beyond the CER model introducing the Dynamic Dividend Growth (DDG) model (for its precise formulation, see Section 4.4.1). When tested on the data, it produces empirical evidence about the horizon dependence of the returns relying on the dividend-price ratio and the excess volatility of returns. It is based on the following log-linearized decomposition of total returns of a stock i:

$$r_{t+1}^{s} = \kappa + \rho(p_{t+1} - d_{t+1}) + \Delta d_{t+1} - (p_t - d_t)$$

where P_t is the stock price at time t and D_t is the dividend paid at time t, $p_t = \ln(P_t), d_t = \ln(D_t), \kappa$ is a constant and $\rho = \frac{P/D}{1+P/D}$, P/D is the average price to dividend ratio. Two considerations are relevant here. First, note that under the CER and a no-bubble condition, the price-dividend ratio should reflect only expected dividend growth. The empirical evidence is strongly against this prediction (see the Campbell and Shiller (1987)). Stock prices are too volatile to be determined only by expected dividends. Campbell and Shiller (1987) illustrate the point by comparing the observed price-dividend ratio and a counterfactual price-dividend ratio which is obtained by assuming constant future expected returns and by using a vector autoregressive model to predict future dividend-growth: the volatility in the price-dividend ratio is much higher than that predicted by the CER model.

Second, once the hypothesis of CER is rejected, the DDG model has interesting implications for the predictability of returns at different horizons. When the price-dividend ratio is a noisy process, such noise dominates the variance of one-period returns and the statistical relation between the price-dividend ratio and one-period returns is weak. However, as the horizon over which returns are defined gets longer, noise tends to be dampened and the predictability of returns given the price-dividend ratio increases. Hence, the DDG model predicts a tighter relation between aggregate stock market returns and the price-dividend ratio as the horizon at which returns are defined increases. The first evidence of the increasing explanatory power of the dividend yield as the investment horizon increases is reported in Table 3.3. Here, we report the slopes, the adjusted R^2, as well as the adjusted t-stats as in Valkanov (2003), of the following predictive

Table 3.3. The predictive power of the dividend-yield.

Horizon k	$\hat{\beta}$	$t/\sqrt{T}$	R^2
1	0.726	0.092	0.007
4	3.369	0.187	0.032
8	7.105	0.269	0.066
16	15.96	0.412	0.144
24	23.59	0.523	0.214
60	54.69	0.976	0.487

Notes: This table reports the OLS estimates of the aggregate US stock market returns on the value-weighted dividend-price ratio. The sample is monthly and goes from 1946:01 to 2012:12. The first column reports the forecasting horizon. The second column reports the slope coefficients while the third the adjusted t-stats, i.e., $t/\sqrt{T}$ as in Valkanov (2003). The last column reports the adjusted R^2.

regression

$$r_{t:t+k} = \alpha_k + \beta_k \log(D_t/P_t) + \sigma\varepsilon_{t+k} \quad \varepsilon_{t+k} \sim N(0,1)$$

where $r_{t:t+k}$ the aggregate US stock market returns from t to $t+k$, D_t the aggregate dividend, P_t the index, ε_{t+k} an idiosyncratic error component and σ its corresponding risk.

The sensitivity of the aggregate cumulative returns on the log dividend-yield β_k increases with the investment horizon. The same is true for the adjusted R^2, meaning, the longer the forecasting term, the higher the predictive power of the value-weighted dividend-yield.

3.9 Conditional Asset Pricing with Predictable Returns

The evidence that the CER model does not provide the best representation of the data opened an interesting debate on the determinants of time-varying expected returns. An immediate motivation for predictability can be found in the process of expectation formation mechanisms that do not efficiently process the available information. Time-varying expected returns can also be understood in the context of a dynamic model that is still derived from the absence of "arbitrage opportunities" (i.e., by the impossibility of making profits without taking risk) but takes into account the unfolding of uncertainty.

This requirement can be satisfied by observing that most of the asset pricing analysis carried out in the previous chapters continues to hold if unconditional expectations are replaced by their conditional counterparts. Consider a situation in which in each period k state of nature can occur and each state has a probability $\pi(k)$, in the absence of arbitrage opportunities the price of an asset i at time t can be written as follows:

$$P_{i,t} = \sum_{s=1}^{k} \pi_{t+1}(s) m_{t+1}(s) X_{i,t+1}(s)$$

where $m_{t+1}(s)$ is the discounting weight attributed to future payoffs, which (as the probability π) is independent from the asset i, $X_{i,t+1}(s)$ are the payoffs of the assets (we have seen that in case of stocks we have $X_{i,t+1} = P_{t+1} + D_{t+1}$), and therefore returns on assets are defined as $1 + R_{s,t+1} = \frac{X_{i,t+1}}{P_{i,t}}$. For the safe asset, whose payoffs do not depend on the state of nature, we have:

$$P_{s,t} = X_{i,t+1} \sum_{s=1}^{k} \pi_{t+1}(s) m_{t+1}(s)$$

$$1 + R_{s,t+1} = \frac{1}{\sum_{j=1}^{m} \pi_{t+1}(s) m_{t+1}(s)}$$

In general, we can write:

$$P_{i,t} = E_t(m_{t+1} X_{i,t+1})$$

$$1 + R_{s,t+1} = \frac{1}{E_t(m_{t+1})}$$

consider now a risky asset:

$$E_t(m_{t+1}(1 + R_{i,t+1})) = 1$$

$$\mathrm{Cov}_t(m_{t+1} R_{i,t+1}) = 1 - E_t(m_{t+1}) E_t(1 + R_{i,t+1})$$

$$E_t(1 + R_{i,t+1}) = -\frac{\mathrm{Cov}_t(m_{t+1} R_{i,t+1})}{E_t(m_{t+1})} + (1 + R_{s,t+1})$$

Turning now to excess returns we can write:

$$E_t(R_{i,t+1} - R_{s,t+1}) = -(1 + R_{s,t+1}) \mathrm{Cov}_t(m_{t+1} R_{i,t+1})$$

Assets whose returns are low when the stochastic discount factor is high (i.e., when agents value payoffs more) require a higher risk premium, i.e., a higher excess return on the risk-free rate. Turning to predictability at different horizons, if you consider the case in which t is defined by taking two points in time very close to each other the safe interest rate will be approximately zero and m will not vary too much across states. The constant expected return model (with expected returns equal to zero) is compatible with the no-arbitrage approach at high frequency. However, consider now the case of low frequency, when t is defined by taking two very distant points in time; in this case, safe interest rate will be different from zero and m will vary sizeably across different states. The constant expected return model is not a good approximation at long horizons. Predictability is not necessarily a symptom of market malfunction but rather the consequence of fair compensation for risk-taking, then it should reflect attitudes toward risk and variation in market risk over time. Different theories on the relationship between risk and asset prices should then be assessed on the basis of their ability to explain the predictability that emerges from the data.

Also, different theories on returns predictability can be interpreted as different theories of the determination of m and/or different mechanism of formation of expectations. On the one hand, we have theories of m based on rational investor behavior and rational expectations, on the other hand, we have alternative approaches based on psychological models of investor behavior. Our main interest is on how the predictability of returns can be used for optimal portfolio allocation purposes, rather than discriminating between the possible sources of predictability.

3.10 Predictive Models in Finance

Predictive models are statistical models of future behavior in which relations between the variables to be predicted and the predictors are specified as functional relation determined by parameters to be estimated. Predictive models can be univariate when there is only one variable of interest, or multivariate when we have a vector of variables of interest. All predictive models we shall analyze are special cases of the following general representation:

$$\mathbf{r}_{t,t+k} = f(X_t^{\mu}, \Theta_t^{\mu}) + \mathbf{H}_{t+k}\epsilon_{t+k}$$
$$\boldsymbol{\Sigma}_{t+k} = \mathbf{H}_{t+k}\mathbf{H}'_{t+k}. \tag{3.8}$$
$$\boldsymbol{\Sigma}_{t+k} = g(X_t^{\sigma}, \Theta_t^{\sigma}) + \sum\nolimits_{j=1}^{q} \mathbf{B}_j \boldsymbol{\Sigma}_{t+k-j}\mathbf{B}'_j,$$
$$\epsilon_{t+k} \sim \mathcal{D}(\mathbf{0}, \mathbf{I}) \tag{3.9}$$

where $\mathbf{r}_{t,t+k}$ is the vector of returns between time t and time $t+k$ in which we are interested, X_t^{μ} is the vector of predictors for the mean of our returns that we observe at time t, f specifies the functional relation (which is potentially time-varying) between the mean returns and the predictors that depend also on a set of parameters Θ_t^{μ}, the matrix $\mathbf{H}_{t+k}$ determines the potentially time varying variance–covariance of the vector of returns. The process for the variance is predictable as there is a functional relation determining the relationship between $\mathbf{H}_{t+k}$ and a vector of predictors X_t^{σ} that is driven by a vector of unknown parameters Θ_t^{σ}.

Chapter 4

From Theory to Practice

Predicting the distribution of returns of financial assets is a task of primary importance for identifying desirable investments, performing optimal asset allocation within a portfolio, as well as measuring and managing portfolio risk. Optimal asset management depends on the statistical properties of returns at different frequencies. Portfolio allocation, i.e., the choice of optimal weights to be attributed to the different (financial) assets in a portfolio is typically based on a long-horizon perspective, while the measurement of risk of a given portfolio takes typically a rather short-horizon perspective. This means that a long-run investor decides the optimal portfolio allocation on the basis of the (joint) distribution of the returns of the relevant (i.e., from some pertinent asset menu from which to choose) financial assets at low frequency. However, the monitoring of daily risk of a portfolio depends on the statistical properties of the distribution of returns at high frequencies.

As the distribution of future returns is not observable, the implementation of the theory of finance requires the estimating distribution of future expected returns. This distribution is derived by using the available data to build a model and then by simulating the model to obtain artificial observations from which a model-based distribution of future returns is derived.

Moving from theory to practice requires knowledge of the statistical techniques to perform the analysis of time series of financial assets and returns at different frequencies and their utilization to build models for asset management and performance evaluation, portfolio allocation, and financial risk management.

The relevant concepts will be introduced and their application will be discussed by using a set of programs written using R, a free software environment for statistical computing and graphics, specifically designed for each chapter. Draft codes for the solutions of the exercises, which are designed to allow the reader to understand how the different econometric techniques could be put to work, are also made available. The main emphasis will be given to the application of econometric techniques, readers interested in the statistical properties of the estimation and the simulation of econometric techniques applied here should refer to appropriate textbooks. All empirical applications will be based on publicly available databases of US data.

4.1 The Econometric Modeling Process

There are three relevant dimensions of the data on financial returns: time series, cross-section and the horizon at which returns are defined. In general, we shall define $r^i_{t,t+k}$ as the returns realized by holding between time t and time $t+k$, the asset i. So, the t index captures the time-series dimension, the i index the cross-sectional dimension, and the k index the horizon dimension.

Consider the problem of the optimal choice at time t of the weights to be given to n risky assets in building an optimal portfolio between time t and time $t+k$. The Portfolio theory illustrated in Chapter 4 has made clear that estimates of the first two moments of the distribution of future returns between time t and time $t+k$ are necessary for the practical implementation of optimal portfolios. Econometrics uses the "past available data" to predict the future distribution of returns. In practice, the information contained in past data is used to build a model that describes the behaviour of returns; a model relates different returns and predictors by using some functional form and some unknown parameters that norm the interaction among relevant variables. The data are used to estimate the unknown parameters, by applying the general principle of minimizing the distance between the value predicted by the model for the variables of interest and those observed. After the unknown parameters have been estimated, the model can be simulated to generate predictions for some moments or the entire distribution of returns. Ex-post comparison of model predictions and realized observation helps model validation. After validation, model simulation can be used for forecasting the distribution of returns for asset allocation and risk measurement. To sum up the Econometric Modeling Process involves several steps:

- Data collection and transformation.
- Graphical and descriptive data analysis.
- Model specification.
- Model estimation.
- Model validation.
- Model simulation.
- Use of the output of simulation for asset allocation and risk measurement.

4.2 The Challenges for Financial Econometrics

In general, financial data are not generated by experiments, what is available to the econometrician are observational data, which are given. A single sample of observations is available. To investigate the effect of a medicine an investigator can take a set of patients and attribute them randomly to a "treatment" group and a "control" group. The medicine is then administered to the treatment group members while a "placebo" is given to the control group members. The effect of the medicine can then be measured by the difference in the average health of the members of the two groups after the treatment administration.

If a researcher is interested in assessing the importance of monetary policy to predict stock market returns, the only available data are those on monetary policy indicators and the stock market returns which are given and not generated by a controlled experiments.

Special issues arise routinely in financial data that are available only for special days (say, for example, the days of the FOMC meetings). They may be affected by seasonality, trends, and cycles. Moreover, rare events affect financial returns and rare events are, by definition, not regularly observed. As Taleb (2012) forcefully stresses in his book Antifragile, the absence of evidence in a given sample of data cannot be taken as evidence of absence.

Econometricians face questions of different natures: sometimes the interest lies in non-causal predictive modeling which can be handled by analyzing conditional expectations, while this is not sufficient to understand causation, to which end correlation and conditional expectations are little informative. One issue is to evaluate if the monetary policy stance helps to predict stock market returns, which is very different from establishing a causation from monetary policy to the stock market, as the evidence of correlation between monetary policy and the stock market might very well reflect the response of monetary policy to stock market fluctuations taken as an indicator of (present and future) economic activity. In the specification of models for financial data, the econometrician must use the same information that is available to agents operating in the market, i.e., model-based predictions should not be affected by the so-called "look-ahead bias". To this end, the sample of available data is usually split into two subsamples: a training sample and a test sample. The training sample is used to get the model ready for simulation and forecasting, i.e., to estimate the unknown parameters, while the test sample is used for model evaluation, simulation and forecasting.

We shall investigate model-based prediction of returns by illustrating first how returns can be defined and their relationships with prices and by then illustrating how returns and prices can be empirically analyzed by using R.

4.3 Returns

Consider an asset that does not pay any intermediate cash income (a zero-coupon bond, such as a Treasury Bill, or a share in a company that pays no dividends). Let P_t be the price of the security at time t.

4.3.1 *Simple and log returns*

The linear or simple return between times t and $t-1$ is defined as[1]:

$$R_t = P_t/P_{t-1} - 1 \tag{4.1}$$

[1]Note that (4.1) defines period returns, there is usually an accrual convention applied to returns according to which they are transformed on a yearly basis.

The log, or continuously compounded, return is defined as:

$$r_t = \ln(P_t/P_{t-1}) = \ln(1 + R_t)$$

Note that, while P_t means "price at time t", r_t is a shorthand for "return between time $t-1$ and t" so that the notation is not really complete, and its interpretation depends on the context. When needed for clarity, we shall specify returns as indexed by the start and the end point of the interval in which they are computed as, for instance, in $r_{t-1,t}$.

The two definitions of return yield different numbers when the ratio between consecutive prices is far from 1.

Consider the Taylor formula for $\ln(x)$ for x in the neighborhood of 1:

$$\ln(x) = \ln(1) + (x-1)/1 - (x-1)^2/2 + \cdots$$

if we truncate the series at the first-order term we have:

$$\ln(x) \cong 0 + x - 1$$

so that if x is the ratio between consecutive prices, then for x close to one the two definitions give similar values. Note however that $\ln(x) \leq x - 1$. In fact, $x-1$ is equal to and tangent to $\ln(x)$ in $x = 1$ and above it anywhere else (in fact, the second derivative of $\ln(x)$ is negative). This implies that if one definition of return is used in place of the other, the approximation errors shall be all of the same sign. This fact has important consequences when multi-period returns are computed as the difference between the two definitions will become larger and larger.

4.3.2 *Statistical models for asset prices and returns*

A standard model for asset prices is the log random walk model with Gaussian residuals

$$\begin{aligned} \ln P_t &= \alpha_0 + \ln P_{t-1} + u_t \\ u_t &\sim N.I.D.[0, \sigma^2] \end{aligned} \tag{4.2}$$

in this case, log returns are normally distributed, this implies that single period gross returns are i.i.d. lognormal variables, as

$r_{t+1} \equiv \log(1 + R_{t+1})$. Note that, under the lognormal model

$$\begin{aligned}
r_{t,t+1} &\sim n.i.d.(\mu, \sigma^2) \\
E(R_{t,t+1}) &= \exp\left(\mu + \frac{1}{2}\sigma^2\right) - 1 \\
\text{Var}(R_{t,t+1}) &= \exp(2\mu + \sigma^2)\left(e^{\sigma^2} - 1\right)
\end{aligned}$$

In the case, we have a vector of log returns that are normally distributed:

$$\begin{aligned}
\mathbf{r}_{t,t+1} &\sim i.i.d.(\mu, \Sigma) \\
E\left(R^i_{t,t+1}\right) &= \exp\left(\mu_i + \frac{1}{2}\sigma_{ii}\right) - 1 \\
\text{Cov}\left(R^i_{t,t+1}, R^j_{t,t+1}\right) &= \exp\left(\mu_i + \mu_j + \frac{1}{2}(\sigma_{ii} + \sigma_{jj})\right)\left(e^{\sigma_{ij}} - 1\right)
\end{aligned}$$

4.3.3 *Multi-period returns and annualized returns*

What are multi-period returns? Multiperiod returns are returns to an investment which is made with a horizon larger than one period. Let us consider the case of the returns to an investment made in time t until time $t + n$. In this case, we define the simple multi-period return as

$$\begin{aligned}
R_{t,t+n} &= P_{t+n}/P_t - 1 \\
&= \frac{P_{t+n}}{P_{t+n-1}}\frac{P_{t+n-1}}{P_{t+n-2}} \cdots \frac{P_{t+1}}{P_t} - 1 \\
&= \prod_{i=1}^{n} (1 + R_{t+i,t+i-1}) - 1 \qquad (4.3)
\end{aligned}$$

in the case of log returns we have instead:

$$\begin{aligned}
r_{t,t+n} &= \ln(P_{t+n}/P_t) \\
&= \ln\left(\frac{P_{t+n}}{P_{t+n-1}}\frac{P_{t+n-1}}{P_{t+n-2}} \cdots \frac{P_{t+1}}{P_t}\right) \\
&= \sum_{i=1}^{n} r_{t+i,t+i-1} \qquad (4.4)
\end{aligned}$$

Consider the case in which the length of our period in one year, given any multiperiod returns one can define its annualized value i.e., as the constant annual rate of return equivalent to the multiperiod returns of an investment in asset i over the period $t, \ldots, t+n$.

In the case of simple returns, we have

$$\begin{aligned}(1+R^A_{t,t+n})^n &= 1+R_{t,t+n}\\ &= \prod_{i=1}^{n}(1+R_{t+i,t+i-1})\\ R^A_{t,t+n} &= \left(\prod_{i=1}^{n}(1+R_{t+i,t+i-1})\right)^{\frac{1}{n}}-1\end{aligned}$$

the annualized simple rate of return is the geometric mean of the annual returns over the period t, $t+n$.

Consider now continuously compounded returns:

$$\begin{aligned}nr^A_{t,t+n} &= r_{t,t+n}\\ &= \sum_{i=1}^{n} r_{t+i,t+i-1}\\ r^A_{t,t+n} &= \frac{1}{n}\sum_{i=1}^{n} r_{t+i,t+i-1}\end{aligned}$$

The annualized log return is the arithmetic mean of annual log returns.

4.3.4 *Working with returns*

Consider the value of a buy-and-hold portfolio invested in shares of k different companies, that pay no dividend, at time t be

$$V_t = \sum_{i=1}^{k} n_i P_{it}$$

The simple one-period return of the portfolio shall be a linear function of the returns of each stock.

$$\begin{aligned} R_t &= \frac{V_t}{V_{t-1}} - 1 = \sum_{i=1..k} \frac{n_i P_{it}}{\sum_{j=1..k} n_j P_{jt-1}} - 1 \\ &= \sum_{i=1..k} \frac{n_i P_{it-1}}{\sum_{j=1..k} n_j P_{jt-1}} \frac{P_{it}}{P_{it-1}} - 1 \\ &= \sum_{i=1..k} w_{it}(R_{it} + 1) - 1 = \left(\sum_{i=1..k} w_{it} R_{it} + \sum_{i=1..k} w_{it} 1 \right) - 1 \\ &= \sum_{i=1}^{k} w_{it} R_{it} \end{aligned}$$

where $w_{it} = \frac{n_i P_{it-1}}{\sum_i n_i P_{it-1}}$ are non negative "weights" summing to 1 which represent the percentage of the portfolio invested in the ith stock at time $t-1$.

This simple result is very useful. Suppose, for instance, that you know at time $t-1$ the expected values for the returns between time $t-1$ and t. Since the expected value is a linear operator (the expected value of a sum is the sum of the expected values, moreover additive and multiplicative constants can be taken out of the expected value) and the weights w_{it} are known, hence non-stochastic, at time $t-1$ we can easily compute the return for the portfolio as

$$E(R_t) = \sum_{i=1..k} w_{it} E(R_{it})$$

Moreover, if we know all the covariances between r_{it} and r_{jt} (if $i = j$ we simply have a variance) we can find the variance of the portfolio return as

$$V(R_t) = \sum_{i=1..k} \sum_{j=1..k} w_i w_j \text{Cov}(R_{it}; R_{jt})$$

This cross-sectional additivity property does not apply to log returns. In fact, we have:

$$
\begin{aligned}
r_t &= \ln\left(\frac{V_t}{V_{t-1}}\right) \\
&= \ln\left(\frac{\sum_{i=1}^{k} n_i P_{it-1}}{\sum_{i=1}^{k} n_i P_{it-1}} \frac{P_{it}}{P_{it-1}}\right) = \ln\left(\sum_{i=1}^{k} w_{it} \exp(r_{it})\right)
\end{aligned}
$$

The log return of the portfolio is not a linear function of the log (and also the linear) returns of the components. In this case assumptions on the expected values and covariances of the components cannot be translated into assumptions on the expected value and the variance of the portfolio by simple use of basic "expected value of the sum" and "variance of the sum" formulas.

On the other hand, log returns are additive when we consider the time series of returns

$$r_{t,t+n} = \sum_{i=1}^{n} r_{t+i,t+i-1}$$

It is then easy, for instance, given the expected values and the covariances of the sub-period returns, to compute the expected value and the variance of the full-period return. Interestingly, additivity does not apply to simple returns.

$$R_{t,t+n} = \prod_{i=1}^{n} R_{t+i,t+i-1} - 1$$

In general, the expected value of a product is difficult to evaluate and does not depend only on the expected values of the terms.

To sum up: the two definitions of returns yield different values when the ratio between consecutive prices is not in the neighborhood of the unit value. The linear definition works very well for portfolios over single periods, in the sense that expected values and variances of portfolios can be derived by expected values variances and covariances of the components, as the portfolio linear return over a time period is a linear combination of the returns of the portfolio components. For analogous reasons, the log definition works very well for single securities over time. However, care must be exercised when long-horizon returns are computed by cumulating continuously compounded returns.

4.4 Stock and Bond Returns

The computation of returns for stock and bonds must take into account the existence of intermediate cash income. In this section we show how this is performed and how linearization can help the empirical analysis of the stock and bond markets.

4.4.1 *Stock returns and the dynamic dividend growth model*

Consider the one-period total holding returns in the stock market, that are defined as follows[2]:

$$H^s_{t+1} \equiv \frac{P_{t+1} + D_{t+1}}{P_t} - 1 = \frac{P_{t+1} - P_t + D_{t+1}}{P_t} = \frac{\Delta P_{t+1}}{P_t} + \frac{D_{t+1}}{P_t} \tag{4.5}$$

where P_t is the stock price at time t, D_t is the (cash) dividend paid at time t, and the superscript s denotes "stock". The last equality decomposes a discrete holding period return as the sum of the percentage capital gain and of (a definition of) the *dividend yield*, D_{t+1}/P_t. Given that one-period returns are usually small, it is sometimes convenient to approximate them with logarithmic, continuously compounded returns, defined as

$$\begin{aligned} r^s_{t+1} &\equiv \log(1 + H^s_{t+1}) = \log\left(\frac{P_{t+1} + D_{t+1}}{P_t}\right) \\ &= \log(P_{t+1} + D_{t+1}) - \log(P_t) \end{aligned} \tag{4.6}$$

Interestingly, while linear returns are additive in the percentage capital gain and the dividend yield components, log returns are not as

$$\log\left(\frac{P_{t+1} + D_{t+1}}{P_t}\right) \neq \log\left(\frac{P_{t+1}}{P_t}\right) + \log\left(\frac{D_{t+1}}{P_t}\right)$$

However, it is still possible to express log returns as a linear function of the log of the price dividend and the (log) dividend growth.

[2]The use of "≡" emphasizes that (4.5) provides a definition. Moreover, ΔX_{t+1} denotes the first difference of a generic variable, or $\Delta X_{t+1} \equiv X_{t+1} - X_t$.

Dividing both sides of (4.5) by $(1+H^s_{t+1})$ and multiplying both sides by P_t/D_t we have:

$$\frac{P_t}{D_t}=\frac{1}{\left(1+H^s_{t+1}\right)}\frac{D_{t+1}}{D_t}\left(1+\frac{P_{t+1}}{D_{t+1}}\right)$$

Taking logs (denoted by lowercase letters, i.e., $x_t \equiv \log X_t$ for a generic variable X_t), we have[3]:

$$p_t-d_t=-r^s_{t+1}+\Delta d_{t+1}+\ln(1+e^{p_{t+1}-d_{t+1}}) \tag{4.7}$$

as $\log(D_{t+1}/D_t)=\log D_{t+1}-\log D_t=\Delta\log D_{t+1}=\Delta d_{t+1}$. Taking a first-order Taylor expansion of the last term about the point $\bar{P}/\bar{D}=e^{\bar{p}-\bar{d}}$ (where the bar denotes a sample average), the logarithm term on the right-hand side can be approximated as:

$$\begin{aligned}\ln(1+e^{p_{t+1}-d_{t+1}}) &\simeq \ln(1+e^{\bar{p}-\bar{d}})+\frac{e^{\bar{p}-\bar{d}}}{1+e^{\bar{p}-\bar{d}}}[(p_{t+1}-d_{t+1})-(\bar{p}-\bar{d})]\\ &=-\ln(1-\rho)-\rho\ln\left(\frac{1}{1-\rho}-1\right)+\rho(p_{t+1}-d_{t+1})\\ &=\kappa+\rho(p_{t+1}-d_{t+1})\end{aligned}$$

where

$$\rho\equiv\frac{e^{\bar{p}-\bar{d}}}{1+e^{\bar{p}-\bar{d}}}=\frac{\bar{P}/\bar{D}}{1+(\bar{P}/\bar{D})}<1 \qquad \kappa\equiv-\ln(1-\rho)-\rho\ln\left(\frac{1}{1-\rho}-1\right)$$

Although $\rho\in(0,1)$ is just a factor that depends on the average price-dividend ratio, in what follows will be used in a way that resembles

---

[3] $-r^s_{t+1}$ follows from

$$\begin{aligned}\log\frac{1}{\left(1+H^s_{t+1}\right)}&=\log 1-\log(1+H^s_{t+1})\\ &=-\log(1+H^s_{t+1})=-r^s_{t+1}\end{aligned}$$

based on our earlier definitions and the fact that $\log 1=0$ for natural logs. Moreover, notice that

$$\frac{P_{t+1}}{D_{t+1}}=e^{\log(P_{t+1}/D_{t+1})}=e^{\log P_{t+1}-\log D_{t+1}}=e^{p_{t+1}-d_{t+1}}$$

a discount factor. At this point, substituting the expression for the approximated term in (4.7), we obtain that the log price-dividend ratio is defined as[4]:

$$p_t - d_t \simeq \kappa - r^s_{t+1} + \Delta d_{t+1} + \rho(p_{t+1} - d_{t+1})$$

Re-arranging this expression shows that total stock market returns can be written as

$$r^s_{t+1} = \kappa + \rho(p_{t+1} - d_{t+1}) + \Delta d_{t+1} - (p_t - d_t)$$

or a constant κ, plus the log dividend growth rate (Δd_{t+1}), plus the (discounted, at rate ρ) change in the log price-dividend ratio, $\rho(p_{t+1} - d_{t+1}) - (p_t - d_t) = \Delta(p_{t+1} - d_{t+1}) - (1 - \rho)(p_{t+1} - d_{t+1})$. Moreover, by *forward* recursive substitution one obtains:

$$\begin{aligned}
(p_t - d_t) &= \kappa - r^s_{t+1} + \Delta d_{t+1} + \rho(p_{t+1} - d_{t+1}) \\
&= \kappa - r^s_{t+1} + \Delta d_{t+1} + \rho(\kappa - r^s_{t+2} + \Delta d_{t+2} + \rho(p_{t+2} - d_{t+2})) \\
&= (\kappa + \rho\kappa) - (r^s_{t+1} + \rho r^s_{t+2}) + (\Delta d_{t+1} + \rho \Delta d_{t+2}) \\
&\quad + \rho^2(p_{t+2} - d_{t+2}) \\
&= (\kappa + \rho\kappa) - (r^s_{t+1} + \rho r^s_{t+2}) + (\Delta d_{t+1} + \rho \Delta d_{t+2}) + \\
&\quad + \rho^2(\kappa - r^s_{t+3} + \Delta d_{t+3} + \rho(p_{t+3} - d_{t+3})) \\
&= \kappa(1 + \rho + \rho^2) - (r^s_{t+1} + \rho r^s_{t+2} + \rho^2 r^s_{t+3}) \\
&\quad + (\Delta d_{t+1} + \rho \Delta d_{t+2} + \rho^2 \Delta d_{t+3}) + \rho^3(p_{t+3} - d_{t+3}) \\
&= \cdots = \kappa \sum_{j=1}^{m} \rho^{j-1} + \sum_{j=1}^{m} \rho^{j-1}(\Delta d_{t+j} - r^s_{t+j}) \\
&\quad + \rho^m(p_{t+m} - d_{t+m})
\end{aligned}$$

Under the assumption that there can be no rational bubbles, i.e., that[5]

$$\lim_{m \longrightarrow \infty} \rho^m(p_{t+m} - d_{t+m}) = 0$$

---

[4]The approximation notation "$\simeq$" appears to emphasize that this expression is derived from an application of a Taylor expansion.

[5]This assumption means that as the horizon grows without bounds, the log price-dividend ratio (hence, the underlying price-dividend ratio) may grow without bounds, but this needs to happen at a speed that is inferior to $1/\rho > 1$, so that when $p_{t+m} - d_{t+m}$ is discounted at the rate ρ^m, the limit of the quantity $\rho^m(p_{t+m} - d_{t+m})$ is zero.

from

$$\lim_{m \longrightarrow \infty} \sum_{j=1}^{m} \rho^{j-1} = \frac{1}{1-\rho}$$

if $\rho \in (0, 1)$, we get

$$(p_t - d_t) = \frac{\kappa}{1-\rho} + \sum_{j=1}^{m} \rho^{j-1} (\Delta d_{t+j} - r^s_{t+j})$$

This result shows that the log price-dividend ratio, $(p_t - d_t)$, measures the value of a very long-term investment strategy (buy and hold) which — apart from a constant $\kappa/(1-\rho)$ — is equal to the stream of future dividend growth discounted at the appropriate rate, which reflects the risk-free rate plus the risk premium required to hold risky assets, $r^s_{t+j} \equiv r^f + (r^s_{t+j} - r^f)$.[6] Therefore, for long investment horizons, econometric methods may hope to infer from the data two different types of "information": information concerning the forecasts of future (continuously compounded) dividend growth rates, i.e., $\Delta d_{t+1}, \Delta d_{t+2}, \ldots, \Delta d_{t+m}$ as $m \longrightarrow \infty$, which are measures of the cash flows paid out by the risky assets (e.g., how well a company will do); information concerning future discount rates, and in particular future risk premia, i.e., $(r^s_{t+1} - r^f), (r^s_{t+2} - r^f), \ldots, (r^s_{t+m} - r^f)$ as $m \longrightarrow \infty$. Note that, under the null hypothesis of constancy of returns, the volatility of the price dividend ratio should be completely explained by that of the dividend process. The empirical evidence is strongly against this prediction (see the Shiller (1981) and Campbell and Shiller (1987)).

If we decompose future variables into their expected component and the unexpected one (an error term) we can write the relationship between the dividend yield and the returns one period ahead and over the long horizon as follows:

$$\begin{aligned} r^s_{t+1} &= \kappa + \rho E_t(p_{t+1} - d_{t+1}) + E_t \Delta d_{t+1} - (p_t - d_t) \\ &\quad + \rho u^{pd}_{t+1} + u^{\Delta d}_{t+1} \end{aligned}$$

[6]Here, we have assumed that the risk-free interest rate is approximately constant. We shall see that, at least as a first approximation, this is an assumption that holds in practice.

$$\sum_{j=1}^{m}\rho^{j-1}r^{s}_{t+j} = \frac{\kappa}{1-\rho} + \sum_{j=1}^{m}\rho^{j-1}E_t(\Delta d_{t+j}) - (p_t - d_t)$$
$$+ \rho^{m}E_t(p_{t+m} - d_{t+m}) + \rho^{m}u^{pd}_{t+m} + \sum_{j=1}^{m}\rho^{j-1}u^{\Delta d}_{t+j}$$

These two expressions illustrate that when the price dividends ratio is a noisy process, such noise dominates the variance of one-period returns and the statistical relation between the price dividend ratio and one-period returns is weak. However, as the horizon over which returns are defined gets longer, noise tends to be dampened and the predictability of returns given the price dividend ratio increases.

4.4.2 *Bond returns: Yields-to-maturity and holding period returns*

We turn now to bonds. We distinguish between two types of bonds: those paying a coupon each given period and those that do not pay a coupon but just reimburse the entire capital upon maturity (zero-coupon bonds).

Zero-coupon bonds

Define the relationship between price and yield to maturity of a zero-coupon bond as follows:

$$P_{t,T} = \frac{1}{(1+Y_{t,T})^{T-t}} \tag{4.8}$$

where $P_{t,T}$ is the price at time t of a bond maturing at time T, and $Y_{t,T}$ is yield to maturity. Taking logs of the left and the right-hand sides of the expression for $P_{t,T}$, and defining the continuously compounded *yield*, $y_{t,T}$, as $\log(1+Y_{t,T})$, we have the following relationship:

$$p_{t,T} = -(T-t)y_{t,T} \tag{4.9}$$

which clearly illustrates that the elasticity of the yield to maturity to the price of a zero-coupon bond is the maturity of the security.

Therefore, the duration of the bond equals maturity as no coupons are paid. The one-period uncertain holding-period return on a bond maturing at time T, $r^T_{t,t+1}$, is then defined as follows:

$$\begin{aligned} r^T_{t,t+1} &\equiv p_{t+1,T} - p_{t,T} = -(T-t-1)y_{t+1,T} + (T-t)y_{t,T} \quad (4.10)\\ &= y_{t,T} - (T-t-1)(y_{t+1,T} - y_{t,T})\\ &= (T-t)y_{t,T} - (T-t-1)\, y_{t+1,T} \quad (4.11)\end{aligned}$$

which means that yields and returns differ by a scaled measure of the change between the yield at time $t+1$, $y_{t+1,T}$, and the yield at time t, $y_{t,T}$.

Coupon bonds

The relationship between price and yield to maturity of a constant coupon (C) bond is given by

$$P^c_{t,T} = \frac{C}{\left(1+Y^c_{t,T}\right)} + \frac{C}{\left(1+Y^c_{t,T}\right)^2} + \cdots + \frac{1+C}{\left(1+Y_{t,T}\right)^{T-t}}$$

When the bond is selling at par, the yield to maturity is equal to the coupon rate. To measure the length of time that a bondholder has invested money for we need to introduce the concept of duration:

$$\begin{aligned} D^c_{t,T} &= \frac{\frac{C}{\left(1+Y^c_{t,T}\right)} + 2\frac{C}{\left(1+Y^c_{t,T}\right)^2} + \cdots + (T-t)\frac{1+C}{\left(1+Y_{t,T}\right)^{T-t}}}{P^c_{t,T}}\\ &= \frac{C\sum_{i=1}^{T-t}\frac{i}{\left(1+Y^c_{t,T}\right)^i} + \frac{(T-t)}{\left(1+Y_{t,T}\right)^{T-t}}}{P^c_{t,T}}\end{aligned}$$

Note that when a bond is floating at par we have

$$D^c_{t,T} = Y^c_{t,T}\sum_{i=1}^{T-t}\frac{i}{\left(1+Y^c_{t,T}\right)^i} + \frac{(T-t)}{\left(1+Y_{t,T}\right)^{T-t}}$$

$$= Y^c_{t,T} \frac{\left((T-t)\frac{1}{1+Y^c_{t,T}} - (T-t) - 1\right)\frac{1}{\left(1+Y^c_{t,T}\right)^{T-t+1}} + \frac{1}{1+Y^c_{t,T}}}{\left(1 - \frac{1}{1+Y^c_{t,T}}\right)^2}$$

$$+ \frac{(T-t)}{(1+Y_{t,T})^{T-t}}$$

$$= \frac{1 - \left(1 + Y^c_{t,T}\right)^{-(T-t)}}{1 - \left(1 + Y^c_{t,T}\right)^{-1}}$$

because when $|x| < 1$,

$$\sum_{k=0}^{n} k x^k = \frac{(nx - n - 1)\, x^{n+1} + x}{(1-x)^2}$$

Duration can be used to find approximate linear relationships between log-coupon yields and holding period returns. Extending the formula of zero-coupon bonds (where duration is equal to maturity) to coupon bonds, we have

$$r^c_{t+1} = D^c_{t,T} y^c_{t,T} - \left(D^c_{t,T} - 1\right) y^c_{t+1,T}$$

Shiller (1979) proposes a *linearization* which takes duration as constant and considers the following approximation in the neighborhood $y_{t,T} = y_{t+1,T} = \bar{y} = C$:

$$H_{t,T} \simeq D_T y_{t,T} - (D_T - 1)\, y_{t+1,T}$$

$$D_T = \frac{1 - \left(1 + \bar{Y}^c_{t,T}\right)^{-(T-t)}}{1 - \left(1 + \bar{Y}^c_{t,T}\right)^{-1}}$$

$$D_T = \frac{1 - \gamma^{T-t-1}}{1 - \gamma} = \frac{1}{1 - \gamma_T}$$

$$\gamma_T = \left\{1 + \bar{Y}^c_{t,T}\left[1 - 1/(1 + \bar{Y}^c_{t,T})^{T-t-1}\right]^{-1}\right\}^{-1}$$

$$\lim_{T \longrightarrow \infty} \gamma_T = \gamma = 1/(1 + \bar{y})$$

Solving this expression forward, we generate the equivalent of the DDG model in the bond market:

$$y_{t,T} = \sum_{j=0}^{T-t-1} \gamma^j (1-\gamma) H_{t+j,T} + \gamma^{T-t} y_{T-1,T}$$

In this case, by equating one-period risk-adjusted returns, we have

$$E\left[\frac{y_{t,T} - \gamma y_{t+1,T}}{1-\gamma} \mid I_t\right] = r_t + \phi_{t,T} \tag{4.12}$$

From the above expression, by recursive substitution, under the terminal condition that at maturity the price equals the principal, we obtain:

$$y_{t,T} = y^*_{t,T} + E[\Phi_T \mid I_t] = \frac{1-\gamma}{1-\gamma^{T-t}} \sum_{j=0}^{T-t-1} \gamma^j E[r_{t+j} \mid I_t] + E[\Phi_T \mid I_t] \tag{4.13}$$

where the constant $\Phi_{t,T}$ is the term premium over the whole life of the bond:

$$\Phi_{t,T} = \frac{1-\gamma}{1-\gamma^{T-t}} \sum_{j=0}^{T-t-1} \gamma^j \phi_{t+j,T}$$

For long-bonds, when $T-t$ is very large, we have:

$$y_{t,T} = y^*_{t,T} + E[\Phi_T \mid I_t] = (1-\gamma) \sum_{j=0}^{T-t-1} \gamma^j E[r_{t+j} \mid I_t] + E[\Phi_T \mid I_t]$$

Subtracting the risk-free rate from both sides of this equation we have

$$\begin{aligned} S_{t,T} = y_{t,T} - r_t &= \sum_{j=1}^{T-1} \gamma^j E[\Delta r_{t+j} \mid I_t] + E[\Phi_T \mid I_t] \\ &= S^*_{t,T} + E[\Phi_T \mid I_t] \end{aligned}$$

4.5 Going to the Data with R

A statistical package is needed to take all the modelling steps in practice. Going from loading the data to transforming them, graphing them, analyzing them, modeling them and using them to estimate parameters and generate model-based simulations and, eventually, producing a report. We will use R and run R through the user interface RStudio. When using R and Rstudio Chat GPT can be used as an online assistant. If you ask Chat GPT "what is R Studio?" you will get an answer similar to the following one.

RStudio is an integrated development environment (IDE) for the R programming language. It provides a user-friendly and feature-rich environment for working with R, making it easier for data scientists, statisticians, and researchers to write, run, and manage R code. Here are some key features and components of RStudio:

- **Script editor:** RStudio includes a script editor with features like syntax highlighting, code completion, and code formatting to enhance your coding experience.
- **Console:** It has an interactive R console that allows you to run R code and see the results in real-time. You can also save your command history for future reference.
- **Data viewer:** RStudio provides a data viewer that lets you examine and manipulate data frames and other data structures visually.
- **Plots and visualization:** You can create and customize plots and charts using R's graphical capabilities. RStudio displays plots within the IDE, making it easier to visualize your data.
- **Package management:** It simplifies the management of R packages, allowing you to install, update, and load packages with ease.
- **Integrated help:** RStudio integrates with R's documentation and help system, making it simple to access information about functions, packages, and syntax.
- **Version control:** It offers version control integration with Git and SVN, allowing you to manage your R projects and code revisions efficiently.
- **Project management:** RStudio supports project organization, making it easy to keep your code, data, and files organized within a project folder.

- **R Markdown:** RStudio supports R Markdown, a format for creating dynamic documents that combine R code, text, and visualizations. This is useful for creating reports, presentations, and publications.
- **Shiny:** RStudio includes Shiny, a web application framework for building interactive web applications with R. This is particularly useful for creating data dashboards and interactive data applications.

4.5.1 *Getting started*

To get started with R and Rstudio you should first install them, then learn what R packages R, how to install them and how to call them. A very useful short piece by Torfs and Brauer (2014) provides all the relevant information to download, install and get started with R and RStudio. You should also be aware of how to get help from the web. The best way to do so Is to ask Chat GPT.

Ask Chat GPT

Here is the Chat GPT answer to the question "How can you help me in using R with RStudio?"

I can assist you in using R with RStudio in various ways, including:

- **Coding and syntax assistance:** I can provide explanations, examples, and code snippets to help you understand and write R code in RStudio. If you encounter errors or have questions about specific functions or packages, feel free to ask for guidance.
- **Data manipulation and analysis:** I can assist you in performing data manipulation, cleaning, and analysis tasks in RStudio. Whether you need help with data frames, statistical analysis, or visualization, I can provide guidance and suggestions.
- **Package recommendations:** If you're looking for R packages to solve specific tasks or problems, I can suggest relevant packages and explain how to install and use them in your RStudio environment.
- **R Markdown and reports:** I can assist you in creating dynamic reports using R Markdown in RStudio. I can provide guidance on

formatting, adding code chunks, and generating documents with embedded R code and output.

- **Plotting and visualization:** I can help you create various types of plots and visualizations in RStudio using packages like ggplot2, base R graphics, and others. I can also explain how to customize and export your plots.
- **Debugging and troubleshooting:** If you encounter errors or bugs in your R code within RStudio, I can help you understand and debug the issues. I can provide strategies for identifying and fixing common programming problems.
- **Version control with git:** I can guide you through the process of using Git for version control within RStudio. This includes initializing repositories, committing changes, and collaborating with others using Git.
- **Project organization:** I can provide advice on organizing your R projects within RStudio, including creating project directories, managing files, and maintaining a tidy project structure.
- **Customization and configuration:** I can help you customize your RStudio environment by explaining how to change themes, set preferences, and install extensions or add-ons that enhance your workflow.
- **Tips and best practices:** I can offer tips and best practices for efficient coding, data analysis, and project management in RStudio to improve your productivity.

To get assistance with any specific R-related task or question you have in RStudio, simply provide me with the details of your problem or topic of interest, and I'll do my best to provide guidance and support.

4.5.2 *Data objects in R*

When working with data in R the first step is to know how to identify them and organize them. R makes available various common **datatypes**: double, integer, complex, logical, character, factor, date and time, and missing data. Data are then organized into datasets that are called **data structures**. The basic data structures we shall use are: vector, matrix, array, dataframes, tibble, time-series, and lists. Chapter 2 of Singh and Allen (2017) provides a good introduction to data objects in R.

Ask Chat GPT

Here is the Chat GPT answer to the question "What is the difference between a data-frame a tibble and a time-series object in R?"[7] In R, dataframes, tibbles, and time-series objects are all data structures used for different purposes, and they have distinct characteristics and functionality:

(1) **Dataframe:** A dataframe is a fundamental data structure in R. It is a two-dimensional tabular data structure where columns can contain different data types (numeric, character, factor, etc.). Dataframes are often used for storing and manipulating structured data, such as data imported from spreadsheets or databases. Dataframes are versatile and widely used for various data analysis tasks.
(2) **Tibble:** A tibble is an enhanced dataframe introduced as part of the tidyverse ecosystem in R, available through the tibble package. Tibbles are designed to be more user-friendly and consistent than traditional dataframes. They have stricter rules, such as not automatically converting strings to factors, which can lead to fewer surprises. Tibbles are particularly well-suited for data wrangling and analysis with tools like dplyr and ggplot2.
(3) **Time-series object:** A time-series object is used specifically for handling time-series data, where data points are associated with specific timestamps or time intervals. Time-series objects can be created using various packages, such as the ts function from base R, or with packages like xts and zoo for more advanced time-series manipulation. Time-series objects have additional attributes and methods for time-based operations, like lagging, differencing, and time-based subsetting. They are essential for time-series analysis and forecasting tasks.

[7]Chat GPT will also provide example codes on how to create dataframe, tibbles and time-series objects.

In summary, the choice between a dataframe, tibble, or time-series object depends on your specific data and analysis needs. Dataframes and tibbles are suitable for general data analysis, while time-series objects are specialized for handling time-dependent data. Tibbles, in particular, provide a more consistent and user-friendly experience for data manipulation tasks, which can be beneficial in many scenarios.

4.5.3 *Data handling in R*

Data handling involves getting the data, import them into R and pre-processing them.

Importing data into R

To get data from the web in R one can use packages, such as *quantmod*, that allow to get data from yahoo.finance or from the online federal reserve database (FRED) (https://fred.stlouisfed.org/). Alternatively, data can be accessed from web provider by providing the appropriate URL or via application program interfaces (API) that can be run within R. Data from Excel or other foreign languages can also be read into R. Time-series Financial Data in Excel format used in this book have been downloaded Robert Shiller's webpage (http://www.econ.yale.edu/~shiller/) and Ken French's webpage (http://mba.tuck.dartmouth.edu/pages/faculty/ken.french/data_library.html). In the website associated to the book several example programmes to download and import data in R are made available.

An illustrative R program

The following code, after preliminaries (such as setting the working directory and running all the relevant packages, after making sure that they are all available, downloads data from Yahoo Finance and the Fred Website illustrates how to change their frequency and how to save them locally in EXCEL format, it also shows how data available from a specific URL can be downloaded and organized.

```
#clear the environment
rm(list=ls())

setwd(dirname(rstudioapi::getActiveDocumentContext()$path))
# packages used
listofpackages <- c("tidyverse","ellipse","reshape2","xts","xlsx","readxl",
"quantmod")
#installation of "xlsx" requires Java

for (j in listofpackages){
  if(sum(installed.packages()[, 1] == j) == 0) {
    install.packages(j)
  }
  library(j, character.only = T)
}

tickers <- c('AXP','AMGN','AAPL','BA','CAT','CSCO','CVX','GS','HD','HON',
             'IBM','INTC','JNJ','KO','JPM','MCD','MMM','MRK','MSFT','NKE',
             'PG','TRV','UNH','CRM','VZ','V','WBA','WMT','DIS','DOW','^DJI')
                  #,'^GSPC',,'^IRX')

#download the historical prices
getSymbols.yahoo(tickers,
                 env = globalenv(),
                 index.class ='Date',
                 from = "1985-01-31",
                 to = "2023-07-31",
                 periodicity ="monthly")

stocks =
    merge(AXP[,6],AMGN[,6],AAPL[,6],BA[,6],CAT[,6],CSCO[,6],CVX[,6],GS[,6],HD[,6],HON[,6],
          IBM[,6],INTC[,6],JNJ[,6],KO[,6],JPM[,6],MCD[,6],MMM[,6],MRK[,6],MSFT[,6],NKE[,6],
          PG[,6],TRV[,6],UNH[,6],CRM[,6],VZ[,6],V[,6],WBA[,6],WMT[,6],DIS[,6],DOW[,6],DJI[,6])

colnames(stocks) <-
    c('AXP','AMGN','AAPL','BA','CAT','CSCO','CVX','GS','HD','HON',
                   'IBM','INTC','JNJ','KO','JPM','MCD','MMM','MRK','MSFT','NKE',
                   'PG','TRV','UNH','CRM','VZ','V','WBA','WMT','DIS','DOW','DJI')

write.xlsx(as.data.frame(stocks), "2023_monthly_stocks.xlsx", row.names =
    TRUE)
rm(list = c('AXP','AMGN','AAPL','BA','CAT','CSCO','CVX','GS','HD','HON',
            'IBM','INTC','JNJ','KO','JPM','MCD','MMM','MRK','MSFT','NKE',
            'PG','TRV','UNH','CRM','VZ','V','WBA','WMT','DIS','DOW','DJI'))

stocks_quarterly = to.quarterly(stocks$AXP)[,4]

for(i in 2:ncol(stocks)){
  x = to.quarterly(stocks[, i])[,4]
  stocks_quarterly = merge(stocks_quarterly, x)
}

colnames(stocks_quarterly) <-
    c('AXP','AMGN','AAPL','BA','CAT','CSCO','CVX','GS','HD','HON',
                     'IBM','INTC','JNJ','KO','JPM','MCD','MMM','MRK','MSFT','NKE',
                     'PG','TRV','UNH','CRM','VZ','V','WBA','WMT','DIS','DOW','DJI')

write.xlsx(as.data.frame(stocks_quarterly), "2023_quarterly_stocks.xlsx",
    row.names = TRUE)

# set tickers
```

```
tickers1 <- c("FEDFUNDS", "DGS10", "GDPPOT")
getSymbols.FRED(tickers1,
                env = globalenv(),
                return.class = "xts",
                index.class ='Date'
                )
# import data from FRED database
quarterly_fedfunds <- apply.quarterly(FEDFUNDS, last)

urlfile="https://raw.githubusercontent.com/pcm-dpc/COVID-19/
master/dati-regioni/dpc-covid19-ita-regioni.csv"
COVID_all<-read_csv(url(urlfile)) #read_csv in package tidyverse
#COVID_all<-read.csv(url(urlfile)) #read.csv in package xlxs
LOMBARDIA=subset(COVID_all,denominazione_regione=="Lombardia",select=c(1:1,4:4,7:20))
VENETO=subset(COVID_all,denominazione_regione=="Veneto",select=c(1:1,4:4,7:20))
```

Pre-processing data

Pre-processing data involves extracting subsets, combining dataframe, and constructing tables. Once the relevant database has been constructed data transformations are necessary to build returns from prices, to construct portfolios and to track their performance over time. R programming and the use of loops, control-flows and functions is very useful when the same operations are iterated for different series, think for example of constructing the returns on the 30 DJ stocks given their prices. Chapter 3 of Singh and Allen (2017) provides a good introduction to R programming and control flow.

4.5.4 *Data exploration and graphics*

Data exploration and graphics of the relevant transformed series complete the initial stage of the modeling process. Data exploration involves the use of descriptive univariate and multivariate statistics while graphics is implemented with the utilization of time-series plots, cross-sectional plots, histograms and QQ-plots. The packages *ggplot* and *highcharter* allow graphical analysis of data respectively formatted as tibble and time-series objects.

Ask Chat GPT

Here is the Chat GPT answer to the question "What can I do with ggplot in R?"

ggplot2 is a powerful data visualization package in R that allows you to create a wide range of high-quality plots and charts. It is based on the "Grammar of Graphics" concept, which means you can build complex plots by specifying their components in a structured and intuitive manner. Here are some of the things you can do with ggplot2 in R:

(1) **Scatter plots:** Create scatter plots to visualize the relationship between two continuous variables.
$ggplot(data = df, aes(x = variable1, y = variable2)) + geom\_point()$

(2) **Line plots:** Generate line plots for time series or continuous data.
$ggplot(data = df, aes(x = time, y = value)) + geom\_line()$

(3) **Bar charts:** Create bar charts to display the distribution of categorical data.
$ggplot(data = df, aes(x = category, y = count)) + geom\_bar(stat = \text{"}identity\text{"})$

(4) **Histograms:** Visualize the distribution of a single continuous variable.
$ggplot(data = df, aes(x = variable)) + geom\_histogram(binwidth = 1, fill = \text{"}blue\text{"}, color = \text{"}black\text{"})$

(5) **Box plots:** Generate box plots to display the distribution of a variable's quartiles and outliers.
$ggplot(data = df, aes(x = category, y = value)) + geom\_boxplot()$

(6) **Density plots:** Create density plots to visualize the distribution of a variable as a smooth curve.
$ggplot(data = df, aes(x = variable)) + geom\_density()$

(7) **Heatmaps:** Generate heatmaps to display patterns in a matrix of data.
$ggplot(data = df, aes(x = variable1, y = variable2, fill = value)) + geom\_tile()$

(8) **Faceting:** Split your data into multiple smaller plots based on a categorical variable.

$ggplot(data = df, aes(x = variable1, y = variable2)) + geom\_point() + facet\_wrap(\ category)$

(9) **Customize aesthetics:** You can customize the appearance of your plots by modifying colors, labels, titles, and more using ggplot2's extensive options.

$ggplot(data = df, aes(x = variable1, y = variable2)) + geom\_point(color = \text{“}red\text{”}) + labs(title = \text{“}MyScatter\ Plot\text{”}, x = \text{“}X - axislabel\text{”}, y = \text{“}Y - axislabel\text{”})$

(10) **Combine layers:** Combine multiple geometric layers to create complex plots.

$ggplot(data = df, aes(x = variable1, y = variable2)) + geom\_point() + geom\_smooth(method = \text{“}lm\text{”})$

These are just some of the things you can do with ggplot2. It offers a flexible and versatile framework for data visualization in R, making it a popular choice for creating informative and visually appealing graphs and charts.

An illustrative R code

```
rm(list=ls())
#Check the working directory before importing else provide full path
#setwd(path)
setwd(dirname(rstudioapi::getActiveDocumentContext()$path))

# packages used
listofpackages <- c("dygraphs",
    "tidyverse","ellipse","reshape2","highcharter","xts","xlsx","readxl","quantmod")

for (j in listofpackages){
  if(sum(installed.packages()[, 1] == j) == 0) {
    install.packages(j)
  }
  library(j, character.only = T)
}

raw_data              = read_xlsx("../data/2023_monthly_stocks.xlsx")
names(raw_data)[1] = 'Date'
typeof(raw_data)
typeof(raw_data$Date)
typeof(raw_data$AXP)
typeof(raw_data$CSCO)

dates <-seq(as.Date("1985-02-01"),length=462, by="months")
params <- c("Date","AXP","AMGN","AAPL","BA","CAT","CSCO", "DJI")
data <- raw_data[, c(params)]
data<- na.omit(data)
```

```
data <- data %>%
  mutate(Date = as.Date(Date, format = "%Y-%m-%d"))

params1 <- c("AXP","AMGN","AAPL","BA","CAT","CSCO", "DJI")
tsdata <- xts(raw_data[, c(params1)], order.by=dates) # creates a time
    series object
tsdata <- na.omit(tsdata) # omitting the rows with NA presence
data<- na.omit(data)
## having created the database with all observation we generate a subset
#tsdata1 <- tsdata["1992-02-01/1993-02-01"]
#data=subset(data,select=c(1:12))

## --------------------
# DATA TRANSFORMATIONS
## --------------------
#1. from prices to returns
# exact monthly returns
t1<-nrow(data)
data$AXP_ret <- data$AMGN_ret <- array(data = NA, dim = t1)
for (i in 2:t1) {
  data[i, "AMGN_ret"][[1]]=(data[i, "AMGN"][[1]]-data[i-1,
      "AMGN"][[1]])/data[i-1, "AMGN"][[1]]
  data[i, "AXP_ret"][[1]]=(data[i, "AXP"][[1]]-data[i-1,
      "AXP"][[1]])/data[i-1, "AXP"][[1]]
}

# the following lines of R apply the same transfromation to
# two series AXP and AMGN available in .xts format in a frame called tsdata.
# Could you do the same transformation in a more parsimonious way  by having
# a loop over the serie names  AXP and AMGN ?

series_names <- c("AAPL","BA","CAT","CSCO","DJI")

for (name in series_names) {
  return_col_name <- paste0(name, "_ret")
  data[, return_col_name] <- array(data = NA, dim = t1)
  for (i in 2:nrow(data)) {
    data[i, return_col_name][[1]] <- (data[i, name][[1]] - data[i - 1,
       name][[1]]) / data[i - 1, name][[1]]
  }
}

# same in .xts
t1<-nrow(tsdata)

tsdata$AXP_ret <- tsdata$AMGN_ret<- tsdata$AAPL_ret<- tsdata$BA_ret<-
    array(data = NA, dim = t1)
tsdata$CAT_ret<-tsdata$CSCO_ret <- tsdata$DJI_ret<- array(data = NA, dim =
    t1)
for (i in 2:t1) {
  tsdata[i, "AMGN_ret"][[1]]=(tsdata[i, "AMGN"][[1]]-tsdata[i-1,
      "AMGN"][[1]])/data[i-1, "AMGN"][[1]]
  tsdata[i, "AXP_ret"][[1]]=(tsdata[i, "AXP"][[1]]-tsdata[i-1,
      "AXP"][[1]])/data[i-1, "AXP"][[1]]
  #   tsdata[i, "AAPL_ret"][[1]]=(tsdata[i, "AAPL"][[1]]-tsdata[i-1,
      "AAPL"][[1]])/data[i-1, "AAPL"][[1]]
  #   tsdata[i, "BA_ret"][[1]]=(tsdata[i, "BA"][[1]]-tsdata[i-1,
      "BA"][[1]])/data[i-1, "BA"][[1]]
  #   tsdata[i, "CAT_ret"][[1]]=(tsdata[i, "CAT"][[1]]-tsdata[i-1, "CAT"][[1]])/data[i-1,
      "CAT"][[1]]
  #   tsdata[i, "CSCO_ret"][[1]]=(tsdata[i, "CSCO"][[1]]-tsdata[i-1,
      "CSCO"][[1]])/data[i-1, "CSCO"][[1]]
```

```
  #   tsdata[i, "DJI_ret"][[1]]=(tsdata[i, "DJI"][[1]]-tsdata[i-1,
      "DJI"][[1]])/data[i-1, "DJI"][[1]]
}

# the loop is a bit different in .xts
series_names <- c("AAPL","BA","CAT","CSCO","DJI")

for (name in series_names) {
  return_col_name <- paste0(name, "_ret")
  temporary_column  <- array(data = NA, dim = t1)

  tsdata <- merge.xts(tsdata, temporary_column) # add last column
  colnames(tsdata)[ncol(tsdata)] = return_col_name # rename it

  for (i in 2:nrow(data)) {
    tsdata[i, return_col_name] <- (tsdata[i, name][[1]] - tsdata[i - 1,
        name][[1]]) / tsdata[i - 1, name][[1]]
  }
}

# buy and hold returns
## what would happen had we invested $1 in the DJI and AXP at t0
## initializing values
data$DJI_cum <- data$AXP_cum <- array(data = NA, dim = nrow(data))

data[1, c("DJI_cum", "AXP_cum")] <- 1
t1<-nrow(data)
for (i in 2:t1) {
  data[i, "DJI_cum"][[1]]=data[i-1, "DJI_cum"][[1]]*(1+data[i,
      "DJI_ret"][[1]])
  data[i, "AXP_cum"][[1]]=data[i-1, "AXP_cum"][[1]]*(1+data[i,
      "AXP_ret"][[1]])
}


tsdata$DJI_cum <- array(data = NA, dim = nrow(tsdata))
tsdata$AXP_cum <- array(data = NA, dim = nrow(tsdata))
tsdata[1, c("DJI_cum", "AXP_cum")] <- 1
t1<-nrow(data)
for (i in 2:t1) {
  tsdata[i, "DJI_cum"][[1]]=tsdata[i-1, "DJI_cum"][[1]]*(1+tsdata[i,
      "DJI_ret"][[1]])
  tsdata[i, "AXP_cum"][[1]]=tsdata[i-1, "AXP_cum"][[1]]*(1+tsdata[i,
      "AXP_ret"][[1]])
}

## -------------------------
# monthly log stock returns
## -------------------------
data$DJI_lp<-log(data$DJI_cum)
data$AXP_lp<-log(data$AXP_cum)
data$DJI_lret <- c(NA,diff(data$DJI_lp))
data$AXP_lret <- c(NA,diff(data$AXP_lp))
# value of a buy-and-hold portfolio using cumulative log returns
data$DJI_cuml  <- array(data = NA, dim = nrow(data))
data[1, c("DJI_cuml")]  <- 1
for (i in 2:t1) {
  data[i, "DJI_cuml"][[1]]=data[i-1, "DJI_cuml"][[1]]*(1+data[i,
      "DJI_lret"][[1]])
      }
```

```
tsdata$DJI_lp<-log(tsdata$DJI_cum)
tsdata$AXP_lp<-log(tsdata$AXP_cum)
tsdata$DJI_lret <- diff(tsdata$DJI_lp)
tsdata$AXP_lret <- diff(tsdata$AXP_lp)
tsdata$DJI_cuml  <- array(data = NA, dim = nrow(tsdata))
tsdata[1, c("DJI_cuml")]  <- 1
for (i in 2:nrow(tsdata)) {
  tsdata[i, "DJI_cuml"][[1]]=tsdata[i-1, "DJI_cuml"][[1]]*(1+tsdata[i,
      "DJI_lret"][[1]])
}

tsdata.df <- as.data.frame(tsdata)
save(data, file='data.Rdata')
save(tsdata, file='tsdata.Rdata')
save(tsdata.df, file='tsdata.df.Rdata')

## ---------------------------
# time-series plots
#-----------------------------
#(1) plot .xts series
plot(tsdata$DJI_ret, col = "blue", lwd = 2, main = "", ylab = "")
lines(tsdata$AXP_ret, col = "green", lwd = 2)
addLegend("topleft",
          legend.names = c("DJI", "AXP"),
          lty = c(1, 1), lwd = c(2, 2),
          col = c("blue", "green"))
dev.copy2pdf(width = 5.72, out.type = "pdf",file="Figure_1xts.pdf")
dev.off()
#(2) use highchart with .xts series
highchart(type = "stock") %>%
  hc_title(text = "Monthly Log Returns") %>%
  hc_add_series(data=tsdata[, "DJI_ret"], name = "DJI_ret")%>%
  hc_add_series(data=tsdata[, "AXP_ret"], name = "AXP_ret")%>%
  hc_add_theme(hc_theme_flat()) %>%
  hc_navigator(enabled = FALSE) %>%
  hc_scrollbar(enabled = FALSE) %>%
  hc_exporting(enabled = TRUE) %>%
  hc_legend(enabled = TRUE)

#(2) use ggplot with the standard dataframe
plot <- ggplot(data, aes(x = Date)) +
  geom_point(aes(y = DJI_ret, color = "DJI"), size = 2) +
  geom_point(aes(y = AXP_ret, color = "AXP"), size = 2) +
  labs(title = "Returns",
       x = "Time", y = " Value") +
  scale_color_manual(values = c("DJI" = "red", "AXP" = "blue")) +
  theme_minimal() +
  theme(axis.line = element_line(color = "black")) #+

print(plot)
ggsave(filename = "Figure_1.pdf", plot = plot, device = "pdf",width =
    5.72,height=3.12)
# dev.copy2pdf(width = 4, out.type = "pdf",file="Figure_1.pdf")
# dev.off()

## ---------------------------
# comparing returns and log-returns
#-----------------------------

plot(tsdata$DJI_ret, ylab = "Returns", main = "S&P500 ", col = "blue", lwd
    = 2)
lines(tsdata$DJI_lret, col = "red")
```

```
# time-series plot of cumulative returns
plot(tsdata$DJI_cum,
     type = "l", col = "red", ylim = c(0, 15),
     ylab = "cumulative return mkt")
lines(tsdata$DJI_cuml, col = "blue",type = "l",ylab = "cumulative log
    return mkt")

# cross-plot of exact and log-linearized returns
plot(x=data$DJI_ret, y=data$DJI_lret, col="red")
lines(x=data$DJI_ret, y=data$DJI_ret,col = "blue")

#cross-plot of returns of AXP and their value predicted from the market
fm1 <- lm(AXP_ret ~ DJI_ret, data=data)
summary(fm1)
data$AXP_retfit<-c(NA,fitted(fm1))
plot(x=data$DJI_ret, y=data$AXP_ret, col="red")
lines(x=data$DJI_ret, y=data$AXP_retfit,col = "blue")

plotactfit <- ggplot(data, aes(x = DJI_ret, y = AXP_ret)) +
  geom_point(color = "red") +
  geom_line(aes(x = DJI_ret, y = AXP_retfit), color = "blue") +
  geom_hline(yintercept = 0, linetype = "dashed", color = "black")  # Adding the zero line

  # Display the plot
  print(plotactfit)



  #--------------------
  #plotting prices
  #--------------------
  sfDJI<- as.numeric(tsdata$DJI[1])
  sfAXP<- as.numeric(tsdata$AXP[1])
  plot(tsdata$DJI/sfDJI,col = "blue",lwd = 2)
  lines(tsdata$AXP/sfAXP, col = "green",lwd = 2)
  addLegend("topleft", on=1,
            legend.names = c("DJIrs", "AXPrs"),
            lty=c(1, 1), lwd=c(2, 1),
            col=c("blue", "green", "red"))

  # you can interact with Chat GPT to improve on this version of the graphs

  #First Question When I run the following sequence in R I get a graph with
      tsdata$DJI
  #written at the top left of it. How do I remove this from the graph ?
  #ANSWER

  plot(tsdata$DJI/3267.70, col = "blue", lwd = 2, main = "", ylab = "")
  lines(tsdata$AXP/3.277914, col = "green", lwd = 2)
  addLegend("topleft",
            legend.names = c("DJI", "AXPrs"),
            lty = c(1, 1), lwd = c(2, 2),
            col = c("blue", "green"))  # Remove "red" from col argument

  #Second Question> I would like to have the same graph in a double scale
  # with DJI on the left hand scale and AXP on the right hand scale
  combined_data <- data.frame(DJI = tsdata$DJI, AXP = tsdata$AXP )
  dygraph(combined_data, main = "Double-Scale Time Series Graph") %>%
    dySeries("DJI", label = "DJI", color = "blue") %>%
    dySeries("AXP", label = "AXP", color = "green", axis = "y2") %>%
    dyAxis("y", label = "DJI") %>%
    dyAxis("y2", label = "AXP", independentTicks = TRUE) %>%
    dyLegend(width = 250)
```

```
#--------------------
#plotting series from a list using GGPLOT
#--------------------
plot <- ggplot(data, aes(x = Date)) +
  geom_line(aes(y = DJI/3267.70, color = "DJI"), size = 2) +
  geom_line(aes(y = AXP/3.277914, color = "AXP"), size = 2) +
  labs(title = "Trends",
       x = "Time", y = " Value") +
  scale_color_manual(values = c("DJI" = "red", "AXP" = "blue")) +
  theme_minimal() +
  theme(axis.line = element_line(color = "black")) +
  scale_x_continuous(breaks = data$Date, labels = data$Date)  # Add this
      line for x-axis labels

# Print the plot
print(plot)

#Ask Chat GPT: When I run the following code in R I get "too many "
   labels on the x axis,
#how can I reduce the number of labels (say one every 5 years) ?
#Answer
#To reduce the number of x-axis labels in your ggplot, you can use the
    scale_x_date() function
#with the date_breaks argument to specify the intervals at which you want
    the labels to appear.
#In your case, you want to display labels every 5 years. Here's how you
    can modify your code to achieve this:
ggplot(data, aes(x = Date)) +
  geom_line(aes(y = DJI/3267.70, color = "DJI"), size = 1) +
  geom_line(aes(y = AXP/3.277914, color = "AXP"), size = 1) +
  labs(title = "Trends",
       x = "Time", y = " Value") +
  scale_color_manual(values = c("DJI" = "red", "AXP" = "blue")) +
  theme_minimal() +
  theme(axis.line = element_line(color = "black")) +
  scale_x_date(date_breaks = "5 years", date_labels = "%Y")
#In the code above:
#scale_x_date() is used to control the x-axis (date) scale.
#date_breaks = "5 years" specifies that you want to display labels every
   5 years.
#date_labels = "%Y" specifies the date format you want to use for the
   labels (in this case, the year only).
#This should result in a plot with x-axis labels appearing every 5 years,
    making the plot more readable when you have a large time series
    dataset. Adjust the date_breaks argument as needed to control the
    spacing of the labels according to your preferences.



## --------------------------------------------------------
#  combine  several plots on one canvas
## --------------------------------------------------------

par(mfrow = c(2, 2))

plot(tsdata$DJI_ret, ylab = "Returns", main = "DJ30 ", col = "blue", lwd
   = 2)

plot(x=data$DJI_ret, y=data$DJI_lret, col="red")
lines(x=data$DJI_ret, y=data$DJI_ret,col = "blue")

plot(x=data$AXP_ret, y=data$AXP_lret, col="red",ylim = c(-0.5, 1))
```

```
lines(x=data$AXP_ret, y=data$AXP_ret,col = "blue")

plot(tsdata$DJI_cum,
     type = "l", col = "red", ylim = c(0, 12),main = "DJ30 ",
     ylab = "cumulative return mkt")

par(mfrow = c(1, 1))

## ------------------------
#  HISTOGRAMS AND QQ PLOTS
## ------------------------

## Histograms
s1 <- na.omit(tsdata$DJI_ret)
hist(s1, breaks = seq(min(s1), max(s1), l = 20+1),prob=TRUE, main =
   "histogram of monthly returns")
curve(dnorm(x,mean=mean(s1),sd=sd(s1)),col='darkblue',lwd=2,add=TRUE)

## Histograms with Highcharter using .xts data

hc_hist <- hist(coredata(tsdata$DJI_lret), breaks = 50, plot = FALSE)
hchart(hc_hist, color = "cornflowerblue")%>%
  hc_title(text =
             paste("DJI",
                   "Log Returns Distribution",
                   sep = " ")) %>%
  hc_add_theme(hc_theme_flat()) %>%
  hc_exporting(enabled = TRUE) %>%
  hc_legend(enabled = FALSE)

hc_hist <- hist(tsdata[, "DJI_lret"], breaks = 50, plot = FALSE)
hchart(hc_hist, color = "cornflowerblue")%>%
  hc_title(text =
             paste("DJI",
                   "Log Returns Distribution",
                   sep = " ")) %>%
  hc_add_theme(hc_theme_flat()) %>%
  hc_exporting(enabled = TRUE) %>%
  hc_legend(enabled = FALSE)
## -----------------------

qqplot(tsdata.df$DJI_ret,
       tsdata.df$DJI_lret,
       ylim = c(-0.15,0.15), xlim = c(-0.15,0.15),
       ylab = "monthly return. log approximation",
       xlab = "monthly return. exact computation",
       main = "Quantile-Quantile plot (Q-Q plot)")
mod5 <- lm(tsdata.df$DJI_ret ~ tsdata.df$DJI_lret)
abline(reg = mod5, col = "red")

# qq-plot versus normal dist
qqnorm(tsdata$DJI_ret,
       ylim = c(-0.15,0.15),ylab = "monthly return. sample quantile",
       xlab = "monthly return. theoretical quantiles",
       main = "Normal (Q-Q plot)")
qqline(tsdata$DJI_ret, datax = FALSE, distribution = qnorm,
       probs = c(0.25, 0.75), qtype = 7)

## --------------------
#  CORRELATION ANALYSIS
## --------------------
tsdata.df <- as.data.frame(tsdata)
```

```
# Select specific columns and observations from the start date onward
selected_cols <- c("AMGN_ret", "AXP_ret", "AAPL_ret", "BA_ret",
    "CAT_ret", "CSCO_ret", "DJI_ret")
datashow <- subset(tsdata.df[, selected_cols])
datashow<-na.omit(datashow)
  # Print the resulting subset
summary(datashow) # this is very useful to get a grip on the data
    structure
mean(datashow[,"AMGN_ret"])
sd(datashow[,"AMGN_ret"])
var(datashow[,"AMGN_ret"])
cor(datashow)
cor.datacor = cor(datashow, use="complete.obs")
cor.datacor

## ---------------------
ord <- order(cor.datacor[1,])
ordered.cor.datacor <- cor.datacor[ord, ord]
plotcorr(ordered.cor.datacor, col=cm.colors(11)[5*ordered.cor.datacor +
    6])


## ---------------------
cormat <- round(cor(datashow),2)
head(cormat)
melted_cormat <- melt(cormat)
head(melted_cormat)
ggplot(data = melted_cormat, aes(x=Var1, y=Var2, fill=value)) +
  geom_tile()
# Get lower triangle of the correlation matrix
get_lower_tri<-function(cormat){
  cormat[upper.tri(cormat)] <- NA
  return(cormat)
}
# Get upper triangle of the correlation matrix
get_upper_tri <- function(cormat){
  cormat[lower.tri(cormat)]<- NA
  return(cormat)
}
upper_tri <- get_upper_tri(cormat)
upper_tri
# Melt the correlation matrix
melted_cormat <- melt(upper_tri, na.rm = TRUE)
# Heatmap
ggplot(data = melted_cormat, aes(Var2, Var1, fill = value))+
  geom_tile(color = "white")+
  scale_fill_gradient2(low = "blue", high = "red", mid = "white",
                       midpoint = 0, limit = c(-1,1), space = "Lab",
                       name="Pearson\nCorrelation") +
  theme_minimal()+
  theme(axis.text.x = element_text(angle = 45, vjust = 1,
                                   size = 12, hjust = 1))+
  coord_fixed()
```

4.5.5 *Interacting with Chat GPT*

There are many ways to use ChatGPT to learn R. The more precise the query, the more precise the answer. But in any case, interaction is fundamental for two reasons: either because ChatCPT may not provide the exact answer to your question or because the snippet you receive in the answer might be "close" to the one that works but non quite there. One can think of three possible ways to interact with ChatGPT (1) Ask to generate a code snippet based on your query (2) Ask ChatGPT to explain a code snippet or a part of it that you do not understand (3) Ask ChatGPT to modify a code snippet of your or suggest improvements. In all three cases, some interaction will be required before converging to a solution. Convergence will be much faster in case (3) than in case (1), case (2) will be intermediate in that you will get a clear explanation but putting it at work in solving the specific problem at your hand will require some more effort. To illustrate a case of interaction with ChatGPT think of a generic USER who has found on the web the following R program that computes the frontier and the efficient frontier for a sample portfolio made of two and three assets.

```
#clear the environment
rm(list=ls())
## -----------------------------------------------------------------
setwd(dirname(rstudioapi::getActiveDocumentContext()$path))
library(data.table)
library(scales)
library(ggplot2)
library(xts)
link <-
   "https://raw.githubusercontent.com/DavZim/Efficient_Frontier/master/data/fin_data.csv"
dt <- fread(link)
dt[, date := as.Date(date)]

# create indexed values
dt[, idx_price := price/price[1], by = ticker]

# plot the indexed values
ggplot(dt, aes(x = date, y = idx_price, color = ticker)) +
  geom_line() +
  # Miscellaneous Formatting
  theme_bw() + ggtitle("Price Developments") +
  xlab("Date") + ylab("Price\n(Indexed 2000 = 1)") +
  scale_color_discrete(name = "Company")
# calculate the arithmetic returns
dt[, ret := price / shift(price, 1) - 1, by = ticker]

# summary table
# take only non-na values
tab <- dt[!is.na(ret), .(ticker, ret)]

# calculate the expected returns (historical mean of returns) and
    volatility (standard deviation of returns)
tab <- tab[, .(er = round(mean(ret), 4),
               sd = round(sd(ret), 4)),
           by = "ticker"]
ggplot(tab, aes(x = sd, y = er, color = ticker)) +
  geom_point(size = 5) +
  # Miscellaneous Formatting
```

```
  theme_bw() + ggtitle("Risk-Return Tradeoff") +
  xlab("Volatility") + ylab("Expected Returns") +
  scale_y_continuous(label = percent, limits = c(0, 0.03)) +
  scale_x_continuous(label = percent, limits = c(0, 0.1))



# load the data
link <-
  "https://raw.githubusercontent.com/DavZim/Efficient_Frontier/master/data/mult_assets.csv"
df <- data.table(read.csv(link))

df_table <- melt(df)[, .(mean = mean(value), sd = sd(value)), by = variable]

er_x <- mean(df$x)
er_y <- mean(df$y)
er_z <- mean(df$z)
sd_x <- sd(df$x)
sd_y <- sd(df$y)
sd_z <- sd(df$z)
cov_xy <- cov(df$x, df$y)
cov_xz <- cov(df$x, df$z)
cov_yz <- cov(df$y, df$z)

# two assets
two_assets_seq <- seq(from = 0, to = 1, length.out = 1000)

two <- data.table(wx = two_assets_seq,
                  wy = 1 - two_assets_seq)

two[, ':=' (er_p = wx * er_x + wy * er_y,
            sd_p = sqrt(wx^2 * sd_x^2 +
                        wy^2 * sd_y^2 +
                        2 * wx * (1 - wx) * cov_xy))]

# plot_two <- ggplot() +
#   geom_point(data = two, aes(x = sd_p, y = er_p, color = wx)) +
#   geom_point(data = df_table[variable != "z"],
#              aes(x = sd, y = mean), color = "red", size = 3, shape = 18) +
#   theme_bw() + ggtitle("Possible Portfolios with Two Risky Assets") +
#   xlab("Volatility") + ylab("Expected Returns") +
#   scale_y_continuous(label = percent, limits = c(0, max(two$er_p) * 1.2))
  +
#   scale_x_continuous(label = percent, limits = c(0, max(two$sd_p) * 1.2))
  +
#   scale_color_continuous(name = expression(omega[x]), labels = percent)
#
# ggsave(plot_two, file = "two_assets.png", scale = 1, dpi = 600)

  ggplot() +
  geom_point(data = two, aes(x = sd_p, y = er_p, color = wx)) +
  geom_point(data = df_table[variable != "z"],
             aes(x = sd, y = mean), color = "red", size = 3, shape = 18) +
  theme_bw() + ggtitle("Possible Portfolios with Two Risky Assets") +
  xlab("Volatility") + ylab("Expected Returns") +
  scale_y_continuous(label = percent, limits = c(0, max(two$er_p) * 1.2)) +
  scale_x_continuous(label = percent, limits = c(0, max(two$sd_p) * 1.2)) +
  scale_color_continuous(name = expression(omega[x]), labels = percent)

# three assets
three_assets_seq <- seq(from = 0, to = 1, length.out = 1000)
```

```
three <- data.table(wx = rep(three_assets_seq, each =
   length(three_assets_seq)),
                    wy = rep(three_assets_seq, length(three_assets_seq)))

three[, wz := 1 - wx - wy]

three[, ':=' (er_p = wx * er_x + wy * er_y + wz * er_z,
              sd_p = sqrt(wx^2 * sd_x^2 +
                          wy^2 * sd_y^2 +
                          wz^2 * sd_z^2 +
                          2 * wx * wy * cov_xy +
                          2 * wx * wz * cov_xz +
                          2 * wy * wz * cov_yz))]

three <- three[wx >= 0 & wy >= 0 & wz >= 0]

plot_three <- ggplot() +
  geom_point(data = three, aes(x = sd_p, y = er_p, color = wx - wz)) +
  geom_point(data = df_table, aes(x = sd, y = mean), color = "red", size =
     3, shape = 18) +
  theme_bw() + ggtitle("Possible Portfolios with Three Risky Assets") +
  xlab("Volatility") + ylab("Expected Returns") +
  scale_y_continuous(label = percent, limits = c(0, max(three$er_p) * 1.2))
    +
  scale_x_continuous(label = percent, limits = c(0, max(three$sd_p) * 1.2))
    +
  scale_color_gradientn(colors = c("red", "blue", "yellow"),
                        name = expression(omega[x] - omega[z]), labels =
                          percent)

ggsave(plot_three, file = "three_assets.png", scale = 1, dpi = 600)
```

The USER, after understanding the code, immediately realizes that the curse of dimensionality applies very rapidly and the procedure becomes very inefficient as the number of assets considered to form the portfolio gets larger.

So an interaction with ChatGPT begins to get a more general version of the code.

USER

I have a database containing sample of returns on five assets, say A, B, C, D, E. I would like to write an R code to derive the efficient frontier and plot it in the space of the mean and the standard deviation of the portfolio together with points identified by the mean and the standard deviation of the five assets. Can you do it?

ChatGPT

Certainly! To derive the efficient frontier and plot it in R, you can follow these steps. I'll provide you with a code template to get you started. Please make sure you have the necessary packages like quantmod and ggplot2 installed:

```r
# Load necessary libraries
library(quantmod)
library(ggplot2)

# Sample returns for five assets (replace with your data)
returns <- data.frame(
  A = c(0.05, 0.06, 0.07, 0.04, 0.03),
  B = c(0.08, 0.09, 0.06, 0.07, 0.05),
  C = c(0.10, 0.12, 0.11, 0.13, 0.09),
  D = c(0.06, 0.05, 0.04, 0.03, 0.07),
  E = c(0.07, 0.08, 0.09, 0.06, 0.05)
)

# Calculate mean and standard deviation of asset returns
mean_returns <- colMeans(returns)
sd_returns <- apply(returns , 2, sd)

# Number of random portfolios to simulate
n_portfolios <- 10000

# Create a function to simulate random portfolios
simulate_portfolios <- function(n_portfolios, returns) {
  portfolio_returns <- numeric(n_portfolios)
  portfolio_volatility <- numeric(n_portfolios)

  for (i in 1:n_portfolios) {
    weights <- runif(ncol(returns))
    weights <- weights / sum(weights)
    portfolio_returns[i] <- sum(weights * mean_returns)
    portfolio_volatility[i] <- sqrt(t(weights) %*% cov(returns) %*% weights)
  }

  portfolio_data <- data.frame(Return = portfolio_returns , Volatility =
      portfolio_volatility)
  return(portfolio_data)
}

# Simulate random portfolios
set.seed(123)  # For reproducibility
portfolios <- simulate_portfolios(n_portfolios, returns)

# Plot the efficient frontier
ggplot(portfolios, aes(x = Volatility, y = Return)) +
  geom_point(alpha = 0.5) +
  geom_point(aes(x = sd_returns , y = mean_returns), color = "red", size =
     3) +
  labs(x = "Standard Deviation (Risk)", y = "Mean Return") +
  ggtitle("Efficient Frontier") +
  theme_minimal()
```

This code first calculates the mean and standard deviation of the returns for the five assets and then simulates a large number of random portfolios to derive the efficient frontier. It finally plots the efficient frontier along with points representing the mean and standard deviation of the five assets in the mean-risk space.

Make sure to replace the sample returns with your actual data for assets A, B, C, D, and E.

USER

this looks good but I doubt it will work with say 20 assets. What would you do if you need to derive exactly the efficient frontier with 20 assets?

ChatGPT

When dealing with a larger number of assets, such as 20, you can still derive the efficient frontier using R, but you might need to use more advanced optimization techniques to find the optimal portfolio weights. Here's an outline of the steps you can take:

(1) **Collect data:** Make sure you have the historical returns of the 20 assets in your dataset.
(2) **Define the objective function:** You'll need to define an objective function that calculates the portfolio return and risk (standard deviation) given a set of portfolio weights.
(3) **Optimization:** Use optimization techniques like the quadratic programming solver in R to find the weights that maximize return for a given level of risk (standard deviation) while satisfying the constraint that the sum of weights equals 1.
(4) **Generate a range of target returns:** To plot the efficient frontier, you'll need to generate a range of target returns and find the portfolio with the minimum risk for each target return.

Here's a high-level code template to help you get started. This example uses the quadprog package for quadratic programming:

```
# Load necessary libraries
library(quadprog)
library(ggplot2)

# Sample returns for 20 assets (replace with your data)
# Ensure you have a matrix of returns with 20 columns
returns_matrix <- read.csv("your_returns_data.csv")  # Replace with your
    data

# Calculate the mean returns and covariance matrix
mean_returns <- colMeans(returns_matrix)
cov_matrix <- cov(returns_matrix)

# Define the objective function to minimize risk (standard deviation)
portfolio.objective <- function(weights, cov_matrix) {
  portfolio_return <- sum(weights * mean_returns)
  portfolio_volatility <- sqrt(t(weights) %*% cov_matrix %*% weights)
  return(portfolio_volatility)
}

# Set up constraints (sum of weights = 1)
A_eq <- matrix(1, 1, ncol(returns_matrix))
b_eq <- 1
```

```
# Generate a range of target returns
target_returns <- seq(min(mean_returns), max(mean_returns), length.out =
    100)

# Initialize vectors to store results
portfolio_returns <- numeric(length(target_returns))
portfolio_volatilities <- numeric(length(target_returns))

# Optimize for each target return
for (i in 1:length(target_returns)) {
  target_return <- target_returns[i]

  # Set up the quadratic programming problem
  Dmat <- cov_matrix
  dvec <- rep(0, ncol(returns_matrix))
  Amat <- matrix(c(mean_returns , 1), nrow = 1)
  bvec <- target_return

  # Solve the optimization problem
  weights <- solve.QP(Dmat, dvec, Amat, bvec, meq = 1)$solution

  # Calculate portfolio risk (volatility)
  portfolio_volatility <- portfolio.objective(weights , cov_matrix)

  # Store results
  portfolio_returns[i] <- target_return
  portfolio_volatilities[i] <- portfolio_volatility
}

# Create a data frame for efficient frontier points
efficient_frontier <- data.frame(Return = portfolio_returns , Volatility =
    portfolio_volatilities)

# Plot the efficient frontier
ggplot(efficient_frontier, aes(x = Volatility, y = Return)) +
  geom_line() +
  labs(x = "Standard Deviation (Risk)", y = "Mean Return") +
  ggtitle("Efficient Frontier") +
  theme_minimal()
```

ChatGPT
In this code, we use a loop to iterate over a range of target returns, solving the quadratic programming problem for each target return to find the corresponding portfolio weights and risk. Finally, we plot the efficient frontier. Make sure to replace "your_returns_data.csv" with the actual file path to your returns data.

Unfortunately, the code provided by ChatGPT has some issues. First, the A_eq and the B_eq are defined but they are never used in the code. Second, the matrices that define the optimization problem and its constraints to run the optimizer are not correctly defined. In fact, some of them are transposed and only one constraint is imposed rather than two (the sum of weight being equal to one and the return being equal to the target). You would need to check the working of the solve.QP function in r by digiting ?solve.QP in the R console and some iteration with ChatGPT to get to the following version of the code that we put at work on the data set of US stocks defined earlier in the chapter.

```
rm(list=ls())
#Check the working directory before importing else provide full path
#setwd(path)
setwd(dirname(rstudioapi::getActiveDocumentContext()$path))

# packages used
listofpackages <- c("dygraphs",
   "tidyverse","ellipse","reshape2","highcharter","xts","xlsx","readxl","quantmod","quadprog")

for (j in listofpackages){
  if(sum(installed.packages()[, 1] == j) == 0) {
    install.packages(j)
  }
  library(j, character.only = T)
}

raw_data             = read_xlsx("../data/2023_monthly_stocks.xlsx")
names(raw_data)[1] = 'Date'
typeof(raw_data)
typeof(raw_data$Date)
typeof(raw_data$AXP)
typeof(raw_data$CSCO)

dates <-seq(as.Date("1985-02-01"),length=462, by="months")
params <- c("Date","AXP","AMGN","AAPL","BA","CAT","CSCO","CVX","GS",
            "HD","HON","IBM","INTC","JNJ","KO","JPM")
data <- raw_data[, c(params)]
data<- na.omit(data)
data <- data %>%
  mutate(Date = as.Date(Date, format = "%Y-%m-%d"))

t1<-nrow(data)
series_names <- c("AXP","AMGN","AAPL","BA","CAT","CSCO","CVX","GS",
                  "HD","HON","IBM","INTC","JNJ","KO","JPM")

for (name in series_names) {
  return_col_name <- paste0(name, "_ret")
  data[, return_col_name] <- array(data = NA, dim = t1)
  for (i in 2:nrow(data)) {
    data[i, return_col_name][[1]] <- (data[i, name][[1]] - data[i - 1,
      name][[1]]) / data[i - 1, name][[1]]
  }
}

params1 <-
    c("AXP_ret","AMGN_ret","AAPL_ret","BA_ret","CAT_ret","CSCO_ret","CVX_ret","GS_ret",
            "HD_ret","HON_ret","IBM_ret","INTC_ret","JNJ_ret","KO_ret","JPM_ret")
returns_data <- data[, c(params1)]
returns_data <- na.omit(returns_data)

returns_matrix<-as.matrix(returns_data)

# Calculate the mean returns and covariance matrix
mean_returns <- colMeans(returns_matrix)
cov_matrix <- cov(returns_matrix)

# Define the objective function to minimize risk (standard deviation)
portfolio.objective <- function(weights, cov_matrix) {
```

```
  portfolio_return <- sum(weights * mean_returns)
  portfolio_volatility <- sqrt(t(weights) %*% cov_matrix %*% weights)
  return(portfolio_volatility)
}
# Set up constraints (sum of weights = 1)
$A_eq <- matrix(1, nrow = 1, ncol = ncol(returns_matrix))
$b_eq <- matrix(1, nrow = 1)

# Generate a range of target returns
target_returns <- seq(min(mean_returns), max(mean_returns), length.out =
    1000)

# Initialize vectors to store results
portfolio_returns <- numeric(length(target_returns))
portfolio_volatilities <- numeric(length(target_returns))

# Optimize for each target return
for (i in 1:length(target_returns)) {
  target_return <- target_returns[i]

  # Set up the quadratic programming problem
  Dmat <- 2*cov_matrix
  dvec <- matrix(rep(0, ncol(returns_matrix)),ncol=1)
  a1mat<- matrix(mean_returns, nrow =ncol(returns_matrix))
  a2mat<-matrix(rep(1, ncol(returns_matrix)), nrow =ncol(returns_matrix))
  Amat <- cbind(a1mat, a2mat)
  bvec <- matrix(c(target_return, 1),ncol=1)

  # Solve the optimization problem
  weights <- solve.QP(Dmat, dvec, Amat, bvec, meq = 2)$solution

  # Calculate portfolio risk (volatility)
  portfolio_volatility <- portfolio.objective(weights, cov_matrix)

  # Store results
  portfolio_returns[i] <- target_return
  portfolio_volatilities[i] <- portfolio_volatility
}

# Create a data frame for efficient frontier points
efficient_frontier <- data.frame(Return = portfolio_returns, Volatility =
    portfolio_volatilities)

# Plot the efficient frontier
ggplot(efficient_frontier, aes(x = Volatility, y = Return)) +
  geom_line() +
  labs(x = "Standard Deviation (Risk)", y = "Mean Return") +
  ggtitle("Efficient Frontier") +
  theme_minimal()
```

4.6 Appendix: The Data

All empirical applications will be based on publicly available databases of US data observed at monthly (and therefore lower) frequency. They have been downloaded from Robert Shiller's webpage

(http://www.econ.yale.edu/~shiller/)

and Ken French's webpage

(http://mba.tuck.dartmouth.edu/pages/faculty/ken.french/data_library.html) and directly form yahoo finance.

The time series made available by Robert Shiller are saved in the successive columns of the EXCELworksheet DATA in the file **IE_DATA.XLS**.

The time-series in the IE_DATA.XLS files

Identifier	Description
P	S&P composite index
D	S&P dividend (at annual rate)
E	S&P earnings
CPI	US consumer price index
GS10	YTM of 10-year US Treasuries
CAPE	cyclically adjusted PE ratio

As described in the section "Online Data" of the webpage these stock market data are those used in the book, *Irrational Exuberance* [Princeton University Press 2000, Broadway Books 2001, 2nd edn., 2005] and cover the period 1871–present. This data set consists of monthly stock price, dividends, and earnings data and the consumer price index (to allow conversion to real values), all starting January 1871. The price, dividend, and earnings series are from the same sources as described in Chapter 26 of the book *Market Volatility* [Cambridge, MA: MIT Press, 1989], although they are observed at monthly, rather than annual frequencies. Monthly dividend and earnings data are computed from the S&P four-quarter totals for the quarter since 1926, with linear interpolation to monthly figures. Dividend and earnings data before 1926 are from Cowles and associates (*Common Stock Indexes*, 2nd edn. [Bloomington, Ind.: Principia Press, 1939]), interpolated from annual data. The CPI-U (Consumer Price Index-All Urban Consumers) published by the US Bureau of Labor Statistics begins in 1913; for years before 1913 1 spliced to the CPI Warren and Pearson's price index, by multiplying it by the ratio of the indexes in January 1913. December 1999 and January 2000 values for the CPI-Uare extrapolated. See George F. Warren and Frank A. Pearson, *Gold and Prices* (New York: John Wiley and Sons, 1935). Data are from their Table 1, pp. 11–14.

The time series made available by Ken French are saved in the successive columns of the EXCELworksheet DATA in the file **FF_DATA.XLS**.

The time-series in the FF_Data.xls files	
Identifier	Description
EXRET_MKT	MKT excess ret
SMB	returns on SMB
HML	returns on HML
RF	returns on the risk-free asset
MOM	returns on MOM
RMW	returns on RMW
CMA	returns on CMA
PR(i,j)	returns on 25 FF portfolios ($i = 1, \ldots 5,\ j = 1, \ldots, 5$)

The construction of the Fama French factors is described at
http://mba.tuck.dartmouth.edu/pages/faculty/ken.french/Data_Library/f-f_5_factors_2x3.html,
while the construction of the FF portfolios is described at
http://mba.tuck.dartmouth.edu/pages/faculty/ken.french/Data_Library/tw_5_ports.html.

Finally, data on the components of the DJ30 and the index have been downloaded from yahoo.finance using the quantmod package in R.

Chapter 5

The Constant Expected Return Model

In this chapter, we shall consider a very basic model for returns and illustrate how model specification, estimation and simulation can be applied to find optimal portfolio weights, measure the risk of a portfolio and backtest the portfolio performance

5.1 Model Specification

Our objective is the specification of a statistical model for asset prices and returns. To this end, consider the (naive) log random walk (LRW) hypothesis on the evolution of prices. The model states that prices evolve approximately according to the stochastic difference equation:

$$\ln P_t = \mu + \ln P_{t-1} + \epsilon_t$$

where the "innovations" ϵ_t are assumed to be uncorrelated across time ($cov(\epsilon_t; \epsilon_{t'}) = 0 \quad \forall t \neq t'$), with constant expected value 0 and constant variance σ^2. Sometimes, a further hypothesis is added and the ϵ_t are assumed to be jointly normally distributed. In this case, the assumption of non correlation becomes equivalent to the assumption of independence.

Since $\ln P_t - \ln P_{t-1} = r^*_{t-1;t}$ the LRW is obviously equivalent to the assumption that log returns are uncorrelated random variables with constant expected value and variance.

A linear random walk in prices was sometimes considered in the earliest times of quantitative financial research, but it does not seem a good model for prices since a sequence of negative innovations may result in negative prices. Moreover, while the hypothesis of constant variance for (log) returns may be a good first-order approximation of what we observe in markets, the same hypothesis for prices is not empirically sound: in general price changes tend to have a variance which is an increasing function of the price level.

If we take prices as inclusive of dividends, then we can write the following model for log-returns

$$r_{t,t+1} = \mu + \sigma\epsilon_t$$
$$\epsilon_t \sim i.i.d.(0,1)$$

This simple specification has some appealing properties for the n period returns $r_{t,t+n}$:

If we assume the LRW and consider a sequence of n log returns r_t^* at times $t, t-1, t-2, \ldots, t-n+1$ (just for the sake of simplicity in notation we suppose each time interval Δ to be of length 1 and drop the generic Δ) we have the following:

$$E(r_{t,t+n}) = E\left(\sum_{i=1}^{n} r_{t+i,t+i-1}\right) = \sum_{i=1}^{n} E(r_{t+i,t+i-1}) = n\mu$$

$$\mathrm{Var}(r_{t,t+n}) = \mathrm{Var}\left(\sum_{i=1}^{n} r_{t+i,t+i-1}\right) = \sum_{i=1}^{n} \mathrm{Var}(r_{t+i,t+i-1}) = n\sigma^2$$

This obvious result, which is a direct consequence of the assumption of constant expected value and variance and of non-correlation of innovations at different times is typically applied, for annualization purposes, also when the LRW is not considered to be valid.

So, for instance, given an evaluation of σ^2 on monthly data, this evaluation is annualized by multiplying it by 12.

This is not a convention, but the correct procedure, if the LRW model holds. In this case, in fact, the variance over n time periods is equal to n times the variance over one time period. If the

LRW model is not believed to hold, for instance, if the expected value and-or the variance of return are not constant over time or if we have correlation among the ϵ_t, this procedure becomes just as a convention.[1]

5.1.1 *Stocks for the long run*

The fact that, under the LRW, the expected value grows linearly with the length of the time period while the standard deviation (square root of the variance) grows with the square root of the number of observations, has created a lot of discussion about the existence of some time horizon beyond which it is always proper to hold a stock portfolio. This problem, conventionally called "time diversification", and more popularly "stocks for the long run", has attracted some considerable attention.

We have three flavors of the "stocks for the long run" argument. The first and the second are a priori arguments depending on the log random walk hypothesis or something equivalent to it, the third is an a posteriori argument based on historical data.

The basic idea of the first version of the argument can be sketched as follows. Assume that single period (log) returns have (positive) expected value μ and variance σ^2. Moreover, assume for simplicity that the investor requires a Sharpe ratio of say S. Under the above hypotheses, plus the log random walk hypothesis, the Sharpe ratio over n time periods is given by

$$S = \frac{n\mu}{\sqrt{n}\sigma} = \sqrt{n}\frac{\mu}{\sigma}$$

so that, if n is large enough, any required value can be reached. Another way of phrasing the same argument, when we add the hypothesis of normality on returns, is that, for any given probability α and any given required return C there is always an

[1] Empirical computation of variances over different time intervals typically results in sequences which increase less than linearly wrt the increase of the time interval between consecutive observations. This could be interpreted as the existence of (small) on average negative correlations between returns.

horizon for which the probability for n period return less than C is less than α.

$$\Pr\left(R^p < C\right) = \alpha.$$

$$\Pr\left(R^p < C\right) = \alpha \Longleftrightarrow \Pr\left(\frac{R^p - n\mu}{\sqrt{n}\sigma} < \frac{C - n\mu}{\sqrt{n}\sigma}\right) = \alpha$$

$$\Longleftrightarrow \Phi\left(\frac{C - \mu_p}{\sigma_p}\right) = \alpha$$

$$C = n\mu + \Phi^{-1}\left(\alpha\right)\sqrt{n}\sigma$$

But $n\mu + \Phi^{-1}\left(\alpha\right)\sqrt{n}\sigma$, for $\sqrt{n} > \frac{1}{2}\frac{\Phi^{-1}(\alpha)}{\mu}\sigma$ is an increasing function in n so that for any α and any chosen value C, there exists a n such that from that n onward, the probability for an n period return less than C is less than α.

The investment implication could be that for a time horizon of an undetermined number n of years, the investment that has the highest expected return per unit of standard deviation is optimal even if the standard deviation is very high. This investment can be very risky in the "short run", but there is always a time horizon for which, the probability of any given loss is as small as you like or, that is the same, the Sharpe ratio as big as you like. Typically, such high return (and high volatility) investment are stocks, so: "stocks for the long run".

Note, however, that the value of n for which this lower bound crosses a given C level is the solution of

$$n\mu + \Phi^{-1}\left(\alpha\right)\sqrt{n}\sigma \geq C$$

In particular, for $C = 0$ the solution is

$$\sqrt{n} \geq -\frac{\Phi^{-1}\left(\alpha\right)\sigma}{\mu}$$

Consider now the case of a stock with σ/μ ratio for one year is of the order of 6. Even allowing for a large α, say 0.25, so that $\Phi^{-1}\left(\alpha\right)$ is near minus one, the required n shall be in the range of 36 which is only slightly shorter than the average working life.

As a matter of fact, based on the analysis of historical prices and risk adjusted returns, stocks have been almost always a good long-run investment. However, some care must be exercised in interpreting this evidence because history is what we have observed and one could doubt the possibility of an institution such as the stock market to survive without providing a sustainable impression of offering some opportunities. Unfortunately, the arrow of time is unidirectional and experimental data for financial time-series are not available.

5.2 Model Estimation

Model specification has led us to the following description for the vector of one-period returns on assets used to build a portfolio:

$$
\begin{aligned}
\mathbf{r}_{t,t+1} &= \mu + \mathbf{H}\epsilon_{t+1} \\
\Sigma &= \mathbf{HH}'. \\
\epsilon_{t+k} &\sim \mathcal{D}\left(\mathbf{0}, \mathbf{I}\right)
\end{aligned}
$$

where $\mathbf{r}_{t,t+k}$ is the vector of returns between time t and time $t+k$ in which we are interested, μ is the vector of mean returns and the matrix $\mathbf{H}$ determines the time invarying variance–covariance matrix of returns.

Model estimation allows to find values for $\mu, \mathbf{\Sigma}$. In the case of CER this step is easily solved by n OLS regressions of the n returns on a constant.

$$
\hat{\mu^i} = \frac{1}{T}\sum_{t=1}^{T} r^i_{t,t+1}
$$

$$
\hat{\sigma}_{ii} = \frac{1}{T}\sum_{t=1}^{T}(r^i_{t,t+1} - \hat{\mu^i})^2
$$

$$
\hat{\sigma}_{ij} = \frac{1}{T-1}\sum_{t=1}^{T}(r^i_{t,t+1} - \hat{\mu^i})(r^j_{t,t+1} - \hat{\mu^j})
$$

5.2.1 *Parameters estimation in a linear model*

The CER is a special case of a linear model, consider the following general representation of a linear model:

$$\mathbf{y} = \mathbf{X}\beta + \epsilon$$

$$\mathbf{y} = \begin{pmatrix} y_1 \\ . \\ . \\ . \\ y_N \end{pmatrix}, \quad \mathbf{X} = \begin{pmatrix} x_{11} & x_{12} & . & . & x_{1k} \\ . & . & . & . & . \\ . & . & . & . & . \\ . & . & . & . & . \\ x_{N1} & x_{N2} & . & . & x_{Nk} \end{pmatrix}$$

$$\beta = \begin{pmatrix} \beta_1 \\ . \\ . \\ . \\ \beta_k \end{pmatrix}, \quad \epsilon = \begin{pmatrix} \varepsilon_1 \\ . \\ . \\ . \\ \varepsilon_N \end{pmatrix}$$

The simplest way to derive estimates of the parameters of interest is the ordinary least squares (OLS) method. Such a method chooses values for the unknown parameters to minimize the magnitude of the non-observable components. The best fit is obtained by minimizing the sum of squared vertical deviations of the data points from the fitted line.

Define the following quantity:

$$\mathbf{e}(\beta) = \mathbf{y} - \mathbf{X}\beta$$

where $\mathbf{e}(\beta)$ is a $(n \times 1)$ vector. If we treat $\mathbf{X}\beta$, as a (conditional) prediction for $\mathbf{y}$, then we can consider $\mathbf{e}(\beta)$ as a forecasting error. The sum of the squared errors is then

$$\mathbf{S}(\beta) = \mathbf{e}(\beta)' \mathbf{e}(\beta)$$

The OLS method produces an estimator of β, $\widehat{\beta}$, defined as follows:

$$\mathbf{S}\left(\widehat{\beta}\right) = \min_{\beta} \mathbf{e}(\beta)' \mathbf{e}(\beta)$$

Given $\widehat{\beta}$, we can define an associated vector of residual $\widehat{\epsilon}$ as $\widehat{\epsilon} = \mathbf{y} - \mathbf{X}\widehat{\beta}$. The OLS estimator is derived by considering the necessary and sufficient conditions for $\widehat{\beta}$ to be a unique minimum for $\mathbf{S}$:

(1) $\mathbf{X}'\widehat{\epsilon} = 0$;
(2) $\text{rank}(\mathbf{X}) = k$.

Condition 1 imposes orthogonality between the $\mathbf{X}$ variables and the OLS residuals, it ensures that residuals have zero mean when a constant is included among the regressors. Condition 2 requires that the columns of the $\mathbf{X}$ matrix are linearly independent.

From 1. we derive an expression for the OLS estimates:

$$\mathbf{X}'\widehat{\epsilon} = \mathbf{X}'\left(\mathbf{y} - \mathbf{X}\widehat{\beta}\right) = \mathbf{X}'\mathbf{y} - \mathbf{X}'\mathbf{X}\widehat{\beta} = 0$$

$$\widehat{\beta} = \left(\mathbf{X}'\mathbf{X}\right)^{-1}\mathbf{X}'\mathbf{y}$$

$$\widehat{\sigma}^2 = \frac{\widehat{\epsilon}'\widehat{\epsilon}}{T-k}$$

OLS in the CER

In the CER we have:

$$\mathbf{y} = \mathbf{X}\beta + \epsilon$$

$$\mathbf{y} = \begin{pmatrix} r_1 \\ . \\ . \\ . \\ r_T \end{pmatrix}, \quad \mathbf{X} = \begin{pmatrix} 1 \\ . \\ . \\ . \\ 1 \end{pmatrix}$$

$$\beta = \mu, \quad \epsilon = \begin{pmatrix} \varepsilon_1 \\ . \\ . \\ . \\ \varepsilon_T \end{pmatrix}$$

From one-period to multi-period returns in the CER

Notice that once one-step ahead returns are known, then also n-step ahead returns are known:

$$E_t(\mathbf{r}_{t,t+n}) = n\hat{\mu}$$

$$\mathrm{Var}(\mathbf{r}_{t,t+n}) = n\hat{\Sigma}$$

As a consequence of these properties of the data, weights in an optimal multi-horizon portfolio coincide with weights in a single-period horizon portfolio:

$$\hat{\mathbf{w}}^T = \frac{\Sigma^{-1}\left(\mu - r^f \mathbf{e}\right)}{\mathbf{e}'\Sigma^{-1}\left(\mu - r^f \mathbf{e}\right)}$$
$$= \frac{\Sigma^{-1}(nn^{-1})\left(\mu - r^f \mathbf{e}\right)}{\mathbf{e}'\Sigma^{-1}(nn^{-1})\left(\mu - r^f \mathbf{e}\right)}$$

5.3 Model Simulation

Once parameters in the CER have been estimated the model can be simulated to derive the distribution of asset returns in the future, this is done by simulating pseudo data from the model. Model can be simply used to create the distribution of returns in the future and derive value-at-risk measures, but they can also evaluated via the following procedure:

- Split the sample into two parts, a training sample and a test sample.
- Use the training sample to estimate model parameters'.
- Use the model to simulate artificial observation for the test sample.
- Evaluate the model by comparing actual data in the test sample with model-simulated data over the same period.

We shall consider two ways of simulating pseudo-data: Monte-Carlo simulation and Bootstrap. To use Monte-Carlo simulation to generate pseudo data from the CER model, some estimates of μ σ are necessary. Given these estimates an assumption must be made on the distribution of ϵ_t. Then an artificial sample for ϵ_t of the length matching that of the available can be computer simulated. The simulated residuals are then mapped into simulated returns via μ, σ. This exercise can be replicated N times (and therefore a Monte-Carlo simulation generates a matrix of computer-simulated returns whose dimensions are defined by the sample size T and by the number of replications N). The distribution of model-predicted returns can be then constructed and one can ask if the observed data can be considered as one draw from this distribution.

One of the possible limitations of the Monte-Carlo approach is the choice of a distribution from which the residuals are to be drawn. It might be very well the case that the model goes wrong because the choice of the statistical distribution is not the correct one. Bootstrap methods overcome this problem by sampling residuals from their empirical distribution. All the steps in a bootstrap simulation are the same as the Monte-Carlo simulation except that different observations for residuals are constructed by taking the deviation of returns from their sample mean putting them in an urn and resampling from the urn with replacement.

5.4 The CER Model at Work with R

In this section, we shall illustrate codes in R that apply model specification, estimation and simulation to the CER model to perform Optimal asset allocation and backtesting.

5.4.1 *Asset allocation with the CER*

The following code runs after the usual preliminaries (setting working directory, upload relevant packages) uses the inbuilt database BERNDINVEST in the package Ecofin to perform optimal asset allocation adopting the CER model for US stocks.

First, Data transformation is applied via a loop to construct, from monthly returns monthly prices, i.e., the value over-time of a buy and hold portfolio in each stock, and monthly log-prices.

Second, descriptive graphical analysis is implemented using the facilities in the package ggplot.

Third, the relevant parameters in the CER are estimated and optimal asset allocation is found by computing weights for the tangency portfolio.

Lastly, the utilization of the package fPortfolio in R is described. Research (2023) is an excellent online guide to Fportfolio. The program illustrates how to get the data in the appropriate format, set constraints for the portfolio optimization, compute efficient frontiers and optimal portfolio weights and provide graphic illustration of the results.

```
# Asset Allocation with CER
# elaboration on the original code produced by E.Zivot by C. Favero
# author: Carlo Favero
# created: August, 2023
# comments: Original Examples are taken from  chapter 11 in Zivot and Wang (2006)

rm(list=ls()) #Removes all items in Environment!
#setwd(path)
setwd(dirname(rstudioapi::getActiveDocumentContext()$path))

# set output options
options(width = 70, digits=4)

#install.packages("fEcofin", repos="http://R-Forge.R-project.org")
library(fEcofin)
# load required packages
listofpackages <- c("ellipse","dygraphs","ggplot2")

for (j in listofpackages){
  if(sum(installed.packages()[, 1] == j) == 0) {
    install.packages(j)
  }
  library(j, character.only = T)
}

install.packages(c("cluster","mvoutlier","pastecs","fPortfolio"),
repos="http://cran.r-project.org")
# load required packages
library(cluster)
library(mvoutlier)
library(pastecs)
library(fPortfolio)

####################################################
# Data Loadings and Transform: Descriptive Analysis
####################################################

# create data frame with dates as rownames
berndt.df = berndtInvest[, -1]
berndt.df$date <- as.Date(berndtInvest[, 1])
rownames(berndt.df) = as.character(berndtInvest[, 1])
colnames(berndt.df)
dimnames(berndt.df)[[2]] #command alternative to the previous one

# transform the data and compute cumulative returns

t0 <- which(berndt.df$date == "1978-01-01")
t1 <- which(berndt.df$date == "1987-12-01")

series_names <-
    c("CITCRP","CONED","CONTIL","DATGEN","DEC","DELTA","GENMIL","GERBER","IBM",
"MARKET","MOBIL","PANAM","PSNH","TANDY","TEXACO","WEYER","RKFREE")

for (name in series_names) {
  P_col_name <- paste0(name,"_P")
  LP_col_name<- paste0("L",P_col_name)
  berndt.df[t0, P_col_name] <- 1
  for (i in (t0+1):(t1)) {
    berndt.df[i, P_col_name][[1]] <- berndt.df[i-1, P_col_name][[1]] *
        (1+berndt.df[i, name][[1]] )
  }
  berndt.df[, LP_col_name] <- log(berndt.df[, P_col_name])
```

```
}
# add a trend to the database
berndt.df$TREND<- array(data = NA, dim = nrow(berndt.df))
berndt.df[t0, c("TREND")] <- 1 # don't need to repeat the value to make the array being assigned be
      of the same length. be careful though as it is one of the few cases of exception

###########################
# Descriptive Analysis
###########################

  #We can now plot, please note the difference with plotting from a time-series object

plot(berndt.df$date[t0:t1],berndt.df$TEXACO[t0:t1],ylab =
    "TEXACO",xlab="year", main = "Monthly Returns", col = "blue", lwd =
    2,type="l")


plot(berndt.df$date[t0:t1],berndt.df$TEXACO[t0:t1], col = 'blue', type =
   "l",
     ylab = "returns TEXACO and MKT", xlab = "date",lwd = 2)
lines(y = rep(mean(berndt.df$TEXACO[t0:t1], na.rm = T),
    length(berndt.df$TEXACO[t0:t1])), x = berndt.df$date[t0:t1], col =
    "red")
lines(y = berndt.df$MARKET[t0:t1], x = berndt.df$date[t0:t1], col =
    "green",lwd = 2)
legend("topleft", legend = c("TEXACO", "MKT"),
       col = c("blue", "green"), lty = 1)

plot(berndt.df$date[t0:t1],berndt.df$LTEXACO_P[t0:t1], col = 'blue', type =
   "l",
     ylab = "portfolios TEXACO and MKT", xlab = "date",ylim = c(-0.5,
        2),lwd = 2)
lines(y = berndt.df$LMARKET_P[t0:t1], x = berndt.df$date[t0:t1], col =
    "green",lwd = 2)
legend("topleft", legend = c("TEXACO", "MKT"),
       col = c("blue", "green"), lty = 1)

# Create the plot using ggplot, as generated by Chat GPT
ggplot(berndt.df, aes(x = date)) +
  geom_line(aes(y = LTEXACO_P), color = "blue", size = 2, linetype =
     "solid") +
  geom_line(aes(y = LMARKET_P), color = "green", size = 2, linetype =
     "solid") +
  labs(x = "Date", y = "Portfolios TEXACO and MKT") +
  ylim(-0.5, 2) +
  theme_minimal() +
  theme(
    legend.position = "topleft",
    legend.title = element_blank(),
    legend.text = element_text(size = 12),
    axis.text = element_text(size = 12),
    axis.title = element_text(size = 14),
    plot.title = element_text(size = 16, hjust = 0.5)
  ) +
  scale_color_manual(
    values = c("blue", "green"),
    guide = guide_legend(override.aes = list(size = 2, linetype = "solid"))
  ) +
  guides(fill = guide_legend(override.aes = list(size = 2)))
```

```
############################
# Asset Allocation with CER
############################
returns.df=berndt.df[, c(1:9,11:16)]
#returns.df = berndt.df[, c(-10, -17)
exreturns.df=returns.df-berndt.df$RKFREE
returns.mat = as.matrix(exreturns.df)
n.obs = nrow(returns.mat)

#Estimation of CER model parameters
cov.sample=var(returns.mat)
mu = matrix(colMeans(returns.mat), nrow = ncol(returns.mat), ncol = 1)

#
# compute tangency portfolio
#

e = matrix(1, nrow = nrow(cov.sample), ncol = 1) # unitary column vector e
w.tan.sample =
    (solve(cov.sample)%*%(mu))/as.numeric(t(e)%*%(solve(cov.sample)%*%(mu)))

colnames(w.tan.sample) = "sample"
barplot(t(w.tan.sample), horiz=F, main="Weights", col="blue", cex.names =
   0.75, las=2)

################################
# Using the fportfolio package
################################

#returns.df=berndt.df[, c(1:9,11:16)]
#exreturns.df=returns.df-berndt.df$RKFREE
companies <- colnames(exreturns.df)
#ts
tsdata <- ts(exreturns.df, start = c(1978, 1), frequency = 12, names =
   companies)
s1 <- window(tsdata[, "TEXACO"], start = c(1978, 1), end = c(1987, 12))
dygraph(s1, ylab = "TEXACO", main = "monthly excess returns")
data01ts <- as.timeSeries(tsdata)
# financial data description
ddown<-drawdowns(data01ts)
ddowndata <- ts(ddown, start = c(1978, 1), frequency = 12, names =
   companies)
s1 <- window(ddowndata[, "TEXACO"], start = c(1978, 1), end = c(1987, 12))
dygraph(s1, ylab = "TEXACO", main = "drawdowns")
drawdownsStats(data01ts[, "TEXACO"])
#----------------------
# Portfolio Allocation
#----------------------

# Step 1 define the data in our case 15 excess returns data in data01ts
showClass("fPFOLIODATA")

lppData <- portfolioData(data = data01ts, spec = portfolioSpec())
# once the data have been defined we can get info on them
str(lppData, width = 65, strict.width = "cut")
print(lppData)
getData(portfolioData(lppData))[-1]
getStatistics(portfolioData(lppData))

# Step 2 Set Portfolio Constraints

showClass("fPFOLIOCON")
```

```
#default constraints: long-only
Data<-data01ts
Spec <- portfolioSpec()
setTargetReturn(Spec) <- mean(Data)
Constraints <- "LongOnly"
defaultConstraints <- portfolioConstraints(Data, Spec, Constraints)
str(defaultConstraints, width = 65, strict.width = "cut")
print(defaultConstraints)

# short constraints
shortConstraints <- "Short"
portfolioConstraints(Data, Spec, shortConstraints)

# box constraints
box.1 <- "minW[1:15] = 0.1"
box.2 <- "maxW[1:15] = 1" # you can have more boxes before combining them
boxConstraints <- c(box.1, box.2)
boxConstraints
portfolioConstraints(Data, Spec, boxConstraints)


# Step 3 Computing Optimal Portfolios

#3.0 A benchmark: equal weight portfolio
ewSpec <- portfolioSpec()
nAssets <- ncol(data01ts)
setWeights(ewSpec) <- rep(1/nAssets, times = nAssets)
ewPortfolio <- feasiblePortfolio(
  data = data01ts,
  spec = ewSpec,
  constraints = "LongOnly")
print(ewPortfolio)

# Efficient Frontier plot
setNFrontierPoints(ewSpec) <- 25
eff_ew_frontier <- portfolioFrontier(data = data01ts, spec = ewSpec,
    constraints = "LongOnly")
tailoredFrontierPlot(object = eff_ew_frontier)

#3.1 Long-Only
tgSpec <- portfolioSpec()
setRiskFreeRate(tgSpec) <- 0
constraints <- "longOnly"
tgPortfolio <- tangencyPortfolio(
  data = data01ts,
  spec = tgSpec, constraints = constraints)
print(tgPortfolio)

#printing the results
col <- seqPalette(ncol(data01ts), "BuPu")
weightsPie(tgPortfolio, box = FALSE, col = col)
mtext(text = "Tangency MV Portfolio", side = 3, line = 1.5,
      font = 2, cex = 0.7, adj = 0)
weightedReturnsPie(tgPortfolio, box = FALSE, col = col)
mtext(text = "Tangency MV Portfolio", side = 3, line = 1.5,
      font = 2, cex = 0.7, adj = 0)
covRiskBudgetsPie(tgPortfolio, box = FALSE, col = col)
mtext(text = "Tangency MV Portfolio", side = 3, line = 1.5,
      font = 2, cex = 0.7, adj = 0)

efficient_frontier <- portfolioFrontier(data = data01ts, spec = tgSpec,
    constraints = constraints)
```

```
print(efficient_frontier)
# Efficient Frontier plot
setNFrontierPoints(tgSpec) <- 25
efficient_frontier <- portfolioFrontier(data = data01ts, spec = tgSpec,
    constraints = constraints)
tailoredFrontierPlot(object = efficient_frontier)

#---------------------
#3.2 Box-Constraints
#---------------------
boxSpec <- portfolioSpec()
setRiskFreeRate(boxSpec) <- 0
boxConstraints <- c("minW[1:15]=0.05", "maxW[1:15]=0.5")
tgPortfolio1 <- tangencyPortfolio(
  data = data01ts,
  spec = boxSpec, constraints = boxConstraints)
print(tgPortfolio1)

#printing the results
col <- seqPalette(ncol(data01ts), "BuPu")
weightsPie(tgPortfolio1, box = FALSE, col = col)
mtext(text = "Tangency MV Portfolio", side = 3, line = 1.5,
      font = 2, cex = 0.7, adj = 0)
weightedReturnsPie(tgPortfolio, box = FALSE, col = col)
mtext(text = "Tangency MV Portfolio", side = 3, line = 1.5,
      font = 2, cex = 0.7, adj = 0)
covRiskBudgetsPie(tgPortfolio, box = FALSE, col = col)
mtext(text = "Tangency MV Portfolio", side = 3, line = 1.5,
      font = 2, cex = 0.7, adj = 0)
```

5.4.2 *Model simulation: Backtesting and VaR*

To illustrate model simulation we consider the application to backtesting and value-at-risk. The following illustrative code starts by building the tangency and the minimum variance portfolio on the stocks considered in the previous section and by implementing within-sample evaluation of the properties of the optimized portfolios. This type of exercise suffers from the well-known problem of "look-ahead bias" as data not available in real time have been used to construct weights. True backtesting, when the available data are divided into a "training Sample" and a test sample, is then implemented using the package fPortfolio. A procedure is used according to which a rolling sample is used to build the allocation that reflects the information available in real-time at the end of the sample, allocations are then evaluated out-of-sample and then re-optimized. The possibility of smoothing optimal weights in the rolling procedure is also considered. Backtesting is then conducted by assessing ex-post the performance of each allocation. Finally, in the last part of the code, the CER model is applied to the Tangency portfolio to simulate, via bootstrap and Monte-Carlo procedures, the distribution of the returns and to produce one-month ahead value-at-risk.

```
# Asset Allocation with CER
# elaboration on the original code produced by E.Zivot by C. Favero
# author: Carlo Favero
# created: August, 2023
#
# comments: Original Examples are taken from  chapter 11 in Zivot and Wang (2006)

rm(list=ls()) #Removes all items in Environment!
#setwd(path)
setwd(dirname(rstudioapi::getActiveDocumentContext()$path))

#install.packages("fEcofin", repos="http://R-Forge.R-project.org")
library(fEcofin)
# load required packages
listofpackages <- c("ellipse","dygraphs","ggplot2","reshape2")

for (j in listofpackages){
  if(sum(installed.packages()[, 1] == j) == 0) {
    install.packages(j)
  }
  library(j, character.only = T)
}

install.packages(c("cluster","mvoutlier","pastecs","fPortfolio"),repos="http://cran.r-project.org")
# load required packages
library(cluster)
library(mvoutlier)
library(pastecs)
library(fPortfolio)


# create data frame with dates as rownames
berndt.df = berndtInvest[, -1]
rownames(berndt.df) = as.character(as.Date(berndtInvest[, 1]))


###############################################################################
# Derive the optimal portfolio weights (i.e. the weights in the tangency portfolio)
# using the CER for (i) the Minimun Variance Portfolio , (ii) the tangency portfolio.
##############################################################################
returns.df=berndt.df[, c(1:9,11:16)]
#returns.df = berndt.df[, c(-10, -17)
exreturns.df=returns.df-berndt.df$RKFREE
returns.mat = as.matrix(exreturns.df)
# using ggplot to plot series in returns
berndt.df$date <- as.Date(row.names(berndt.df))

# Create the time series plot using ggplot
ggplot(data = berndt.df, aes(x = date, y = WEYER)) +
  geom_line() +                        # Add a line plot
  labs(x = "Date", y = "WEYER")  # Label the axes



#
# compute global min variance portfolio
#
# use CER model: estimate the relevant unknown parameters with the sample covariances
returns.mat = as.matrix(exreturns.df)
n.obs = nrow(returns.mat)
```

```
cov.sample=var(returns.mat)
mu = matrix(colMeans(returns.mat), nrow = ncol(returns.mat), ncol = 1)
e = matrix(1, nrow = nrow(cov.sample), ncol = 1) # unitary column vector e
#
# compute GMIN portfolio
#
w.gmin.sample = solve(var(returns.mat))%*%rep(1,nrow(cov.sample))
w.gmin.sample = w.gmin.sample/sum(w.gmin.sample)
berndt.df$GMIN<-returns.mat%*%w.gmin.sample

barplot(t(w.gmin.sample), horiz=F, main="Weights", col="blue", cex.names =
    0.75, las=2)

ggplot(data = berndt.df, aes(x = date, y = GMIN)) +
  geom_line() +                    # Add a line plot
  labs(x = "Date", y = "GMIN")  # Label the axes

#
# compute tangency portfolio
#
w.tan.sample = (solve(cov.sample)%*%as.numeric(mu))
w.tan.sample =w.tan.sample/as.numeric(t(e)%*%(solve(cov.sample)%*%(mu)))

berndt.df$TAN<-returns.mat%*%w.tan.sample

# visualize the differences
par(mfrow=c(1,2))
barplot(t(w.tan.sample), horiz=T, main="Tangency Port CER", col="blue",
    cex.names = 0.75, las=1)
barplot(t(w.gmin.sample), horiz=T, main="Min Var Port CER", col="red",
    cex.names = 0.75, las=1)
par(mfrow=c(1,1))

plot <- ggplot(data= berndt.df, aes(x = date)) +
  geom_line(aes(y = TAN, color = "TAN"), size = 1) +
  geom_line(aes(y = GMIN, color = "GMIN"), size = 1) +
  labs(title = "Returns",
       x = "Time", y = "Monthly Returns") +
  scale_color_manual(values = c("TAN" = "red", "GMIN" = "blue")) +
  theme_minimal() +
  theme(axis.line = element_line(color = "black"))

print(plot)


##################################################
# Graphs the value over-time of 1 dollar invested in 1978:1 until the end of the
# available sample in the two alternative tangency portfolios and in the market
##################################################
berndt.df$Port_mkt <- berndt.df$Port_TAN<- berndt.df$Port_GMIN <-
    array(data = NA, dim = nrow(berndt.df))

berndt.df[1, c("Port_mkt", "Port_TAN","Port_GMIN")] <- 1
t1<-nrow(berndt.df)
for (i in 2:t1) {
  berndt.df[i, "Port_mkt"][[1]]=berndt.df[i-1,
     "Port_mkt"][[1]]*(1+berndt.df[i, "MARKET"][[1]])
  berndt.df[i, "Port_TAN"][[1]]=berndt.df[i-1,
     "Port_TAN"][[1]]*(1+berndt.df[i, "TAN"][[1]])
  berndt.df[i, "Port_GMIN"][[1]]=berndt.df[i-1,
     "Port_GMIN"][[1]]*(1+berndt.df[i, "GMIN"][[1]])
}
```

```
# time series Plot of the three Portfolios

plot <- ggplot(data= berndt.df, aes(x = date)) +
  geom_line(aes(y = Port_mkt, color = "Port_mkt"), size = 1) +
  geom_line(aes(y = Port_GMIN, color = "Port_GMIN"), size = 1) +
  geom_line(aes(y = Port_TAN, color = "Port_TAN"), size = 1) +
  labs(title = "Returns",
       x = "Time", y = "Monthly Returns") +
  scale_color_manual(values = c("Port_mkt" = "red", "Port_GMIN" =
      "blue","Port_TAN" = "green")) +
  theme_minimal() +
  theme(axis.line = element_line(color = "black"))


# compare means and sd values on global min variance portfolios

mu.gmin.sample = as.numeric(colMeans(berndt.df$GMIN))
mu.tan.sample = as.numeric(colMeans(berndt.df$TAN))
sd.gmin.sample = as.numeric(apply(berndt.df$GMIN,2,sd))
sd.tan.sample = as.numeric(apply(berndt.df$TAN,2,sd))
cbind(mu.tan.sample,mu.gmin.sample, sd.tan.sample, sd.gmin.sample)

## ------------------------------
#  BACKTESTING   with fPortfolio
## ------------------------------
companies <- colnames(berndt.df)
#getting the data in ts format
tsdata <- ts(berndt.df, start = c(1978, 1), frequency = 12, names =
   companies)
data01ts <- as.timeSeries(tsdata)
ddown<-drawdowns(data01ts)
ddowndata <- ts(ddown, start = c(1978, 1), frequency = 12, names =
   companies)
s1 <- window(ddowndata[, "TAN"], start = c(1978, 1), end = c(1987, 12))
dygraph(s1, ylab = "TAN", main = "drawdowns")
drawdownsStats(data01ts[, "TAN"])
## ------------------------------
#  out-of-sample BACKTESTING
## ------------------------------

Data <- data01ts
Spec <- portfolioSpec()
Constraints <- "LongOnly"
Backtest <- portfolioBacktest()
setWindowsHorizon(Backtest) <- "60m"
equidistWindows(data = Data, backtest = Backtest)


#Specify assets for backtesting
#Formula <- MARKET ~ CITCRP + CONED + CONTIL + DATGEN + DEC + DELTA +
# +      GENMIL + GERBER +IBM+MOBIL+PANAM+PSNH+TANDY+TEXACO+WEYER
Formula <- MARKET ~ CITCRP + CONED + CONTIL + DATGEN + DEC + DELTA +
  GENMIL + GERBER + IBM + MOBIL + PANAM + PSNH + TANDY + TEXACO + WEYER

#Optimize rolling portfolios and run backtests
#btportfolios <- portfolioBacktesting(formula = Formula,
#                                     +data = data01ts, spec = Spec, constraints = Constraints,
#                                     + backtest = Backtest, trace = FALSE)

btportfolios <- portfolioBacktesting(formula = Formula,
```

```
                                    data = data01ts, spec = Spec,
                                        constraints = Constraints,
                                    backtest = Backtest, trace = FALSE)


#Weights are rebalanced on a monthly basis
Weights <- round(100 * btportfolios$weights, 2)[1:60, ]
Weights

setSmootherLambda(btportfolios$backtest) <- "1m"
SmoothPortfolios <- portfolioSmoothing(object = btportfolios,trace = FALSE)
smoothWeights <- round(100 * SmoothPortfolios$smoothWeights,2)[1:60, ]
smoothWeights

backtestPlot(SmoothPortfolios, cex = 0.6, font = 1, family = "mono")

netPerformance(SmoothPortfolios)

## --------------------
#  MODEL-SIMULATION
## --------------------

## ----------------------------------
# model specification and estimation
mod_TAN <- lm(berndt.df$TAN ~ 1)
summary(mod_TAN)


## ----------------------------------
# parameter calibration and choice of the number of replications in the simulation and of the sample size for simulated data
vol <- sd(mod_TAN$residuals)
alpha <- mod_TAN$coefficients[[1]]
nrep <- 1000
TT <- nrow(berndt.df)
# here I create the containers to be filled with the generated data.
y_bt <- y_mc <- array(1, c(TT, nrep))
x_bt <- x_mc <- array(alpha, c(TT, nrep))

# now, the loop

for (i in 1:nrep){
  u <- rnorm(TT)
  res <- sample(mod_TAN$residuals, replace = T) # this (re)samples from the data

  x_mc[, i] <- alpha + vol * u # the Monte Carlo way
  x_bt[, i] <- alpha+res             # the bootstrap way

  # now we simply construct and store the bootstrapped and MC cumulative returns
  for (j in 2:TT){
    y_mc[j, i] <- y_mc[j-1, i] * (1 + x_mc[j, i])
    y_bt[j, i] <- y_bt[j-1, i] * (1 + x_bt[j, i])
  }
}

# now we want to construct the series of means and quantiles of the resulting collection of drawn series
for (i in 1:TT){
  # obtaining the means
  berndt.df$y_bt_mean[i] <- mean(y_bt[i, ])
  berndt.df$x_bt_mean[i] <- mean(x_bt[i, ])
  berndt.df$y_mc_mean[i] <- mean(y_mc[i, ])
```

```
  berndt.df$x_mc_mean[i] <- mean(x_mc[i, ])

  # and the quantiles
  berndt.df$y_bt_q05[i] <- quantile(y_bt[i, ], 0.05)
  berndt.df$x_bt_q05[i] <- quantile(x_bt[i, ], 0.05)
  berndt.df$y_mc_q05[i] <- quantile(y_mc[i, ], 0.05)
  berndt.df$x_mc_q05[i] <- quantile(x_mc[i, ], 0.05)

  berndt.df$y_bt_q95[i] <- quantile(y_bt[i, ], 0.95)
  berndt.df$x_bt_q95[i] <- quantile(x_bt[i, ], 0.95)
  berndt.df$y_mc_q95[i] <- quantile(y_mc[i, ], 0.95)
  berndt.df$x_mc_q95[i] <- quantile(x_mc[i, ], 0.95)

}

## ----------------------------------------------
# plotting
plot <- ggplot(data= berndt.df, aes(x = date)) +
  geom_line(aes(y = TAN, color = "TAN"), size = 1) +
  geom_line(aes(y = x_mc_mean, color = "x_mc_mean"), size = 1) +
  geom_line(aes(y = x_mc_q05, color = "x_mc_q05"), size = 1) +
  geom_line(aes(y = x_mc_q95, color = "x_mc_q95"), size = 1) +
  labs(title = "Simulation",
       x = "Time", y = "Monthly Returns") +
  scale_color_manual(values = c("TAN" = "blue", "x_mc_q05" =
     "red","x_mc_q95" = "red","x_mc_mean" = "green")) +
  theme_minimal() +
  theme(axis.line = element_line(color = "black"))

## ---------------------------------------------
# Value at Risk  via Monte Carlo simulation
## ---------------------------------------------
s1_mc=x_mc[2,]
hist(s1_mc, breaks = seq(min(s1_mc), max(s1_mc), l = 20+1),prob=TRUE, main
   = "histogram of monthly returns")
curve(dnorm(x,mean=mean(s1_mc),sd=sd(s1_mc)),col='darkblue',lwd=2,add=TRUE)
VaR_mc <- quantile(s1_mc, 0.05)
VaR_mc
```

Chapter 6

Factor Models

The traditional approach to asset allocation among N risky assets requires the prediction of their future distribution $\mathbf{r} \sim \mathcal{D}(\mu, \Sigma)$. One of the most relevant problems in the implementation of the traditional approach to portfolio allocation is dimensionality. The implementation of asset allocation and risk measurement among n assets requires the estimation of a large number of parameters: $\frac{n(n+1)}{2} + n$. Factor models allow to reduce of the dimensionality of the number of parameters to be estimated to derive the predictive distribution of returns. Moreover, linear multi-factor models (e.g., Fama and French, 1993, 2015; Ang, 2014; Hou *et al.*, 2018) represent the workhorse of empirical asset pricing. These models have been also successfully employed to parsimoniously characterize the cross-section of average one-period (often monthly) returns.

6.1 Time-Series Representation

The statistical distribution of excess returns on N assets ($i = 1, \ldots, n$) can be conditioned on a vector of K factors $\mathbf{f}$ (where N is large and K is small)

$$r^i_{t,t+k} = \gamma^i_0 + \gamma^{i\prime}_1 \mathbf{f}_{t,t+k} + v^i_{t,t+k} \tag{6.1}$$

$$\mathbf{f}_{t,t+k} = \mu^f + \mathbf{H}^f \epsilon_{t,t+k}$$

$$\Sigma^f = \mathbf{H}^f \mathbf{H}^{f\prime}.$$

$$\mathbf{E}\left(v^i_{t,t+k}, v^j_{t,t+k}\right) = 0$$

$$\mathbf{E}\left(v^i_{t,t+k}, \epsilon^j_{t,t+k}\right) = 0$$

$$\epsilon_{t+k} \sim \mathcal{D}\left(\mathbf{0}, \mathbf{I}\right)$$

Note that the projection of the large number of N excess returns on the small number K of factors allows decomposing the compensation for risk into two orthogonal components: a common risk component captured by the factors $\gamma_1^{i\prime}\mathbf{f}$ and an idiosyncratic component captured by the residuals of the projection of returns on factors $v^i_{t,t+k}$. By their nature, idiosyncratic components are not correlated with each other and therefore while the variance–covariance matrix of N excess returns contains $N(N+1)/2$ parameters the variance–covariance matrix of the residuals of the projections of excess returns on factors is diagonal and contains only N parameters to be estimated. The application of the CER model for asset allocation to select a portfolio from N assets requires the estimation of $N + N(N+1)/2$ parameters, while the adoption of a structure of K factors requires the estimation of $(2N+NK)+(K+K(K+1)/2)$ parameters. Think, for example, of an asset allocation problem with 30 assets and four factors. The CER would require the estimation of 505 parameters, the factor model would reduce that number to 194. The traditional factor model results from a combination of the application of the CER to factors and of the projection of returns to factors. the constancy of conditional expectations of factors implies the absence of predictability for them which immediately translates into the absence of predictability for returns. In the traditional factor model, we have:

$$\begin{aligned} E\left(\mathbf{f}_{t,t+k}\right) &= \mu^f \\ E\left(r^i_{t,t+k}\right) &= \gamma^i_0 + \gamma_1^{i\prime} E\left(\mathbf{f}_{t,t+k}\right) \\ &= \gamma^i_0 + \gamma_1^{i\prime} \mu^f \end{aligned} \tag{6.2}$$

and the model rules out predictability both for factors and returns.

6.2 Cross-Sectional Representation

If we consider the cross-section of returns rather than their time-series, the multifactor model has the following cross-sectional representation for the $(N \times 1)$ vector of returns between time t and time $t+k$ as a linear projection of factors between time t and time $t+k$

$$\underset{(Nx1)}{\mathbf{r}_{t,t+k}} = \underset{(Nx1)}{\alpha} + \underset{(NxK)}{B}\underset{(Kx1)}{\mathbf{f}_{t,t+k}} + \underset{(Nx1)}{\mathbf{v}_t} \tag{6.3}$$

$$\underset{(Kx1)}{\mathbf{f}_{t,t+k}} = \underset{(Kx1)}{\mu^f} + \underset{(KxK)}{\mathbf{H}^f}\underset{(Kx1)}{\epsilon^f}$$

$$\Sigma^v = \begin{bmatrix} \sigma_1 & 0 & 0 & 0 \\ 0 & \sigma_2 & 0 & 0 \\ .. & .. & .. & .. \\ 0 & 0 & 0 & \sigma_n \end{bmatrix}$$

$$\Sigma^f = \mathbf{H}^f\mathbf{H}^{f\prime}.$$

The specification and estimation of a factor model allow the computation of optimal portfolio weights. We have

$$\underset{(Nx1)}{E}\,\mathbf{r}_{t,t+k} = \underset{(Nx1)}{\alpha} + \underset{(NxK)}{B}\underset{(Kx1)}{\mu^f} \tag{6.4}$$

$$\underset{(NxN)}{\Sigma}{}^r = \underset{(NxK)}{B}\underset{(KxK)}{\Sigma}{}^f\underset{(KxN)}{B'} + \underset{(NxN)}{\Sigma}{}^v$$

from which optimal weights are derived for the different specifications of the optimal portfolio.

6.3 Factor-Based Portfolios and Factor Exposures

After optimal portfolio weights have been set using a specific criterion, the portfolio exposures to factors can be assessed by computing the share of the total portfolio variance attributable to each factor. Define the returns of an optimal portfolio obtained by combining

n assets as $r^p_{t+1} = \sum_{i=1}^N w_i r^i_{t+1}$

$$
\begin{aligned}
r^p_{t+1} &= \alpha_1 + \beta_{f^1} f^1_{t+1} + \beta_{f^2} f^2_{t+1} + \cdots + \beta_{f^k} f^k_{t+1} + v_{t+1} \\
\operatorname{Var}\left(r^p_{t+1}\right) &= \operatorname{Cov}\left(r^p_{t+1}, r^p_{t+1}\right) \\
&= \beta_{f^1} \operatorname{Cov}\left(f^1_{t+1}, r^p_{t+1}\right) + \cdots \beta_{f^k} \operatorname{Cov}\left(f^k_{t+1}, r^p_{t+1}\right) \\
&\quad + \operatorname{Cov}\left(v_{t+1}, r^p_{t+1}\right)
\end{aligned}
$$

The factor exposure can then be computed as the share of the total variance portfolio attributable to each factor:

$$
\mathrm{EXP}^p_{f^i} = \frac{\beta_{f^i} \operatorname{Cov}\left(f^i_{t+1}, r^p_{t+1}\right)}{\operatorname{Var}\left(r^p_{t+1}\right)}
$$

The above decomposition resembles the risk parity approach. As risk parity can be considered as an alternative method to allocate assets, "smart beta" strategies can be implemented through alternative weighting methods that emphasize the exposures to specific factors.

6.4 Asset Allocation with the CER and the CAPM in R

We shall illustrate factor models with the most famous single factor model for asset returns: the CAPM (Sharpe, 1964; Lintner, 1965). In the CAPM the common factor to all asset returns is identified with the market. The CAPM has the following time-series representation for the return of the ith assets to be included in the portfolio

$$
\begin{aligned}
\left(r^i_t - r^{rf}_t\right) &= \beta_{0,i} + \beta_{1,i}\left(r^m_t - r^{rf}_t\right) + u_{i,t} \\
\left(r^m_t - r^{rf}_t\right) &= \mu_m + u_{m,t} \\
u_{i,t} &\sim n.i.d.\left(0, \sigma^2_i\right) \\
\begin{pmatrix} u_{i,t} \\ u_{m,t} \end{pmatrix} &\sim n.i.d.\left[\begin{pmatrix} 0 \\ 0 \end{pmatrix}, \begin{pmatrix} \sigma_{ii} & 0 \\ 0 & \sigma_{mm} \end{pmatrix}\right]
\end{aligned}
$$

The hypothesis of crucial importance for the validity of the factor representation is that of orthogonality between the common shock

$u_{m,t}$ and all the idiosyncratic shocks $u_{i,t}$. The cross-sectional representation of the vectors of N returns in the CAPM is then:

$$\begin{aligned}\mathbf{r}_t &= \boldsymbol{\beta_0} + \boldsymbol{\beta_1} r_t^m + \mathbf{u}_t \\ r_t^m &= E\left(r^m\right) + \sigma_m \mathbf{u}_{m,t} \\ \Sigma &= \boldsymbol{\beta_1}\boldsymbol{\beta_1}'\sigma_m^2 + \Sigma_u \\ \mu &= \beta_0 + \beta_1 E\left(r^m\right)\end{aligned}$$

Note that while if a CER model is adopted for all returns the total number of parameters to be estimated is $N + \frac{N(N+1)}{2}$ (the parameters in the mean vector + the parameters in the variance-covariance matrix of returns), while μ, Σ can be obtained with the estimation of $3N + 2$ parameters when the CAPM is adopted.

The following R code allows uploading a data set of US stock market returns, performing descriptive and graphical analysis of the performance of the single index model applied to returns, and tracking the capability of the model for returns to track prices in the case of a specific stock, implementing optimal portfolio allocation with the CER model, implementing optimal portfolio allocation with the CAPM model, comparing the results, and checking the validity of the CAPM model by comparing the correlation matrix of returns with the correlation matrix of their estimated idiosyncratic components. The code also exploits alternative approaches to run CAPM regressions for many assets using first multivariate least squares and then iterating OLS regressions for all available returns.

```
# elaboration on the original produced by E.Zivot by C. Favero
# author: Carlo Favero
# created: July, 2021
#
# comments: Original Examples follow chapter 11 in Zivot and Wang (2006)


rm(list=ls()) #Removes all items in Environment!
#setwd(path)
setwd(dirname(rstudioapi::getActiveDocumentContext()$path))

# set output options
# options(width = 70, digits=4)
listofpackages <- c("dygraphs",
    "dplyr","ellipse","reshape2","ggplot2","PerformanceAnalytics","zoo")

for (j in listofpackages){
  if(sum(installed.packages()[, 1] == j) == 0) {
    install.packages(j)
  }
```

```
  library(j, character.only = T)
}
install.packages("fEcofin", repos="http://R-Forge.R-project.org")
# load required packages
library(fEcofin)              # various data sets

########################
# Data Loadings and Transform Descriptive Analysis
########################

# create data frame with dates as rownames
berndt.df = berndtInvest[, -1]
berndt.df$date <- as.Date(berndtInvest[, 1])
rownames(berndt.df) = as.character(berndtInvest[, 1])
colnames(berndt.df)
dimnames(berndt.df)[[2]] #command alternative to the previous one

# transform the data and compute cumulative returns

t0 <- which(berndt.df$date == "1978-01-01")
t1 <- which(berndt.df$date == "1987-12-01")

series_names <-
    c("CITCRP","CONED","CONTIL","DATGEN","DEC","DELTA","GENMIL","GERBER","IBM",
"MARKET","MOBIL","PANAM","PSNH","TANDY","TEXACO","WEYER","RKFREE")

for (name in series_names) {
  P_col_name <- paste0(name,"_P")
  LP_col_name<- paste0("L",P_col_name)
  berndt.df[t0, P_col_name] <- 1
  for (i in (t0+1):(t1)) {
    berndt.df[i, P_col_name][[1]] <- berndt.df[i-1, P_col_name][[1]] *
        (1+berndt.df[i, name][[1]] )
  }
  berndt.df[, LP_col_name] <- log(berndt.df[, P_col_name])
}
# add a trend to the database
berndt.df$TREND<- array(data = NA, dim = nrow(berndt.df))
berndt.df[t0, c("TREND")] <- 1 # don't need to repeat the value to make the array being assigned be
      of the same length. be careful though as it is one of the few cases of exception

##################################
# Descriptive Analysis of prices and returns
##################################
# plot log prices
ggplot(berndt.df, aes(x = date)) +
  geom_line(aes(y = LTEXACO_P), color = "blue", size = 1, linetype =
     "solid") +
  geom_line(aes(y = LMARKET_P), color = "green", size = 1, linetype =
     "solid") +
  labs(x = "Date", y = "Portfolios TEXACO and MKT") +
  ylim(-0.5, 2) +
  theme_minimal() +
  theme(
    legend.position = "topleft",
    legend.title = element_blank(),
    legend.text = element_text(size = 12),
    axis.text = element_text(size = 12),
    axis.title = element_text(size = 14),
    plot.title = element_text(size = 16, hjust = 0.5)
  ) +
  scale_color_manual(
```

```
      values = c("blue", "green"),
      guide = guide_legend(override.aes = list(size = 2, linetype = "solid"))
    ) +
    guides(fill = guide_legend(override.aes = list(size = 2)))
  # plot returns
  ggplot(berndt.df, aes(x = date)) +
    geom_line(aes(y = TEXACO), color = "blue", size = 1, linetype = "solid") +
    geom_line(aes(y = MARKET), color = "green", size = 1, linetype = "solid")
      +
    labs(x = "Date", y = "Portfolios TEXACO and MKT") +
    ylim(-0.45, 0.45) +
    theme_minimal() +
    theme(
      legend.position = "topleft",
      legend.title = element_blank(),
      legend.text = element_text(size = 12),
      axis.text = element_text(size = 12),
      axis.title = element_text(size = 14),
      plot.title = element_text(size = 16, hjust = 0.5)
    ) +
    scale_color_manual(
      values = c("blue", "green"),
      guide = guide_legend(override.aes = list(size = 2, linetype = "solid"))
    ) +
    guides(fill = guide_legend(override.aes = list(size = 2)))



################################
# CAPM FOR TEXACO
################################
capm_tex<-lm(TEXACO ~ MARKET, data=berndt.df)
summary(capm_tex)
berndt.df$TEXACO_fitted<-capm_tex$fitted.values

#fitting returns

plot(berndt.df$date[t0:t1],berndt.df$TEXACO[t0:t1], col = 'blue', type =
   "l",
     ylab = " actual and fitted returns", xlab = "date",lwd = 2,)
lines(y = rep(mean(berndt.df$TEXACO[t0:t1], na.rm = T),
    length(berndt.df$TEXACO[t0:t1])), x = berndt.df$date[t0:t1], col =
     "red")
lines(y = berndt.df$TEXACO_fitted[t0:t1], x = berndt.df$date[t0:t1], col =
    "green",lwd = 2)
legend("topright", legend = c("TEXACO ACTUAL", "TEXACO FITTED"),
       col = c("blue", "green"), lty = 1)
grid(nx = 6, ny = 7, col = "lightgray", lty = "dotted",
     lwd = par("lwd"), equilogs = TRUE)

#fitting prices
berndt.df$TEXACO_P_FITTED <-  array(data = NA, dim = nrow(berndt.df))
berndt.df$TEXACO_P_FITTED[t0] <- 1
for (i in (t0+1):(t1)) {
  berndt.df$TEXACO_P_FITTED[i] <- berndt.df$TEXACO_P_FITTED[i-1] * (1 +
     berndt.df$TEXACO_fitted[i])}

plot(berndt.df$date[t0:t1],berndt.df$TEXACO_P[t0:t1], col = 'blue', type =
    "l",
     ylab = " actual and fitted prices", xlab = "date",lwd =
        2,ylim=c(0.9,5))
```

```
#lines(y = rep(mean(berndt.df$TEXACO[t0:t1], na.rm = T), length(berndt.df$TEXACO[t0:t1])), x =
      berndt.df$date[t0:t1], col = "red")
lines(y = berndt.df$TEXACO_P_FITTED[t0:t1], x = berndt.df$date[t0:t1], col
   = "green",lwd = 2)
legend("topleft", legend = c("TEXACO ACTUAL", "TEXACO FITTED"),
       col = c("blue", "green"), lty = 1)
grid(nx = 6, ny = 7, col = "lightgray", lty = "dotted",
     lwd = par("lwd"), equilogs = TRUE)
#dev.copy2pdf(width = 8.5, out.type = "pdf",file="CAPM.pdf")
#dev.off()
###################
# Optimal Portfolio weights with the CER approach
###################

returns.df=berndt.df[, c(1:9,11:16)]
#returns.df = berndt.df[, c(-10, -17)
exreturns.df=returns.df-berndt.df$RKFREE
returns.mat = as.matrix(exreturns.df)
n.obs = nrow(returns.mat)

#Estimation of CER model parameters
cov.sample=var(returns.mat)
mu = matrix(colMeans(returns.mat), nrow = ncol(returns.mat), ncol = 1)
#
# compute global min variance portfolio
#
w.gmin.sample = solve(var(returns.mat))%*%rep(1,nrow(cov.sample))
w.gmin.sample = w.gmin.sample/sum(w.gmin.sample)
colnames(w.gmin.sample) = "sample"
barplot(t(w.gmin.sample), horiz=F, main="Weights", col="blue", cex.names =
   0.75, las=2)
################################
# A Single index model: the CAPM
################################

##
## use multivariate regression and matrix algebra
##
returnsmkt.df=berndt.df[, c(10:10,17:17)]
#returns.df = berndt.df[, c(-10, -17)
returnsmkt.df$EXRETMKT=returnsmkt.df$MARKET-returnsmkt.df$RKFREE
market.mat = as.matrix(returnsmkt.df[,3, drop=F])
n.obs = nrow(returns.mat)
X.mat = cbind(rep(1,n.obs),market.mat)
colnames(X.mat)[1] = "intercept"
XX.mat = crossprod(X.mat)

# multivariate least squares
G.hat = solve(XX.mat)%*%crossprod(X.mat,returns.mat)
# can also use solve(qr(X.mat), returns.mat)
beta.hat = G.hat[2,]
E.hat = returns.mat - X.mat%*%G.hat
#D.hat=crossprod(E.hat)
diagD.hat = diag(crossprod(E.hat)/(n.obs-2))
# compute R2 values from multivariate regression
sumSquares = apply(returns.mat, 2, function(x) {sum( (x - mean(x))^2 )})
R.square = 1 - (n.obs-2)*diagD.hat/sumSquares

# print and plot results
cbind(beta.hat, diagD.hat, R.square)

par(mfrow=c(1,2))
```

```
barplot(beta.hat, horiz=T, main="Beta values", col="blue", cex.names =
   0.75, las=1)
barplot(R.square, horiz=T, main="R-square values", col="blue", cex.names =
   0.75, las=1)
par(mfrow=c(1,1))

# compute single index model covariance/correlation matrices
cov.si = as.numeric(var(market.mat))*beta.hat%*%t(beta.hat) +
   diag(diagD.hat)
cor.si = cov2cor(cov.si)
#
# COMPARE CORRELATIONS
#
# FACTOR MODEL BASED CORRELATION MATRIX using plotcorr() from ellipse package
#
rownames(cor.si) = colnames(cor.si)
ord <- order(cor.si[1,])
ordered.cor.si <- cor.si[ord, ord]
plotcorr(ordered.cor.si, col=cm.colors(11)[5*ordered.cor.si + 6])
plotcorr(cor.si, col=cm.colors(11)[5*cor.si + 6])
#
# SAMPLE CORRELATION MATRIX
#
cor.sample = cor(returns.mat)
ord <- order(cor.sample[1,])
ordered.cor.sample <- cor.sample[ord, ord]
plotcorr(ordered.cor.sample, col=cm.colors(11)[5*ordered.cor.sample + 6])
plotcorr(cor.sample, col=cm.colors(11)[5*cor.sample + 6])
#
# CAPM residuals  CORRELATION MATRIX
#
cor.resid = cor(E.hat)
ord <- order(cor.resid[1,])
ordered.cor.resid <- cor.resid[ord, ord]
plotcorr(ordered.cor.resid, col=cm.colors(11)[5*ordered.cor.resid + 6])
#
# compute global min variance portfolio
#
# use CAPM covariance (1-factor model)
w.gmin.si = solve(cov.si)%*%rep(1,nrow(cov.si))
w.gmin.si = w.gmin.si/sum(w.gmin.si)
colnames(w.gmin.si) = "single.index"


#par(mfrow=c(2,1))
#barplot(t(w.gmin.si), horiz=F, main="Single Index Weights", col="blue", cex.names = 0.75, las=2)
#barplot(t(w.gmin.sample), horiz=F, main="Sample Weights", col="blue", cex.names = 0.75, las=2)
#par(mfrow=c(1,1))


#compare weights delivered by the two alternative methods
pdf("output.pdf", width = 10, height = 8)
par(mfrow = c(2, 1))
barplot(t(w.gmin.si), horiz=F, main="Single Index Weights", col="blue",
   cex.names = 0.75, las=2)
barplot(t(w.gmin.sample), horiz=F, main="Sample Weights", col="blue",
   cex.names = 0.75, las=2)
par(mfrow = c(1, 1))
dev.off()
```

```
# compare means and sd values on global min variance portfolios
mu.vals = colMeans(returns.mat)
mu.gmin.si = as.numeric(crossprod(w.gmin.si, mu.vals))
sd.gmin.si = as.numeric(sqrt(t(w.gmin.si)%*%cov.si%*%w.gmin.si))
mu.gmin.sample = as.numeric(crossprod(w.gmin.sample, mu.vals))
sd.gmin.sample =
    as.numeric(sqrt(t(w.gmin.sample)%*%var(returns.mat)%*%w.gmin.sample))
cbind(mu.gmin.si,mu.gmin.sample, sd.gmin.si, sd.gmin.sample)


########################################
## AN ALTERNATIVE APPROACH to compute parameters in CAPM:
## use lm function to compute single index model regressions for each asset
########################################

asset.names = colnames(returns.mat)
asset.names

# initialize list object to hold regression objects

reg.list = list()
# loop over all assets and estimate time series regression
for (i in asset.names) {
 reg.df = berndt.df[, c(i, "MARKET")]
 si.formula = as.formula(paste(i,"~", "MARKET", sep=" "))
 reg.list[[i]] = lm(si.formula, data=reg.df)
}

# examine the elements of reg.list  - they are lm objects!
names(reg.list)
class(reg.list$CITCRP)
reg.list$CITCRP
summary(reg.list$CITCRP)

# plot actual vs. fitted over time
# use chart.TimeSeries() function from PerformanceAnalytics package

dataToPlot = cbind(fitted(reg.list$CITCRP), berndt.df$CITCRP)
colnames(dataToPlot) = c("Fitted","Actual")
dev.off()

# Verify the data
str(dataToPlot)
summary(dataToPlot)

# Create the time series chart
chart.TimeSeries(dataToPlot, main = "Single Index Model for CITCRP",
                 colorset = c("black", "blue"), legend.loc = "bottomleft")


# scatterplot of the single index model regression
plot(berndt.df$MARKET, berndt.df$CITCRP, main="SI model for CITCRP",
     type="p", pch=16, col="blue",
     xlab="MARKET", ylab="CITCRP")
abline(h=0, v=0)
abline(reg.list$CITCRP, lwd=2, col="red")

## extract beta values, residual sd's and R2's from list of regression objects
## brute force loop
reg.vals = matrix(0, length(asset.names), 3)
rownames(reg.vals) = asset.names
colnames(reg.vals) = c("beta", "residual.sd", "r.square")
```

```
for (i in names(reg.list)) {
    tmp.fit = reg.list[[i]]
    tmp.summary = summary(tmp.fit)
    reg.vals[i, "beta"] = coef(tmp.fit)[2]
    reg.vals[i, "residual.sd"] = tmp.summary$sigma
    reg.vals[i, "r.square"] = tmp.summary$r.squared
}
reg.vals

# alternatively use R apply function for list objects - lapply or sapply
extractRegVals = function(x) {
# x is an lm object
 beta.val = coef(x)[2]
 residual.sd.val = summary(x)$sigma
 r2.val = summary(x)$r.squared
 ret.vals = c(beta.val, residual.sd.val, r2.val)
 names(ret.vals) = c("beta", "residual.sd", "r.square")
 return(ret.vals)
}
reg.vals = sapply(reg.list, FUN=extractRegVals)
t(reg.vals)
```

6.5 Validating Factor Models

In the previous section, we have seen that a first validation of a factor model can be implemented by exploiting the fact that the diagonality of the variance–covariance matrix of the residuals coming from projecting asset returns on factors is a necessary — and testable — requirement for the validity of any factor model. However, further validation can be based on testing restrictions on the estimated coefficients in any given factor model.

Consider once again the time-series representation of a factor model

$$r_{t+1}^{i} = \alpha_1 + \beta_i^{f^1} f_{t+1}^{1} + \beta_i^{f^2} f_{t+1}^{2} + \cdots + \beta_i^{f^k} f_{t+1}^{k} + v_{t+1} \qquad (6.5)$$

After having estimated N equations for the N assets you have available the following k vectors of coefficients, each of length N:

$\boldsymbol{\beta}^{f1}, \boldsymbol{\beta}^{f2}, \ldots, \boldsymbol{\beta}^{fk}$. Using the sample of t observations on the returns of the N assets you can compute the vector of length N of average sample returns for the assets: $E(\mathbf{r})$.

You can now run the affine expected return-beta cross-sectional regression:

$$E(\mathbf{r}) = \gamma_0 + \gamma_1 \boldsymbol{\beta}_{f1} + \gamma_2 \boldsymbol{\beta}_{f2} + \cdots + \gamma_k \boldsymbol{\beta}_{fk} + \mathbf{u}$$

A two-step test Fama and MacBeth (1973) for the validity of any factor model can be run by considering the following null hypothesis:

$$\hat{\gamma}_0 = \bar{r}^f, \quad \hat{\gamma}_i = E\left(f^i\right)$$

care must be exercised in the test as the variance-covariance matrix of the residuals in the cross-sectional regression will not be diagonal and corrections for heteroscedasticity should be implemented. Note also that, if both test assets and factors are excess returns, the validity of the model can be simply tested by evaluating the null that all intercepts in the time-series model for excess returns are zero. This null is inevitably rejected in the single-factor CAPM model. Two industries have emerged (i) the factors "zoo", that looks for omitted factors (ii) the performance evaluation industry that classifies fund manager performance according to their alphas.

6.5.1 *Which factors?*

Many different set of factors have been considered in the literature:

- Fundamental factors:
  - Fama–French five factors with observable characteristics and estimated betas (MKT, SMB, HML, RMW, CMA and momentum MOM.
  - BARRA factors with known time-invariant betas and unobservable factor realizations estimated by cross-sectional regressions.
- Macroeconomic factors (inflation, growth and uncertainty).
- Statistical factors (for example principal components).

6.6 Factor Models with Predictability

Factor models are commonly used to characterize parsimoniously the predictive distribution of asset returns. Specifically, multi-factor models in which k factors characterize in a lower parametric dimension the distribution of n asset returns, have the following general form:

$$r_{i,t+1} = \alpha_i + \beta_i' \mathbf{f}_{t+1} + v_{i,t+1}, \tag{6.6}$$

$$\mathbf{f}_{t+1} = E\left(\mathbf{f}_{t+1} \mid I_t\right) + \epsilon_{t+1} \quad \text{with } \epsilon_{t+1} \sim \mathcal{D}\left(\mathbf{0}, \boldsymbol{\Sigma}\right) \tag{6.7}$$

where $\text{Cov}(v_{i,t+1}, v_{j,t+1}) = 0$ for $i \neq j$, $\mathbf{f}_{t+1}$ is a k-dimensional vector of factors at time $t+1$, $r_{i,t+1}$ is the return on the ith of the n assets at time $t+1$, and the vector β_i' contains the loadings for asset i on the k factors. Equation (6.6) specifies the conditional distribution of returns on factors, while Eq. (6.7) specifies the predictive distribution for factors at time $t+1$ conditioning on information available at time t. A baseline specification for this system assumes away factors predictability thus implying that conditional expectations of factors have no variance (i.e., $E(\mathbf{f}_{t+1} \mid I_t) = \mu$).

In Eq. (6.6) it is often assumed without further qualification that returns and factors are stationary variables. The model, however, leaves prices undetermined: the long-run forecast for asset prices is independent from the long-run forecast of factors. A factor model that leaves asset prices undetermined does not exploit information in the data that can be used for (i) factor selection, and (ii) asset allocation.

Consider an asset i and denote its log one-period return by $r_{i,t}$. We define the log price of this asset as

$$\ln P_{i,t} = \ln P_{i,t-1} + \mathbf{r}_{i,t} \tag{6.8}$$

i.e., prices of any asset are cumulative returns. The analogous of the (log) price for an asset can be constructed for any given factor. We define as factor (log) price the cumulative returns of a portfolio investing in standard factors (e.g., the aggregate market return). The generic prices associated to factors with a log period returns of $\mathbf{f}_t$ evolve according to the following process:

$$\ln \mathbf{F}_t = \ln \mathbf{F}_{t-1} + \mathbf{f}_t \tag{6.9}$$

If returns to test assets and factors are stationary, then portfolio prices and factor-prices are non-stationary. In fact, imagine simulating data using the model given by Eqs. (6.6)–(6.9). The simulated data will deliver a linear relationship between returns and factors but no relationship between asset prices and factor prices. Asset prices and factor prices will follow two *unrelated* stochastic trends. In technical jargon, the model given by (6.6)–(6.9) rules out the hypothesis of the existence of a long-run relation (cointegration) between asset prices and factor prices by assumption. The presence of co-integration which is, at least in some cases, borne out by the data it is not tested for, nor it is reflected in the factor model specification when appropriate. This has two implications. First, in the absence of cointegration, the opportunity of discarding factor models that do not explain the long-run trends in prices is not exploited. Second, in the presence of cointegration, its implications for portfolio returns predictability are left unexplored.

In fact, if factor prices are the non-stationary variables that drive the non-stationary dynamics of portfolio prices, then a linear combination of prices and risk drivers should be stationary, i.e., asset and factor prices should be cointegrated.

Consider the following model describing the exposure of a given portfolio price $P_{i,t}$ to factor prices $\mathbf{F}_t$:

$$\ln P_{i,t} = \alpha_{0,i} + \alpha_{1,i}t + \beta_i' \ln \mathbf{F}_t + u_{i,t}$$

The estimation of such regression delivers stationary residuals $u_{i,t}$ anytime the chosen set of factor prices captures the stochastic trend that determines the long-run dynamics of prices. In this case, the linear combination of the right-hand side variables of the equation defines the long-run equilibrium value determined by the factor prices and $u_{i,t}$ captures temporary deviations of asset prices from it. Thus, it is natural to refer to the residuals $u_{i,t}$ as the "equilibrium correction term" (ECT) associated with asset i at time t. Formally, we define the residual from the long-run cointegrating relationship as

$$\text{ECT}_{i,t} \equiv \ln P_{i,t} - \hat{\alpha}_{0,i} - \hat{\alpha}_{1,i}t - \hat{\beta}_i' \ln \mathbf{F}_t \tag{6.10}$$

For expository purposes, it is useful to specify the error term $u_{i,t}$ as an AR(1) process. In sum, we model the joint distribution of asset prices, factor prices, asset returns and factors as follows:

$$\begin{aligned}
\ln P_{i,t+1} &= \alpha_{0,i} + \alpha_{1,i}t + \beta_i' \ln \mathbf{F}_{t+1} + u_{i,t+1} \qquad (6.11)\\
u_{i,t+1} &= \rho_i u_{i,t} + v_{i,t+1}\\
\mathbf{f}_{t+1} &= E\left(\mathbf{f}_{t+1} \mid I_t\right) + \epsilon_{t+1}\\
\ln P_{i,t} &= \ln P_{i,t-1} + r_{i,t}\\
\ln \mathbf{F}_t &= \ln \mathbf{F}_{t-1} + \mathbf{f}_t
\end{aligned}$$

where $\epsilon_{t+1} \sim \mathcal{D}(\mathbf{0}, \mathbf{\Sigma})$, $u_{i,t+1}$ and $v_{i,t+1}$ have zero mean and variance $\sigma^2_{u,i}$ and $\sigma^2_{v,i}$, respectively, and $\text{Cov}\left(v_{i,t+1}, v_{j,t+1}\right) = 0$ for $i \neq j$.

By taking first differences of our model in (6.11) we obtain a novel specification for returns and factors, where asset returns relate to factors *plus* the ECT:

$$r_{i,t+1} = \alpha_{1,i} + \beta_i' \mathbf{f}_{t+1} + \underbrace{(\rho_i - 1)}_{\delta_i} \underbrace{u_{i,t}}_{\equiv \mathrm{ECT}_{i,t}} + v_{i,t+1} \tag{6.12}$$

Equation (6.12) represents the factor error correction model (FECM).[1]

Two comments are in order. First, we include a linear trend in Eq. (6.11) since it allows us to recover the standard short-run specification — returns are regressed on factors plus a constant — when taking first-differences. In other words, a positive α_1 in the long-run relation (6.11) generates "alpha" in returns.[2]

Second, when $\mathrm{ECT}_{i,t}$ is stationary, then asset and factor prices are cointegrated. The stationarity of $\mathrm{ECT}_{i,t}$ implies that, in the relation (6.12) linking returns to factors, this term appears with a coefficient δ_i capturing the speed with which the system eliminates disequilibria with respect to the long-run relationship. Indeed, δ_i is related to the persistence ρ_i of $\mathrm{ECT}_{i,t}$, see Eq. (6.12).

When factor prices explain the buy-and-hold value of a portfolio, cointegration implies that portfolio returns respond to the ECT so far omitted in the empirical asset pricing literature. The inclusion of the ECT ensures that the specification for returns is consistent with the long-run relationship between asset and factor prices. The omission of the ECT leads to a misspecification of the factor model, in the sense that the factor model leaves price dynamics undetermined.

Interestingly, a traditional factor model would not be affected by omitting the disequilibrium term only if factor prices and asset prices are not cointegrated (i.e., when $\mid \rho_i \mid = 1$). However, this restriction also implies that a given factor model is unable to price the buy-and-hold portfolios since asset prices do not track factor prices in the long-run. The significance of the ECM terms generates

[1] The equilibrium correction representation (6.12) of cointegrated time-series (see the system of equations in (6.11)) is warranted by the Engle and Granger (1987) representation theorem.

[2] Moreover, as discussed by Engle and Yoo (1987) and MacKinnon (2010), the inclusion of a trend is a simple way to avoid the dependence of the distribution of test statistics for residuals on α_1.

predictability that is relevant for computing optimal portfolio weights. The standard cross-sectional representation of 1-period ahead returns becomes now

$$\underset{(Nx1)}{\mathbf{r}_{t,t+1}} = \underset{(Nx1)}{\alpha} + \underset{(NxK)}{B}\underset{(Kx1)}{\mathbf{f}_{t,t+1}} + \underset{(NxN)}{\Gamma}\underset{(Nx1)}{\mathbf{u}_t} + \underset{(Nx1)}{\mathbf{v}_t} \tag{6.13}$$

$$\underset{(Kx1)}{\mathbf{f}_{t,t+1}} = \underset{(Kx1)}{\mu^f} + \underset{(KxK)}{\mathbf{H}^f}\underset{(Kx1)}{\epsilon^f}$$

$$\Sigma^v = \begin{bmatrix} \sigma_1 & 0 & 0 & 0 \\ 0 & \sigma_2 & 0 & 0 \\ .. & .. & .. & .. \\ 0 & 0 & 0 & \sigma_n \end{bmatrix}$$

$$\Sigma^f = \mathbf{H}^f\mathbf{H}^{f\prime}.$$

Predictability emerges as the conditional expectations of one-period ahead expected returns is time varying, the relevant conditional variance–covariance matrix of predicted asset returns also changes as the variance of the one-period ahead predictive error is different for the variance of asset returns. In fact, we have

$$\underset{(Nx1)}{E}\,\mathbf{r}_{t,t+1} = \underset{(Nx1)}{\alpha} + \underset{(NxK)}{B}\underset{(Kx1)}{\mu^f} + \underset{(NxN)}{\Gamma}\underset{(Nx1)}{\mathbf{u}_t} \tag{6.14}$$

$$\underset{(NxN)}{\Sigma}{}^{r} = \underset{(NxK)}{B}\underset{(KxK)}{\Sigma}{}^{f}\underset{(KxN)}{B'} + \underset{(NxN)}{\Sigma}{}^{v}$$

where Γ is a diagonal matrix when asset returns depend exclusively on their own price disequilibria. The analysis of the long-run (cointegrating) relationship between asset prices and factor prices provides an opportunity to validate factor models that is left unexploited by the standard factor model specification in Eqs. (6.6)–(6.7). Furthermore, looking at the short-run FECM specification in (6.12), the omission of the ECT omits a source of predictability of the conditional distribution of test assets returns that has relevant consequences for asset allocation and risk management. For example, consider the situation in which the portfolio price is aligned with the long-run value determined by the risk drivers, and assume a negative shock (to price) occurs. The returns predictive distribution based on the ECT is then shifted to the right. This shift represents an opportunity to be exploited for asset allocation and relevant information for risk measurement.

6.6.1 *An illustration with R*

The following R code considers the assets in the previous asset allocation example runs the long runs regressions of asset prices and factor prices and concentrates on a case study on TEXACO to show the relevance of predictability and illustrate how the CAPM can be modified to derive a factor model with returns predictability

---

```

# The effect of omitting long-run trends from factor models

rm(list=ls()) #Removes all items in Environment!
#setwd(path)
setwd(dirname(rstudioapi::getActiveDocumentContext()$path))

# set output options
options(width = 70, digits=4)
listofpackages <- c("dygraphs",
    "dplyr","ellipse","reshape2","ggplot2","PerformanceAnalytics ","zoo")

for (j in listofpackages){
  if(sum(installed.packages()[, 1] == j) == 0) {
    install.packages(j)
  }
  library(j, character.only = T)
}
install.packages("fEcofin", repos="http://R-Forge.R-project.org")

# load required packages
library(fEcofin)              # various data sets

########################
# Data Loadings and Transform Descriptive Analysis
########################

# create data frame with dates as rownames
berndt.df = berndtInvest[, -1]
berndt.df$date <- as.Date(berndtInvest[, 1])
rownames(berndt.df) = as.character(berndtInvest[, 1])
colnames(berndt.df)
dimnames(berndt.df)[[2]] #command alternative to the previous one

# transform the data and compute cumulative returns

t0 <- which(berndt.df$date == "1978-01-01")
t1 <- which(berndt.df$date == "1987-12-01")

series_names <-
    c("CITCRP","CONED","CONTIL","DATGEN","DEC","DELTA","GENMIL","GERBER",
"IBM","MARKET","MOBIL","PANAM","PSNH","TANDY","TEXACO","WEYER","RKFREE")

for (name in series_names) {
  P_col_name <- paste0(name,"_P")
  LP_col_name<- paste0("L",P_col_name)
```

```
  berndt.df[t0, P_col_name] <- 1
  for (i in (t0+1):(t1)) {
    berndt.df[i, P_col_name][[1]] <- berndt.df[i-1, P_col_name][[1]] *
        (1+berndt.df[i, name][[1]] )
  }
  berndt.df[, LP_col_name] <- log(berndt.df[, P_col_name])
}
# add a trend to the database
berndt.df$TREND<- array(data = NA, dim = nrow(berndt.df))
berndt.df[t0, c("TREND")] <- 1 # don't need to repeat the value to make the array being assigned be of the same length. be careful though as it is one of the few cases of exception
for (i in (t0+1):(t1)) {
  berndt.df[i, "TREND"][[1]] <- berndt.df[i-1, "TREND"][[1]] +1
}

#########################
# Descriptive Analysis
#########################
ggplot(berndt.df, aes(x = date)) +
  geom_line(aes(y = LTEXACO_P, color = "TEXACO"), size = 1, linetype =
    "solid") +
  geom_line(aes(y = LMARKET_P, color = "MARKET"), size = 1, linetype =
    "solid") +
  labs(x = "Date", y = "Portfolios TEXACO and MKT") +
  ylim(-0.5, 2) +
  theme_minimal() +
  theme(
    legend.position = c(0.15, 0.95),  # Set the legend position (top-left)
    legend.title = element_blank(),
    legend.text = element_text(size = 8),
    axis.text = element_text(size = 8),
    axis.title = element_text(size = 10),
    plot.title = element_text(size = 12, hjust = 0.5)
  ) +
  scale_color_manual(
    values = c("blue", "green"),
    labels = c("TEXACO", "MARKET")
  )


# plot returns
ggplot(berndt.df, aes(x = date)) +
  geom_line(aes(y = TEXACO, color = "TEXACO"), size = 1, linetype =
    "solid") +
  geom_line(aes(y = MARKET, color = "MARKET"), size = 1, linetype =
    "solid") +
  labs(x = "Date", y = "Returns TEXACO and MKT") +
  ylim(-0.45, 0.45) +
  theme_minimal() +
  theme(
    legend.position = c(0.15, 0.95),  # Set the legend position (top-left)
    legend.title = element_blank(),
    legend.text = element_text(size = 8),
    axis.text = element_text(size = 8),
    axis.title = element_text(size = 8),
    plot.title = element_text(size = 12, hjust = 0.5)
  ) +
  scale_color_manual(
    values = c("blue", "green"),
    labels = c("TEXACO", "MARKET")
  )
```

```
###############################
# Standard CAPM Factor Models
###############################

## use lm function to compute single index model regressions for each asset
##
returns.mat = as.matrix(berndt.df[, c(1:9,11:16)])
asset.names = colnames(returns.mat)
asset.names

# initialize list object to hold regression objects

reg.list = list()
# loop over all assets and estimate time series regression
for (i in asset.names) {
 reg.df = berndt.df[, c(i, "MARKET")]
 si.formula = as.formula(paste(i,"~", "MARKET", sep=" "))
 reg.list[[i]] = lm(si.formula, data=reg.df)
}

# examine the elements of reg.list  - they are lm objects!
names(reg.list)
class(reg.list$TEXACO)
reg.list$TEXACO
summary(reg.list$TEXACO)

# plot actual vs. fitted over time
# use chart.TimeSeries() function from PerformanceAnalytics package
dataToPlot = cbind(fitted(reg.list$TEXACO), berndt.df$TEXACO)
colnames(dataToPlot) = c("Fitted","Actual")
chart.TimeSeries(dataToPlot, main="Single Index Model for TEXACO",
                 colorset=c("black","blue"), legend.loc="bottomleft")

# scatterplot of the single index model regression
plot(berndt.df$MARKET, berndt.df$TEXACO, main="SI model for CITCRP",
     type="p", pch=16, col="blue",
     xlab="MARKET", ylab="TEXACO")
abline(h=0, v=0)
abline(reg.list$TEXACO, lwd=2, col="red")

## extract beta values, residual sd's and R2's from list of regression objects

reg.vals = matrix(0, length(asset.names), 3)
rownames(reg.vals) = asset.names
colnames(reg.vals) = c("beta", "residual.sd", "r.square")
for (i in names(reg.list)) {
    tmp.fit = reg.list[[i]]
    tmp.summary = summary(tmp.fit)
    reg.vals[i, "beta"] = coef(tmp.fit)[2]
    reg.vals[i, "residual.sd"] = tmp.summary$sigma
    reg.vals[i, "r.square"] = tmp.summary$r.squared
}
reg.vals

# print regression results

par(mfrow=c(1,2))
barplot(reg.vals[,1], horiz=T, main="Beta values", col="blue", cex.names =
   0.75, las=1)
barplot(reg.vals[,3], horiz=T, main="R-square values", col="blue",
   cex.names = 0.75, las=1)
par(mfrow=c(1,1))
```

```
########################
# CAPM in levels
########################

## use lm function to compute single index model regressions for each asset
##
selected_columns <-
    c("LCITCRP_P","LCONED_P","LCONTIL_P","LDATGEN_P","LDEC_P","LDELTA_P","LGENMIL_P",
"LGERBER_P","LIBM_P","LMOBIL_P","LPANAM_P","LPSNH_P","LTANDY_P","LTEXACO_P","LWEYER_P")

# Extract the specified columns and store them in a matrix
lprices.mat <- as.matrix(berndt.df[, selected_columns])

asset.names = colnames(lprices.mat)
asset.names

# initialize list object to hold regression objects

reg1.list = list()
# loop over all assets and estimate time series regression
for (i in asset.names) {
  #reg.df = berndt.df[, c(i, "LMARKET_P")]
  si.formula = as.formula(paste(i,"~", "LMARKET_P+TREND", sep=" "))
  reg1.list[[i]] = lm(si.formula, data=berndt.df)
}

# examine the elements of reg.list  - they are lm objects!
names(reg1.list)
class(reg1.list$LTEXACO_P)
reg1.list$LTEXACO_P
summary(reg1.list$LTEXACO_P)

# plot actual vs. fitted over time
# use chart.TimeSeries() function from PerformanceAnalytics package
dataToPlot = cbind(fitted(reg1.list$LTEXACO_P), berndt.df$LTEXACO_P)
colnames(dataToPlot) = c("Fitted","Actual")
chart.TimeSeries(dataToPlot, main="Single Index Model for price TEXACO",
                 colorset=c("black","blue"), legend.loc="bottomleft")

# scatterplot of the single index model regression
plot(berndt.df$LMARKET_P, berndt.df$LTEXACO_P, main="SI model for
   LTEXACO_P",
     type="p", pch=16, col="blue",
     xlab="MARKET", ylab="TEXACO")
abline(h=0, v=0)
abline(reg.list$TEXACO, lwd=2, col="red")

## extract beta values, residual sd's and R2's from list of regression objects

reg.vals1 = matrix(0, length(asset.names), 3)
rownames(reg.vals1) = asset.names
colnames(reg.vals1) = c("beta", "residual.sd", "r.square")
for (i in names(reg1.list)) {
  tmp.fit = reg1.list[[i]]
  tmp.summary = summary(tmp.fit)
  reg.vals1[i, "beta"] = coef(tmp.fit)[2]
  reg.vals1[i, "residual.sd"] = tmp.summary$sigma
  reg.vals1[i, "r.square"] = tmp.summary$r.squared
}
reg.vals1
```

```
# print regression results

par(mfrow=c(1,2))
barplot(reg.vals1[,1], horiz=T, main="Beta values", col="blue", cex.names =
   0.75, las=1)
barplot(reg.vals1[,3], horiz=T, main="R-square values", col="blue",
   cex.names = 0.75, las=1)
par(mfrow=c(1,1))

########################################
# a Single Factor Model with Predictability : an illustration with TEXACO
#######################################

#Log Level linear model between LCITCRP_P TREND an MARKET
model_TEXACO_P=lm(berndt.df$LTEXACO_P ~ berndt.df$LMARKET_P+berndt.df$TREND)
summary(model_TEXACO_P)

ggplot(berndt.df, aes(x = date)) +
  geom_line(aes(y = LTEXACO_P, color = "TEXACO"), size = 1, linetype =
     "solid") +
  geom_line(aes(y = fitted(model_TEXACO_P), color = "Fitted"), size = 1,
     linetype = "solid") +
  labs(x = "Date", y = "Actual and Fitted") +
  ylim(-0.5, 2) +
  theme_minimal() +
  theme(
    legend.position = c(0.15, 0.95),  # Set the legend position (top-left)
    legend.title = element_blank(),
    legend.text = element_text(size = 8),
    axis.text = element_text(size = 8),
    axis.title = element_text(size = 10),
    plot.title = element_text(size = 12, hjust = 0.5)
  ) +
  scale_color_manual(
    values = c("blue", "green"),
    labels = c("TEXACO", "Fitted")
  )


#store log level residuals as u and test for their stationarity
u_TEXACO=as.matrix(model_TEXACO_P$residuals)
DuTEXACO=diff(u_TEXACO,lag=1)
model_DuTEXACO=lm(DuTEXACO ~  u_TEXACO[1:(nrow(u_TEXACO)-1)]-1)
summary(model_DuTEXACO)
D12uTEXACO=diff(u_TEXACO,lag=12)
model_D12uTEXACO=lm(D12uTEXACO ~  u_TEXACO[1:(nrow(u_TEXACO)-12)]-1)
summary(model_D12uTEXACO)
##############################

#Compute Log Returns for 1M ahead timespan (1 months)
logret1M_TEXACO=diff(berndt.df$LTEXACO_P,lag=1)
logret1M_MARKET=diff(berndt.df$LMARKET_P,lag=1)

#Compute Log Returns for 1Y ahead timespan (12 months)
logret1Y_TEXACO=diff(berndt.df$LTEXACO_P,lag=12)
logret1Y_MARKET=diff(berndt.df$LMARKET_P,lag=12)

#############################

#model the regression on log returns appending the u residuals as another variable
model_d_TEXACO_1M=lm(logret1M_TEXACO ~
    logret1M_MARKET+u_TEXACO[1:(nrow(u_TEXACO)-1)])
```

```
summary(model_d_TEXACO_1M)

model_d_TEXACO_1Y=lm(logret1Y_TEXACO ~
    logret1Y_MARKET+u_TEXACO[1:(nrow(u_TEXACO)-12)])
summary(model_d_TEXACO_1Y)

model_d_TEXACO_1Y_CAPM=lm(logret1Y_TEXACO ~ logret1Y_MARKET)
summary(model_d_TEXACO_1Y_CAPM)
```

Chapter 7

Models for Risk Measurement

7.1 Risk Measurement

Once the portfolio weights ($\hat{\mathbf{w}}$) are chosen, possibly exploiting the predictability of the distribution of the relevant future returns, the distribution of portfolio returns can be described as follows:

$$R^p \sim \mathcal{D}\left(\mu_p, \sigma_p^2\right)$$
$$\mu_p = \mu'\hat{\mathbf{w}} \qquad \sigma_p^2 = \hat{\mathbf{w}}'\mathbf{\Sigma}\hat{\mathbf{w}}$$

Having solved the portfolio problem and having committed to a given allocation described by $\hat{\mathbf{w}}$, there is a further role that econometrics can play: measuring portfolio risk Christoffersen (2011). Note that even if portfolio weights can be decided at a low frequency with a horizon of one or more years, the risk management is run at a high frequency. Hence, what matters for risk measurement is the predictive distribution of returns at high frequencies. The question "What is the risk of my portfolio tomorrow?" is relevant even if the portfolio is built with a 10-year perspective.

7.1.1 *Value at risk (VaR)*

A natural measure of risk is Value at Risk (VaR). The VaR is the percentage loss obtained with a probability at most of α percent:

$$\Pr\left(R_{t+1}^p < -\mathrm{VaR}_\alpha\right) = \alpha$$

VaR depends on the predictive distribution of returns at high frequency, once α is chosen, VaR_α is defined by the predictive distribution of returns.

7.2 VaR without Predictability

We start our discussion of risk measurement by illustrating how the standard models used so far, which imply no predictability for the distribution of returns, can be used to compute VaR.

7.2.1 *VaR with the CER*

Applying the CER model to the univariate distribution of portfolio returns, we have

$$\begin{aligned} \mathbf{r}_{t,t+1}^P &= \mu + \sigma\epsilon_{t+1} \\ \epsilon_{t+1} &\sim \mathcal{D}(0,1) \end{aligned}$$

Given some estimates of the unknown parameters in the model (μ σ in our case), the distribution of returns at $t+1$ (say tomorrow) can be simulated either by specifying a parametric distribution of $\hat{\epsilon}_{t+1}$ and resampling from it (Monte-Carlo), or by re-sampling from the estimated residuals of the model (Bootstrap). In both cases an artificial sample for $\hat{\epsilon}_{t+1}$ of the desired length can be generated. Simulated residuals are then mapped into simulated returns via the model's parameters. This exercise can be replicated N times to construct the distribution of model-predicted returns. Once the distribution is derived, then VaR is available.

7.2.2 *VaR with the CAPM*

Factor models can also be simulated to derive VaR. Suppose you are invested in a specific portfolio and apply the CAPM to derive the distribution of its future returns

$$\begin{aligned} R_{t+1}^{Port} &= \gamma_0 + \gamma_1 R_{t+1}^{Mkt} + \sigma^{Port} v_{1,t+1} \\ R_{t+1}^{Mkt} &= \mu + \sigma^{Mkt} z_{t+1} \\ v_{i,t+1} &\sim \text{IID } \mathcal{N}(0,1) \\ z_{t+1} &\sim \text{IID } \mathcal{N}(0,1) \end{aligned}$$

After parameter estimation, get residuals for a training sample. Then, at each point in time generate an artificial sample for the residuals. The model has two residuals: the common risk component and the idiosyncratic risk component. By their nature these two residuals can be simulated independently, drawing them independently from their marginal distribution rather than drawing them simultaneously from their joint distribution. Simulated residuals can then be mapped into simulated returns via the model, to construct the distribution of model-predicted returns and derive the VaR for the portfolio. Note that both in the case of the VaR with CER and the VaR with CAPM the absence of predictability will imply that the VaR is constant over time. A model with no predictability rules out variability and/or persistence in the VaR measures.

7.3 The Evidence from High-Frequency Data

Figure 7.1 illustrated the behavior of one-day linear and squared returns for the SP500. High-frequency data show:

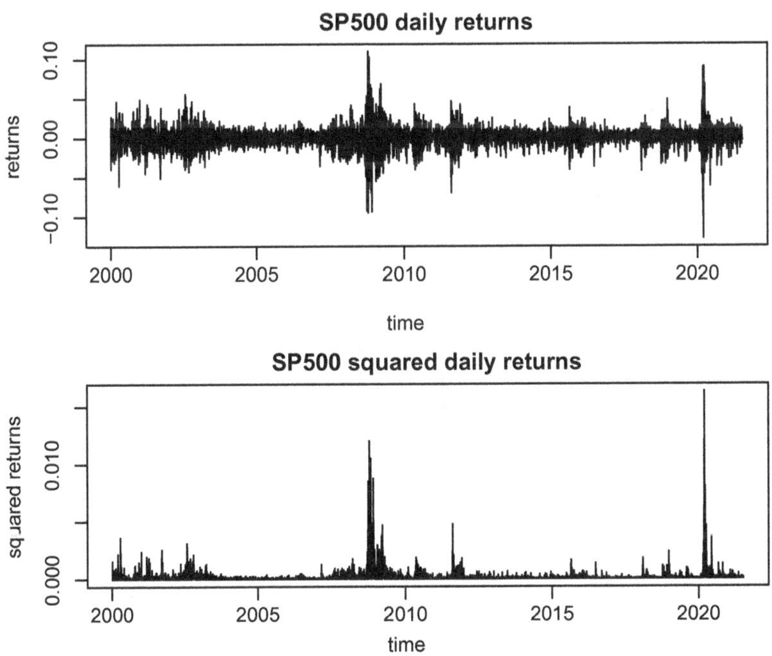

Figure 7.1. Daily SP500 returns and squared returns.

- very little or no persistence in the first moments,
- persistence in the variance,
- non-normality,
- volatility "clusters" in time: high (low) volatility tends to be followed by high (low) volatility.

These data features can be used to build appropriate models with predictability in the distribution of future returns driven by the predictability in the second moments and use them to construct time-varying measures of VaR.

7.4 A General Model for High-Frequency Data

The data at high frequency suggest a different modeling framework from the standard models with no-predictability:

$$\begin{aligned} R_{t+1} &= \sigma_{t+1} u_{t+1} \\ \sigma_{t+1}^2 &= f(\mathcal{I}_t) \qquad u_{t+1} \sim \text{IID } \mathcal{D}(0,1) \end{aligned}$$

The following features of the model are noteworthy:

(1) The distribution of returns is centered around a mean of zero, and the zero mean model dominates any alternative model based on predictors.
(2) The variance is time-varying and predictable, given the information set, $\mathcal{I}_t$, available at time t.
(3) The distribution of returns at high frequency is not normal, i.e., $\mathcal{D}(0,1)$ may often differ from $\mathcal{N}(0,1)$.

7.4.1 *GARCH models for heteroscedasticity*

Generalizing the seminal contribution of modeling time-varying volatility by Engle (1982), Bollerslev (1986) proposed a parsimonious model capable of capturing all the features of high-frequency returns:

$$\begin{aligned} R_{t+1} &= \mu_t + \sigma_{t+1} z_{t+1} \quad z_{t+1} \sim \text{IID } \mathcal{N}(0,1) \\ \sigma_{t+1}^2 &= \omega + \alpha \left(R_t - \mu_t\right)^2 + \beta \sigma_t^2 \\ \alpha + \beta &< 1 \end{aligned}$$

where returns have a constant mean (that is usually zero) and a time-varying GARCH(1,1) structure.

In a model like this the innovation $\epsilon_t \equiv \sigma_t z_t$ has zero mean and is serially uncorrelated at all lags $j \geqslant 1$. Where μ_t is often, but not necessarily, set to 0.

7.4.2 *GARCH properties*

R_{t+1} has a finite unconditional long-run variance of $\frac{\omega}{1-\alpha-\beta}$

$$\begin{aligned}\sigma^2 = E\left(\sigma_{t+1}^2\right) &= \omega + \alpha E\left(R_t - \mu\right)^2 + \beta\sigma^2 \\ &= \omega + \alpha\sigma^2 + \beta\sigma^2 \\ &= \frac{\omega}{1-\alpha-\beta}\end{aligned}$$

Substituting ω out of the GARCH expression:

$$\begin{aligned}\sigma_{t+1}^2 &= \left(1-\alpha-\beta\right)\sigma^2 + \alpha R_t^2 + \beta\sigma_t^2 \\ &= \sigma^2 + \alpha\left(\left(R_t-\mu\right)^2 - \sigma^2\right) + \beta\left(\sigma_t^2 - \sigma^2\right)\end{aligned}$$

which illustrates the relation between predicted variance and long-run variance in a GARCH model.

7.4.3 *GARCH forecasting*

$$\begin{aligned}\sigma_{t+1|t}^2 &= \sigma^2 + \alpha\left[\left(R_t-\mu_t\right)^2 - \sigma^2\right] + \beta\left(\sigma_t^2 - \bar{\sigma}^2\right) \\ \sigma_{t+2|t}^2 &= \sigma^2 + \left(\alpha+\beta\right)\sigma_{t+1|t}^2 \\ \sigma_{t+n+1|t}^2 &= \sigma^2 + \left(\alpha+\beta\right)^n\sigma_{t+1|t}^2\end{aligned}$$

7.4.4 *Testing for GARCH*

The presence of a (G)ARCH in returns/disturbances can be tested via the Lagrange multiplier test proposed by Engle (1982) the test is implemented in the following two steps: First, use simple OLS to estimate the most appropriate regression equation or ARMA model on asset returns and let $\{\hat{z}_t^2\}$ denote the squares of the standardized returns (residuals), for instance, coming from a homoskedastic model, $\hat{z}_t^2 = R_t^2/\hat{\sigma}^2$; Second, regress these squared residuals on a constant and on q lagged values $\hat{z}_{t-1}^2, \hat{z}_{t+2}^2, \ldots, \hat{z}_{t-q}^2$ (e_t is a white noise shock):

$$\hat{z}_t^2 = \xi_0 + \xi_1 \hat{z}_{t-1}^2 + \xi_2 \hat{z}_{t-2}^2 + \cdots + \xi_q \hat{z}_{t-q}^2 + e_t$$

If there are no ARCH effects, the estimated values of ξ_1 through ξ_q should be zero, $\xi_1 = \xi_2 = \cdots = \xi_q$.

7.5 Estimation of GARCH Models

Standard OLS estimation cannot be applied to GARCH models as σ_{t+1} is not observed. Maximum likelihood methods are necessary in this case. These methods are promptly available in R and we shall describe their working in a simple case. Think of the following Data Generating Process for returns

$$\begin{aligned}
R_{t+1} &= \sigma_{t+1} z_{t+1} \quad z_{t+1} \sim \text{IID } \mathcal{N}(0,1) \\
\sigma_{t+1}^2 &= \omega + \alpha R_t^2 + \beta \sigma_t^2 \\
\alpha + \beta &< 1
\end{aligned}$$

The assumption of IID normal shocks (z_t), implies (from normality and identical distribution of z_{t+1}) that the density of the time t observation is

$$l_t \equiv \Pr(R_t; \boldsymbol{\theta}) = \frac{1}{\sigma_t(\boldsymbol{\theta})\sqrt{2\pi}} \exp\left(-\frac{1}{2}\frac{R_t^2}{\sigma_t^2(\boldsymbol{\theta})}\right)$$

where the notation $\sigma_t^2(\boldsymbol{\theta})$ emphasizes that conditional variance depends on $\boldsymbol{\theta} \in \Theta$, $\boldsymbol{\theta} = (\alpha, \beta, \omega)$.

Because each shock is independent of the others (from independence over time of z_{t+1}), the total probability density function (PDF) of the entire sample is then the product of T such densities:

$$L(R_1, R_2, \ldots, R_T; \boldsymbol{\theta}) \equiv \prod_{t=1}^{T} l_t = \prod_{t=1}^{T} \frac{1}{\sigma_t(\boldsymbol{\theta})\sqrt{2\pi}} \exp\left(-\frac{1}{2}\frac{R_t^2}{\sigma_t^2(\boldsymbol{\theta})}\right)$$

taking logs

$$\mathcal{L}(R_1, R_2, \ldots, R_T; \boldsymbol{\theta}) = -\frac{T}{2}\log 2\pi - \frac{1}{2}\sum_{t=1}^{T} \log \sigma_t^2(\boldsymbol{\theta}) - \frac{1}{2}\sum_{t=1}^{T} \frac{R_t^2}{\sigma_t^2(\boldsymbol{\theta})}$$

Substituting an expression for $\sigma_t^2(\boldsymbol{\theta})$ (given by the chosen GARCH specification) given the observations on the returns and given an initial observation for variance

$$\mathcal{L}(R_1, R_2, \ldots, R_T; \boldsymbol{\theta}) = -\frac{T}{2}\log 2\pi - \frac{1}{2}\sum_{t=1}^{T}\log\left[\omega + \alpha R_{t-1}^2 + \beta\sigma_{t-1}^2\right]$$
$$-\frac{1}{2}\sum_{t=1}^{T}\frac{R_t^2}{\omega + \alpha R_{t-1}^2 + \beta\sigma_{t-1}^2}$$
$$\sigma_0^2 = \frac{\omega}{1-\alpha-\beta}$$

maximizing the log-likelihood to select the unknown parameters will deliver the MLE, denoted as $\hat{\boldsymbol{\theta}}_T^{ML}$.

7.5.1 *Quasi MLE estimation*

The QMLE result says that we can still use MLE estimation *based on normality assumptions* even when the shocks are not normally distributed, if our choices of conditional mean and variance functions are defendable, at least in empirical terms (i.e. conditional mean and conditional variance are correctly specified). However, because the maintained model still has that $R_{t+1} = \sigma_{t+1}z_{t+1}$ with $z_{t+1} \sim$ IID $\mathcal{D}(0,1)$, the shocks will have to be anyway IID: you can just do without normality, but the convenience of $z_{t+1} \sim$ IID $\mathcal{D}(0,1)$ To illustrate QMLE consider the following example.

Because we know that the long-run (ergodic) variance from a GARCH(1,1) is $\bar{\sigma}^2 = \omega/(1-\alpha-\beta)$, instead of jointly estimating ω, α, and β, you simply set

$$\tilde{\omega} = (1-\alpha-\beta)\left[\frac{1}{T}\sum_{t=1}^{T}R_t^2\right]$$

for whatever values of α and β. Note that (i) you impose the long-run variance estimate on the GARCH model directly and avoid that the model may yield nonsensical estimates; (ii) you have reduced the number of parameters to be estimated in the model by one. These benefits must be carefully contrasted with the well-known costs, the loss of efficiency caused by QMLE.

7.6 From GARCH to VaR

After estimation a GARCH model can be simulated using bootstrap or Monte-Carlo to derive the distribution of returns and the relevant VaR

$$
\begin{aligned}
R_{t+1} &= \mu + \sigma_{t+1} z_{t+1} \quad z_{t+1} \sim \text{IID } \mathcal{N}(0,1) \\
\sigma_{t+1}^2 &= \omega + \alpha \left(R_t - \mu_t\right)^2 + \beta \sigma_t^2 \\
\alpha + \beta &< 1
\end{aligned}
$$

Given estimation, derive $\hat{z}_t = \frac{R_t}{\hat{\sigma}_t}$. At time t you can now predict σ_{t+1}^2 and the distribution of R_{t+1} can now be simulated via the preferred method.

Recursion can then be applied to derive the distribution of R_{t+n} with $n > 1$.

7.6.1 *GARCH with factors*

Think of modeling the returns of many assets at a high frequency with a (single) factor model

$$
\begin{aligned}
R_{t+1}^i &= \gamma_0 + \gamma_1 f_{t+1} + \sigma^i v_{i,t+1} \\
f_{t+1} &= \mu_t + \sigma_{t+1} z_{t+1} \\
\sigma_{t+1}^2 &= \omega + \alpha \left(R_t - \mu_t\right)^2 + \beta \sigma_t^2 \\
v_{i,t+1} &\sim \text{IID } \mathcal{N}(0,1), \\
z_{t+1} &\sim \text{IID } \mathcal{N}(0,1), \\
\alpha + \beta &< 1
\end{aligned}
$$

one GARCH estimation will allow to model many returns distribution. Again factor models allow parsimonious parameterization.

7.7 Measuring Risk: An Illustration with R

The following programme illustrates how to construct VaR in models with and without predictability. A data set on monthly returns on the Dow Jones index and Bank of America is extracted to estimate the model for a training sample up to December 2005 and the to compute one-step ahead Var over the period 2006:1 2015:1. The Var is computed using the CAPM model with a CER for the market and the CAPM model with a GARCH for the market. While the first measure of risk is constant through the sample the second one reflects the predictability of the volatility fitted with a GARCH(1,1).

```
rm(list=ls())
setwd(dirname(rstudioapi::getActiveDocumentContext()$path))
# packages used
listofpackages <- c("tidyverse","dygraphs", "rugarch",
      "forecast","dplyr","ellipse","reshape2","ggplot2","xts","xlsx","readxl")

for (j in listofpackages){
  if(sum(installed.packages()[, 1] == j) == 0) {
    install.packages(j)
  }
  library(j, character.only = T)
}

# setting the seed for replication
set.seed(77)

raw_data            = read_xlsx("../data/2023_monthly_stocks.xlsx")
names(raw_data)[1] = 'Date'
typeof(raw_data)
typeof(raw_data$Date)
typeof(raw_data$AXP)
typeof(raw_data$CSCO)

dates <-seq(as.Date("1985-02-01"),length=462, by="months")
params <- c("Date","BA", "DJI")
data <- raw_data[, c(params)]
data<- na.omit(data)
data <- data %>%
  mutate(Date = as.Date(Date, format = "%Y-%m-%d"))

params1 <- c("BA", "DJI")
tsdata <- xts(raw_data[, c(params1)], order.by=dates) # creates a time series object
tsdata <- na.omit(tsdata) # omitting the rows with NA presence
data<- na.omit(data)
## having created the database with all observation we generate a subset
#tsdata1 <- tsdata["1992-02-01/1993-02-01"]
#data=subset(data,select=c(1:12))

## --------------------
# DATA TRANSFORMATIONS
## --------------------
#1. from prices to returns
# exact monthly returns
t1<-nrow(data)
data$BA_ret <- data$DJI_ret <- array(data = NA, dim = t1)
for (i in 2:t1) {
  data[i, "BA_ret"][[1]]=(data[i, "BA"][[1]]-data[i-1,
     "BA"][[1]])/data[i-1, "BA"][[1]]
  data[i, "DJI_ret"][[1]]=(data[i, "DJI"][[1]]-data[i-1,
     "DJI"][[1]])/data[i-1, "DJI"][[1]]
}


# same in .xts
```

```
t1<-nrow(tsdata)

tsdata$BA_ret <- tsdata$DJI_ret<- array(data = NA, dim = t1)

for (i in 2:t1) {
  tsdata[i, "BA_ret"][[1]]=(tsdata[i, "BA"][[1]]-tsdata[i-1,
     "BA"][[1]])/data[i-1, "BA"][[1]]
  tsdata[i, "DJI_ret"][[1]]=(tsdata[i, "DJI"][[1]]-tsdata[i-1,
     "DJI"][[1]])/data[i-1, "DJI"][[1]]

}

## ----------------------------------
## VAR with CER-CAPM
## ----------------------------------


## -----------------------------------
## MODEL SPECIFICATION AND ESTIMATION
## -----------------------------------
start_date <- as.Date("1992-03-01")  # Replace with your start date
end_date <- as.Date("2005-12-01")    # Replace with your end date

# Extract observations between 'start_date' and 'end_date'

data_est <- subset(x = data,  Date >= start_date & Date <= end_date)

# estimation
cer_mkt <- lm(data_est$DJI_ret ~ 1)
capm_BA <- lm(data_est$BA_ret ~ data_est$DJI_ret)
summary(cer_mkt)
summary(capm_BA)

## ------------------
## MODEL SIMULATION
## ------------------

tt <- as.Date("2006-01-01")
tT <- as.Date("2015-12-01")
data_sim <- subset(x = data,  Date >= tt & Date <= tT)

# creating the containers
nrep <- 1000
BA_bt_2 <- mkt_bt_2 <- array(0, c(length(data_sim$DJI_ret), nrep))

# resampling the residuals
res_mkt_bt_2 <- matrix(sample(resid(cer_mkt), size =
    length(data_sim$DJI_ret) * nrep, replace = T),
                     nrow = length(data_sim$DJI_ret), ncol = nrep)
res_BA_bt_2 <- matrix(sample(resid(capm_BA), size =
    length(data_sim$DJI_ret) * nrep, replace = T),
                    nrow = length(data_sim$DJI_ret), ncol = nrep)


# the loop
for (i in 1:nrep){
  for (j in 1:length(data_sim$DJI_ret)){
    mkt_bt_2[j, i] <- coef(cer_mkt)[1] + res_mkt_bt_2[j, i]
    BA_bt_2[j, i] <- coef(capm_BA)[1] + coef(capm_BA)[2] * mkt_bt_2[j, i] +
        res_BA_bt_2[j, i]
  }
}
```

```
# the quantiles
var_BA_capm <- array(0, length(data_sim$DJI_ret))
for (j in 1:length(data_sim$DJI_ret)){
  var_BA_capm[j] <- quantile(BA_bt_2[j, ], probs = 0.05)
}
data_sim$var_BA_capm<-var_BA_capm
# plotting
ggplot(data_sim, aes(x = Date)) +
  geom_line(aes(y = BA_ret, color = "BA"), size = 1, linetype = "solid") +
  geom_line(aes(y = var_BA_capm, color = "VaR"), size = 1, linetype =
      "solid") +
  labs(x = "Date", y = "Returns and VaR") +
  ylim(-0.15, 0.15) +
  theme_minimal() +
  theme(
    legend.position = c(0.15, 0.95),  # Set the legend position (top-left)
    legend.title = element_blank(),
    legend.text = element_text(size = 8),
    axis.text = element_text(size = 8),
    axis.title = element_text(size = 10),
    plot.title = element_text(size = 12, hjust = 0.5)
  ) +
  scale_color_manual(
    values = c("blue", "green"),
    labels = c("BA", "VaR")
  )



## -------------------
## GARCH MODELLING
## -------------------

# the market GARCH regression
## specification
mkt_garch <- ugarchspec(variance.model = list(garchOrder = c(1, 1)),
                        mean.model = list(armaOrder = c(0, 0)))
## estimation
mkt_garchfit <- ugarchfit(mkt_garch, data = data_est$DJI_ret)
mkt_garchfit


# forecasting and plotting the results
horizon <- 10*12 # ten years
mygarchforecast <- ugarchforecast(mkt_garchfit, n.ahead = 10*12)

plotdata <- cbind(mygarchforecast@forecast$seriesFor,
                  mygarchforecast@forecast$seriesFor +
                     mygarchforecast@forecast$sigmaFor*1.96,
                  mygarchforecast@forecast$seriesFor -
                     mygarchforecast@forecast$sigmaFor*1.96)
colnames(plotdata) <- c("mean", "upper", "lower")
dygraph(ts(plotdata, start = c(2006,1), frequency = 12), main = "Forecast
    of the mean") %>%
  dySeries(c("lower", "mean", "upper"))

plotdata2 <- as.matrix(mygarchforecast@forecast$sigmaFor^2)
colnames(plotdata2) <- "var"
dygraph(ts(plotdata2, start = c(2006, 1), frequency = 12), main = "Forecast
    of the variance")
```

```
## ---------------------
## GARCH SIMULATION
## ---------------------

## coefficients
gamma0 <- coef(mkt_garchfit)[1]
omega0 <- coef(mkt_garchfit)[2]
omega1 <- coef(mkt_garchfit)[3]
omega2 <- coef(mkt_garchfit)[4]
sigma2 <- sigma(mkt_garchfit) # this constructs the series of standard deviations conditional on
      information at "t-1". Is thus a vector.

# the CAPM
## estimation
capm_BA <- lm(data_est$BA_ret ~ data_est$DJI_ret)
summary(capm_BA)

beta0 <- coef(capm_BA)[1]
beta1 <- coef(capm_BA)[2]



## -----------------
# simulation
# output containers
nrep <- 1000
BA_bt <- mkt_bt<- sigma<- array(0, c(length(data_sim$DJI_ret), nrep))

# extracting the errors and resampling

res_mkt <- as.numeric(residuals(mkt_garchfit, standardize = T)) # the standardized residuals from the
      market equation

res_mkt_bt <- matrix(sample(res_mkt, size = length(data_sim$DJI_ret) *
    nrep, replace = T),
                        nrow = length(data_sim$DJI_ret), ncol = nrep)
res_BA_bt <- matrix(sample(resid(capm_BA), size = length(data_sim$DJI_ret)
    * nrep, replace = T),
                       nrow = length(data_sim$DJI_ret), ncol = nrep)

# initial values
mkt_bt[1, ] <- data_sim$DJI_ret[1]
BA_bt[1, ] <- beta0 + beta1*mkt_bt[1, ]
sigma[1, ]<- ugarchforecast(mkt_garchfit)@forecast$sigmaFor[1] #takes the first value (the one step
      ahead)
# the loop
for (i in 1:nrep){
  for (j in 2:length(data_sim$DJI_ret)){
    sigma[j, i] <- sqrt(omega0+omega1*( data_sim$DJI_ret[j-1]- gamma0)^2 +
        omega2*(sigma[j-1, i])^2)
    mkt_bt[j, i] <- gamma0 + res_mkt_bt[j, i] * sigma[j,i]
    BA_bt[j, i] <- beta0 + beta1 * mkt_bt[j, i] + res_BA_bt[j, i]
  }
}

# getting the quantiles
var_BA_garch <- array(0, length(data_sim$DJI_ret))
for (j in 1:length(data_sim$DJI_ret)){
  var_BA_garch[j] <- quantile(BA_bt[j, ], probs = 0.05)
}
```

```
data_sim$var_BA_garch<-var_BA_garch

# plotting
tt <- as.Date("2006-02-01")
tT <- as.Date("2015-12-01")
data_simplot <- subset(x = data_sim,  Date >= tt & Date <= tT)
ggplot(data_simplot , aes(x = Date)) +
  geom_line(aes(y = BA_ret, color = "BA"), size = 1, linetype = "solid") +
  geom_line(aes(y = var_BA_capm, color = "Var CAPM"), size = 1, linetype =
     "solid") +
  geom_line(aes(y = var_BA_garch, color = "VaR GARCH"), size = 1, linetype
     = "solid") +
  labs(x = "Date", y = "Returns and VaR") +
  ylim(-0.30, 0.20) +
  theme_minimal() +
  theme(
    legend.position = c(0.15, 0.95),  # Set the legend position (top-left)
    legend.title = element_blank(),
    legend.text = element_text(size = 8),
    axis.text = element_text(size = 8),
    axis.title = element_text(size = 10),
    plot.title = element_text(size = 12, hjust = 0.5)
  ) +
  scale_color_manual(
    values = c("blue", "green", "red"),
    labels = c("BA", "VaR CAPM", "Var GARCH")
  )

save(data_simplot,file="VaRdata.Rdata")
```

7.8 Backtesting VaR

How do we test the validity of a VaR model? The relevant evidence to judge a VaR model are violations:

$$\text{Min}(R_{t+1} - \text{VaR}^p_{t+1}, 0)$$

(a) A good VaR model should not feature neither too few nor too many violations.
(b) We have too few violations when a VaR at the confidence level of alpha shows less than 100*alpha violations in a sample of 100 observations. In this case, the VaR model is too conservative.
(c) When we have violations there are two interesting aspects of that: their number and their timing. A five per cent VaR that features 5 violations in five successive periods cannot be taken as a valid VaR model as violations are not independent. Clustering of violations is a problem that should lead to reject specific VaR models. Kupiec (2002) proposed a formal test of VaR validity based on these two aspects.

7.8.1 *Unconditional coverage testing*

Given a time-series of VaR and observed returns the "hit sequence" of VaR violations is defined as follows:

$$I_{t+1} = 1, if\ R_{t+1} > \mathrm{VaR}_{t+1}^{p}$$
$$I_{t+1} = 0, if\ R_{t+1} > \mathrm{VaR}_{t+1}^{p}$$

If the VaR is a valid model violations should not be predictable: the probability of a VaR violation should be p every day. The hit sequence in this case should be distributed over time as a Bernoulli variable that takes the value 1 with probability p and the value 0 with probability $1-p$. So

$$H_0 \ : \ I_{t+1} \sim i.i.d.\ \text{Bernoulli}\,(p)$$
$$f\,(I_{t+1}, p) = (1-p)^{1-I_{t+1}}\, p^{I_{t+1}}$$

The first test of the validity of a VaR is therefore constructed as follows. Take a Bernoulli distribution (I_{t+1}, x) for the that the number of violations, derive a maximum likelihood estimator $\hat{x}$ of x, and test using a likelihood ratio test that $\hat{x}$ is not statistically different from p.

$$L\,(I_{t+1}, x) = \prod_{i=1}^{T} (1-x)^{1-I_{t+1}}\, x^{I_{t+1}}$$
$$= (1-x)^{T_0}\, x^{T_1}$$

where T_1 is the number of violations of the VaR observed in the sample, and $T_0 = T - T_1$.

The maximum likelihood estimator $\hat{x} = \frac{T_1}{T}$.

A likelihood ratio test of the null hypothesis $\hat{x} = p$, can then be constructed as follows:

$$\mathrm{LR}_{uc} = -2\ln\left[\frac{L\,(p)}{L\,(\hat{x})}\right]$$

which is distributed as a χ^2 with one degree of freedom.

Note that usually the number of violations and the number of observations available will not be large, so rather than relying upon the χ^2 distribution, it is advisable to use Monte-Carlo simulations to build the relevant distribution to conduct the test. In this case the simulated P-values would be obtained by drawing an artificial sample of the relevant size from the null, and using as a P-value the share of simulated test that are larger than the observed ones.

7.8.2 *Independence testing*

We concentrate now on a test able to reject a VaR with clustered violations. In this case the hit sequence is dependent over time and its evolution over time can be described by a so-called Markov sequence where the transition from the relevant states (violation and no violation) can be described by the following transition probability matrix

$$X_1 = \begin{bmatrix} x_{00} & 1 - x_{00} \\ 1 - x_{11} & x_{11} \end{bmatrix}$$

where:

$$\begin{aligned} x_{00} &= \Pr\left(I_{t+1} = 0 \mid I_t = 0\right) \\ 1 - x_{00} &= \Pr\left(I_{t+1} = 1 \mid I_t = 0\right) \\ x_{11} &= \Pr\left(I_{t+1} = 1 \mid I_t = 1\right) \\ 1 - x_{11} &= \Pr\left(I_{t+1} = 0 \mid I_t = 1\right) \end{aligned}$$

If we observe a sample of T observations the likelihood function of the first order Markov process can be written as follows:

$$L\left(X_1, I_{t+1}\right) = x_{00}^{T_{00}} \left(1 - x_{00}\right)^{T_{01}} \left(1 - x_{11}\right)^{T_{10}} x_{11}^{T_{11}}$$

The maximum likelihood estimates of the relevant parameters are then

$$\begin{aligned} \hat{x}_{00} &= \frac{T_{00}}{T_{00} + T_{01}} \\ \hat{x}_{11} &= \frac{T_{11}}{T_{10} + T_{11}} \end{aligned}$$

and so

$$\hat{X}_1 = \begin{bmatrix} \frac{T_{00}}{T_{00}+T_{01}} & \frac{T_{01}}{T_{00}+T_{01}} \\ \frac{T_{10}}{T_{10}+T_{11}} & \frac{T_{11}}{T_{10}+T_{11}} \end{bmatrix}$$

Independence Testing

Under independence

$$\hat{X}_1^{id} = \begin{bmatrix} 1 - \hat{x} & \hat{x} \\ 1 - \hat{x} & \hat{x} \end{bmatrix}$$

and therefore the independence hypothesis $(1 - \hat{x}_{00}) = \hat{x}_{11}$ can be tested using a likelihood ratio test

$$\mathrm{LR}_{\mathrm{ind}} = -2 \ln \left[\frac{L\left(\hat{X}_1^{id}\right)}{L\left(\hat{X}_1\right)} \right] \sim \chi_1^2$$

As for the unconditional coverage test, small sample problems can be fixed by Monte Carlo simulation of the critical values, moreover samples in which $\mathrm{T}_{11} = 0$ are often observed. In this cases, the likelihood function is computed as

$$L\left(X_1, I_{t+1}\right) = x_{00}^{T_{00}} \left(1 - x_{00}\right)^{T_{01}}$$

7.8.3 *Conditional coverage testing*

Conditional Coverage Testing

Having constructed the test for independence we can test jointly the hypothesis of conditional coverage and independence via the following likelihood ratio test:

$$\mathrm{LR}_{cc} = -2 \ln \left[\frac{L\left(p\right)}{L\left(\hat{X}_1\right)} \right] \sim \chi_2^2$$

note that

$$\mathrm{LR}_{cc} = \mathrm{LR}_{uc} + \mathrm{LR}_{\mathrm{ind}}$$

7.8.4 *Backtesting VaR in R*

The following program implements the Kupiec (2002) test on the Var measures derived in Section 7.7.

```
rm(list=ls())
setwd(dirname(rstudioapi::getActiveDocumentContext()$path))
# packages used
listofpackages <- c("tidyverse","dygraphs", "rugarch",
      "forecast","dplyr","ellipse","reshape2","ggplot2","xts","xlsx","readxl")

for (j in listofpackages){
  if(sum(installed.packages()[, 1] == j) == 0) {
    install.packages(j)
  }
  library(j, character.only = T)
}

# loading the  databases
load("VaRdata.Rdata")
ggplot(data_simplot, aes(x = Date)) +
  geom_line(aes(y = BA_ret, color = "BA"), size = 1, linetype = "solid") +
  geom_line(aes(y = var_BA_capm, color = "Var CAPM"), size = 1, linetype =
     "solid") +
  geom_line(aes(y = var_BA_garch, color = "VaR GARCH"), size = 1, linetype
     = "solid") +
  labs(x = "Date", y = "Returns and VaR") +
  ylim(-0.30, 0.20) +
  theme_minimal() +
  theme(
    legend.position = c(0.15, 0.95),  # Set the legend position (top-left)
    legend.title = element_blank(),
    legend.text = element_text(size = 8),
    axis.text = element_text(size = 8),
    axis.title = element_text(size = 10),
    plot.title = element_text(size = 12, hjust = 0.5)
  ) +
  scale_color_manual(
    values = c("blue", "green", "red"),
    labels = c("BA", "VaR CAPM", "Var GARCH")
  )
## ---------------
# VaR tail
alpha <- 0.1


## --------------
violations <- (data_simplot$BA_ret - data_simplot$var_BA_capm) < 0
table(violations)
plot(y = violations*runif(length(violations), min = 0.99, max = 1.01), x =
    data_simplot$Date, main = "VaR violations",
     ylab = "violations", xlab = "time") # adding jitter to make sure that adjacent observations
           don't overlap

## testing
### Unconditional coverage
p <- alpha
T1 <- sum(violations)
T0 <- length(violations) - sum(violations)

x <- T1/(T1+T0) # violations as fraction of sample length, which is also the test statistic estimate

L_p <- (1-p)^T0 * p^T1
L_x <- (1-x)^T0 * x^T1

{\rm LR}_uc <- -2 * log(L_p/L_x) # test statistic
critical <- qchisq(p = 0.95, df = 1) # the 5% critical value
```

```
{\rm LR}_uc; critical
LR_uc > critical

### Independence testing
temp1 <- abs(diff(violations)) # to identify moments of change
temp2 <- violations[2:length(violations)] # to identify the ending points
T01 <- sum(temp2 * temp1) # those that finish with 1 and had a change
T11 <- sum(temp2 * (1-temp1)) # those that finish with 1 and had no change
T10 <- sum((1 - temp2) * temp1) # those finishing with 0 and having a change
T00 <- sum((1-temp2) * (1-temp1)) # finishing with 0 and no change

xhat <- x # from before
x00 <- T00/(T00 + T01)
x11 <- T11/(T11 + T10)

L_x_different <- x00^T00 * (1-x00)^T01 * (1-x11)^T10 * x11^T11
L_x_equal <- (1-xhat)^T00 * xhat^T01 * (1-xhat)^T10 * xhat^T11

LR_ind <- -2 * log(L_x_equal/L_x_different)
critical <- qchisq(p = 0.95, df = 1) # the 5% critical value
LR_ind; critical
LR_ind > critical
```

Bibliography

Ang, A. (2014) *Asset Management: A Systematic Approach to Factor Investing*. Oxford University Press, USA.

Banz, R. W. (1981) "The relationship between return and market value of common stocks," *Journal of Financial Economics*, 9(1), 3–18.

Basu, S. (1983) "The relationship between earnings' yield, market value and return for NYSE common stocks: Further evidence," *Journal of Financial Economics*, 12(1), 129–156.

Battigalli, P., E. Catonini, and N. De Vito (2023) "Game theory: Analysis of strategic thinking," Bocconi University, Milan.

Bhandari, L. C. (1988) "Debt/equity ratio and expected common stock returns: Empirical evidence," *The Journal of Finance*, 43(2), 507–528.

Billingsley, P. (2017) *Probability and Measure*. John Wiley & Sons, Germany.

Black, F. (1972) "Capital market equilibrium with restricted borrowing," *The Journal of Business*, 45 (3), 444–455.

Bollerslev, T. (1986) "Generalized autoregressive conditional heteroskedasticity," *Journal of Econometrics*, 31(3), 307–327.

Bordalo, P., N. Gennaioli, and A. Shleifer (2012) "Salience theory of choice under risk," *The Quarterly Journal of Economics*, 127(3), 1243–1285.

Bordalo, P., N. Gennaioli, and A. Shleifer (2022) "Salience," *Annual Review of Economics*, 14(1), 521–544.

Brennan, M. J. (1971) "Capital market equilibrium with divergent borrowing and lending rates," *Journal of Financial and Quantitative Analysis*, 6(5), 1197–1205.

Campbell, J. Y. and R. J. Shiller (1987) "Cointegration and tests of present value models," *Journal of Political Economy*, 95(5), 1062–1088.

Chan, L. K. C., Y. Hamao, and J. Lakonishok (1991) "Fundamentals and stock returns in Japan," *The Journal of Finance*, 46(5), 1739–1764.

Christoffersen, P. (2011) *Elements of Financial Risk Management.* Academic Press, London.

Cieslak, A., A. Morse, and A. Vissing-Jorgensen (2019) "Stock returns over the FOMC cycle," *The Journal of Finance*, 74(5), 2201–2248.

Cochrane, J. H. (1999) "New facts in finance," *Economic Perspectives* 23(3), 36+. Gale Academic OneFile. https://link.gale.com/apps/doc/A56973779/AONE?u=anon?c3c3deb8&sid=googleScholar&xid=2dfb5fe4, Accessed on December 29, 2024.

Di Tella, S., B. M. Hébert, P. Kurlat, and Q. Wang (2023) The zero-beta interest rate. Technical Report, National Bureau of Economic Research, Working Paper 31596, DOI 10.3386/w31596.

Ellsberg, D. (1961) "Risk, ambiguity, and the Savage axioms," *The Quarterly Journal of Economics*, 75(4), 643–669.

Elton, E. J., M. J. Gruber, S. J. Brown, and W. N. Goetzmann (2009) *Modern Portfolio Theory and Investment Analysis.* John Wiley & Sons, Hoboken, NJ.

Engle, R. F. (1982) "Autoregressive conditional heteroscedasticity with estimates of the variance of United Kingdom inflation," *Econometrica: Journal of the Econometric Society*, 55(2), 987–1007.

Engle, R. F. and C. W. J. Granger (1987) "Co-integration and error correction: Representation, estimation, and testing," *Econometrica*, 55(2), 251–276.

Engle, R. F. and B. S. Yoo (1987) "Forecasting and testing in co-integrated systems," *Journal of Econometrics*, 35(1), 143–159.

Fama, E. F. (1970) "Efficient capital markets: A review of theory and empirical work," *The Journal of Finance*, 25(2), 383–417.

Fama, E. F. and K. R. French (1993) "Common risk factors in the returns on stocks and bonds," *Journal of Financial Economics*, 33(1), 3–56, https://doi.org/10.1016/0304-405X(93)90023-5.

Fama, E. F. and K. R. French (2015) "A five-factor asset pricing model," *Journal of Financial Economics*, 116(1), 1–22.

Fama, E. F. and J. D. MacBeth (1973) "Risk, return, and equilibrium: Empirical tests," *Journal of Political Economy*, 81(3), 607–636.

Frazzini, A. and L. H. Pedersen (2014) "Betting against beta," *Journal of Financial Economics*, 111(1), 1–25.

Hou, K., H. Mo, C. Xue, and L. Zhang (2018) "Which factors?" *Review of Finance*, 23(1), 1–35.

Jegadeesh, N. and S. Titman (2011) "Momentum," *Annual Review Financial Economic*, 3(1), 493–509.

Jensen (Deceased), M. C. and F. Black, M. S. Scholes (1972). "The capital asset pricing model: Some empirical tests," in M. C. Jensen (ed.), *Studies in the Theory of Capital Markets*. Praeger Publishers Inc. Available at SSRN: https://ssrn.com/abstract=908569.

Kothari, S. P., E. So, and R. Verdi (2016) "Analysts' forecasts and asset pricing: A survey," *Annual Review of Financial Economics*, 8, 197–219.

Kupiec, P. (2002) "Stress-testing in a value at risk framework," *Risk Management: Value at Risk and Beyond*, 10, 76–99.

Lintner, J. (1965) "Security prices, risk, and maximal gains from diversification," *The Journal of Finance*, 20(4), 587–615.

Lucca, D. O. and E. Moench (2015) "The pre-FOMC announcement drift," *The Journal of Finance*, 70(1), 329–371.

Maccheroni, F., M. Marinacci, and A. Rustichini (2006) "Ambiguity aversion, robustness, and the variational representation of preferences," *Econometrica*, 74(6), 1447–1498.

MacKinnon, J. G. (2010) Critical values for cointegration tests. Technical report, Queen's Economics Department.

Mas-Colell, A., M. D. Whinston, J. R. Green *et al.* (1995) *Microeconomic Theory*, Vol. 1. Oxford University Press, New York.

Novy-Marx, R. and M. Velikov (2022) "Betting against betting against beta," *Journal of Financial Economics*, 143(1), 80–106.

Research, Milton Financial Market (2023) "The complete guide to portfolio optimization in R," https://miltonfmr.com/the-complete-guide-to-portfolio-optimization-in-r-part1/, Accessed on September 2023.

Rosenberg, B., K. Reid, and R. Lanstein (1985) "Persuasive evidence of market inefficiency," *Journal of Portfolio Management*, 11(3), 9–16.

Ross, S. A. (1973) *Return, Risk and Arbitrage*. Rodney L. White Center for Financial Research, The Wharton School.

Sharpe, W. F. (1964) "Capital asset prices: A theory of market equilibrium under conditions of risk," *The Journal of Finance*, 19(3), 425–442.

Shiller, R. J. (1979) "The volatility of long-term interest rates and expectations models of the term structure," *Journal of Political Economy*, 87(6), 1190–1219.

Shiller, R. J. (1981) "Do stock prices move too much to be justified by subsequent changes in dividends?" *The American Economic Review*, June, 421–436.

Singh, Abhay Kumar and David Edmund Allen (2017) *R in Finance and Economics: A Beginner's Guide*: World Scientific, Allen Lane, London, UK.

Taleb, N. N. (2012) *Antifragile: How to Live in a World We Don't Understand*, Vol. 3. Allen Lane, London.

Taylor, S. E. and S. C. Thompson (1982) "Stalking the elusive" vividness" effect," *Psychological Review*, 89(2), 155.

Torfs, P. and C. Brauer (2014) "A (very) short introduction to R," https://cran.r-project.org/doc/contrib/Torfs+Brauer-Short-R-Intro.pdf, Accessed on September 2023.

Valkanov, R. (2003) "Long-horizon regressions: Theoretical results and applications," *Journal of Financial Economics*, 68(2), 201–232.

Vasicek, O. A. (1973) "A note on using cross-sectional information in Bayesian estimation of security betas," *The Journal of Finance*, 28(5), 1233–1239.

Von Neumann, J. and O. Morgenstern (2007) "Theory of games and economic behavior: 60th anniversary commemorative edition," *Theory of Games and Economic Behavior*. Princeton University Press, Princeton, NJ.

Index

A

absolute risk aversion coefficient, 16
anomalies, 116
arbitrage pricing theory, 89
asset allocation, 189
asymmetric information, 5

B

backtesting, 182
  VaR models, 223

C

capital market line, 75
certainty equivalent, 18
chat GPT, 142–143, 145, 148, 158, 160–163
cointegration, 202

D

duration, 139
dynamic dividend growth model, 134

E

efficient frontier, 54
efficient market hypothesis, 101
equilibrium correction term, 202
estimation
  maximum likelihood, 216
  ordinary least squares (OLS), 175
  quasi maximum likelihood, 217
expected loss, 21
expected utility, 9

F

factor exposures, 192
factor models, 189
  cross-sectional representation, 191
  Fama-French, 114
  time-series representation, 189
  validation, 199
factor models with predictability, 200
factor-based portfolios, 191
fair lottery, 12
fair price, 27, 51
feasible set, 54
financial literacy, 1
first order condition, 22

I

insurance pricing, 19

L

lexicographic preference, 7
look-ahead-bias, 128, 182
lottery, 12

M

maturity, 139
minimum variance frontier, 54
model
  CAPM, 73, 101
  constant expected return, 101
  dynamic dividend growth, 137
  factor error correction (FECM), 203
  GARCH, 215
  GARCH with factors, 218
  lognormal, 130
  random walk, 169
  zero-beta CAPM, 79
models for asset returns, 126

N

non-satiation, 16

O

optimal portfolio allocation, 21

P

portfolio
  optimal weights, 72
  risk parity, 55
  smart beta, 192
  tangency, 73
portfolio allocation, 125
predictability, 122
preference relation, 6
present value relationship, 25
price deflator, 25
pricing kernel, 25
probability space, 4

R

R
  backtesting VaR models, 226
  data-handling, 146
  dataframes, 145
  datatypes, 145
  estimation, 177
  importing data, 146
  measuring risk, 218
  model simulation, 182
  models with predictability, 205
  optimal portfolio alllocation, 193
  package fPortfolio, 177
rare event, 52
rational expectations, 122
rational preference, 8
relative risk aversion coefficient, 16
returns
  anomalies, 118
  continuously compounded, 129
  coupon-bonds, 140
  high-frequency, 117
  linear, 128
  multi-period, 130
  predictability, 122
  stock and bond, 134
  volatility, 116
  zero-coupon bonds, 138
risk aversion, 13
risk compensation, 21
risk lover, 15
risk measurement, 125, 211
risk neutral, 15
risk premium, 18
risk-neutral measure, subjective, 26
Roll's critique, 81

S

security market line, 75
Sharpe ratio, 171
simulation, 176
  bootstrap, 176
  Monte-Carlo, 176
strategic interaction, 5

T

time-diversification, 171
two-fund separation theorem, 74
two-funds theorem, 67

U

utility function, 8

V

value-at-risk, 116, 182, 211
value at risk with factor models, 212
value at risk with predictability, 214
value at risk without predictability, 212

www.ingramcontent.com/pod-product-compliance
Lightning Source LLC
LaVergne TN
LVHW011812200926
848484LV00005B/1162

* 9 7 8 9 8 1 9 8 1 1 5 9 5 *